NORTH AMERICA'S MARITIME FUNNEL:

The Ships that Brought the Irish
1749 - 1852

THE MARITIME FUNNEL

Imagine using a funnel in reverse. You want to pour honey into a jar, but you are putting it in at the narrow end. Some spills, some sticks, but most eventually swirls around the bowl of the funnel and drips out the wide end. Consider that the honey was Ireland's emigrants, and that the narrow end of the funnel was Atlantic Canada. Some of them fell by the wayside, perishing at sea or in quarantine stations after reaching port. Some stuck to the narrow end, and settled in the Canadian Maritimes. Most spread out the wide end across America, from Ontario south to Louisiana. That is the Maritime funnel.

NORTH AMERICA'S MARITIME FUNNEL:

The Ships that Brought the Irish

1749 - 1852

Terrence M. Punch, CM, FRSAI, FIGRS

Genealogical Publishing Company

Published by Genealogical Publishing Company
3600 Clipper Mill Rd., Suite 260
Baltimore, MD 21211-1953

Library of Congress Catalogue Card Number 2012945584
ISBN 978-0-8063-1965-0
Made in the United States of America

CONTENTS

ABOUT THIS BOOK

The Maritime Provinces of Canada – New Brunswick, Nova Scotia, and Prince Edward Island – were a convenient destination for tens of thousands of Irish between 1749 and 1852. Thanks to the availability of timber vessels and relatively low fares, the region attracted Irish emigrants as a first step towards the United States and the Canadas. People converged through the narrow aperture of fewer than a dozen significant ports, then dispersed widely across the North American continent: north and west to what became Ontario and Québec, south and south-west to the eastern seaboard of the United States, thence inland to the opening mid-west and beyond. This geographical pattern suggested to me the image of the Maritimes as the neck of a funnel whose wide end was the American continent.

Ireland had too many people by the early nineteenth century. That fact alone, together with economic, social and political issues, prompted mass migration which, in turn, brought about a form of industry, where emigrants and ships met through the agency of men whose business it was to find vessels for emigrants and human cargoes for empty holds. After an Introduction, the book delves into the demographic crisis that Ireland faced (Section II).

People leaving Ireland could not take a train or coach to a harbour of choice. Either they lived near a navigable harbour such as Dublin or Cork, or they could follow a river system to a seaport like Londonderry or Waterford, which meant they inhabited a catchment, or hinterland, behind a seaport (Section III). Then we take a brief glimpse at each of the several Irish ports mentioned in this study (Section IV).

The largest part of the book is Section V, which offers a year-by-year listing of known voyages between an Irish port and a harbour in the Maritimes. By the use of hundreds of footnotes, the reader can discover whether a complete or partial passenger list for each voyage is known, or whether the names of some passengers can be gleaned anywhere. These are cited in the footnotes. Passenger lists survive for 123 of 1050 voyages, about 11%.[1] Then follow a survey of the annual number of voyages (Section VI), a discussion of how many Irish emigrants reached the Maritimes between 1749 and 1852(Section VII), and a presentation of the emigration in terms of where the ships arrived at a Maritime port (Section IX).

Since passenger lists can be difficult to read, and since transcribers bring different intentions, skills and motivation to their work, the published results can be confusing. To alert genealogists to this, two versions of the passenger list of the *Envoy* in 1847 have been compared to each other and to other contemporary documentation (Section X).

There are five appendixes which present information of interest. Appendix I is a selection of probable Irish people among the founding party in 1749 of Halifax, Nova Scotia, the first town established in the Maritimes by the British. Appendix II is an attempt to sort out the Irish who came into the area between 1761 and 1773. It is not a complete project, but it offers a step towards a resolution. Appendix III is intended to show Irish emigrants were arriving between 1792 and 1825, when there is no record of the ships which brought them. Appendix IV is a compilation of Irish emigrants found in the Ordnance Survey Memoirs from two northern counties in the 1830s. The four appendixes identify 1,523 people. Appendix V talks about the voyage of the *Aldebaran* in 1847 as an example of what historians have termed "coffin ships" because of the high mortality experienced by their passengers.

Page iii explains the Irish subdivisions of land, so readers will not find them confusing.

---

[1] Most of these we have from the Customs House at Saint John in the 1830s and the Cooke line lists published by Brian Mitchell and associates. Partial lists were gleaned from newspaper notices, Alms House records and deaths reported at the Quarantine station at Partridge Island in Saint John Harbour.

SUBDIVISIONS OF IRELAND

The land mass of Ireland was divided for administrative or other purposes in a descending series of units. From largest to smallest these were the provinces, counties, baronies, civil parishes and townlands.[1]

There were four **provinces** in Ireland in the year 1800: Munster (Clare, Cork, Kerry, Limerick, Tipperary, Waterford); Connacht (Sligo, Mayo, Roscommon, Galway, Leitrim); Ulster (Antrim, Armagh, Cavan, Donegal, Down, Fermanagh, Londonderry or Derry, Monaghan, Tyrone); and Leinster (Carlow, Dublin, Kildare, Kilkenny, Leix or Queens, Longford, Louth, Meath, Offaly or Kings, Westmeath, Wexford, Wicklow).

There were thirty-two **counties** (named above), which were major land divisions created for local government purposes by the English in imitation of their system of shires presided over by a sheriff and responsible for tax collection, road maintenance and courts.

Each county was divided into **baronies**, of which there were 331 in all. The barony was a major division of a county, but sometimes their boundaries crossed county and parish lines. There were as few as five baronies in counties Leitrim and Monaghan, and over thirty in County Cork. Baronies probably matter less in terms of genealogical documentation than either counties or civil parishes.

A **civil parish** (there were 2,508 of them) was not a church parish but a civil administrative division, one or several of which might coincide with a Church of Ireland (Anglican) parish or not. Roman Catholic parishes seldom had the same bounds and sometimes had different names than the civil parish designation. Civil parishes might cross barony or county lines and some existed in two or more separated sections.[2]

A **townland**, of which Ireland had well over 60,000, was the smallest governmental administrative land division. These were often named from topographic natural or cultural characteristics, or reflect the name of a family or clan once powerful in the vicinity. A townland might amount to a family farm in size or include a group of farms. The largest townland – Sheskin, Kilcommon parish, County Mayo – contained 7,012 acres, while the smallest – Old Church Yard, Termonmagurk parish, County Tyrone – was just over half an acre in extent.[3]

---

[1] A helpful mentor for this subject is James R. Reilly, *Richard Griffith and His Valuation of Ireland* (Baltimore: Clearfield Company, Inc., 2000), particularly pp. 72 - 73.

[2] Instances of parishes that existed in separate sections would be Castleventry, County Kerry, or Bovevagh, County Londonderry. Parishes that cross county lines include Crecrin which is partly in Carlow and partly in Wicklow, or Shankill Parish, which straddles the borders of the counties Antrim and Down. An example of name difference would be the civil parish of Kilmore, County Mayo, coterminus with the Roman Catholic parish of Moygownagh.

[3] Examples of townlands whose names are geographically descriptive would be Ardmore (24 of them; the name means 'big hill'), Ballyglass (over 50 of these; the name denotes 'green town/settlement'); or Rathmoyle (7 of this name, which means 'dilapidated or fallen fort'). Certain words are generic, e.g., 'bally' indicating a local settlement, 'inish(h)/inch' denoting an island or river meadow that floods, etc. Many places in Leinster and Munster recall early Norman and Welsh settlers of mediæval times, e.g., Keatingstown, Kilkenny; Punchestown, Kildare; Rochestown, Wexford. For more on this interesting topic the reader is referred to the works of P. W. Joyce, such as *Irish Local Names Explained*, reprinted at Dublin in 1979.

I - INTRODUCTION

A significant share of emigration from the British Isles to North America from about 1750 until 1850 flowed through what is now Atlantic Canada. As this book and volume three of *Some Early Scots in Maritime Canada*[1] demonstrate, almost 2,300 voyages were made from Scotland and Ireland to ports in Maritime Canada (Prince Edward Island, Nova Scotia and New Brunswick).[2] Even at a modest estimate of one hundred souls per voyage, that would represent the arrival of 230,000 emigrants between 1749 and 1852. The numbers were probably twice that. From two to as many as 685 passengers embarked in sailing vessels for voyages that took four weeks when fortune smiled, and two or three times as long when conditions were adverse.[3]

It is difficult to determine or even to estimate accurately the true number of emigrants being carried. There are several reasons for this, most notably the attempts by ship masters and their owners to maximize profits while seeking ways to circumvent officialdom and its rules.[4] In several cases presented in this book, it is apparent that skippers took on board additional passengers after clearing their port of origin. There seems to have been uncertainty whether the officers and crew counted as part of the number legally permitted to be in the vessel; sometimes they were, at others, not. The permitted number of souls in the vessel was predicated upon the ship's tonnage, so the decision of whether to count crewmen in the totals offered a tempting loophole to some masters. Since tonnage was determined differently in the later part of the period than previously, and since regulations sometimes changed the definition of "passenger", it was relatively easy to interpret the computations to one's advantage.[5]

Other factors make it almost impossible to estimate reliably the exact numbers of emigrants. In some cases, no primary source document tells whether the vessel carried passengers. There was a tendency to round off numbers, making it difficult in the absence of passenger lists to know whether to interpret "150 passengers" as being precisely that or a little above or below that figure. In some cases we know that there were passengers but not their number.

---

[1] Terrence M. Punch, *Some Early Scots in Maritime Canada* (Baltimore: Genealogical Publishing Company, 2012), Vol. III, pp. 11 - 38.

[2] Punch, p. 7, found 1,183 voyages of ships from Scotland reached the Maritimes. A further 58 may be added, giving a total of 1,241 from Scotland. The sources of these additional numbers are volume IV of David Dobson's *Ships from Scotland to America 1628 - 1828* (Baltimore: Genealogical Publishing Company, 2011), and the website www.rootsweb.ancestry.com/~pictou/passlist The present book counts 1,057 voyages from Ireland, giving a total of about 2,300 potential emigrant voyages. In her recent book, *Planters, Paupers, and Pioneers; English Settlers in Atlantic Canada* (Toronto: Natural Heritage Books, 2010), Lucille H. Campey records approximately 700 voyages of ships from English ports to Maritime Canada, 1772 - 1852. This may add between 50,000 and 75,000 to the total emigration from the British Isles to Maritime ports.

[3] The *Margaret Pollock* from Belfast took 685 Irish to Pictou, Nova Scotia, in 1841. The *Dunkeld* sailed from the Hebrides of Scotland to Pictou, Nova Scotia in 1791 with 650 Catholic Highlanders from the Western Isles. At the time, a mortality of 3 or 4% of the passengers in an emigrant voyage was more or less considered the norm.

[4] Punch, pp. 41 - 44.

[5] When children were counted as fractions of a passenger, the absence of a nominal list of those on board a vessel leaves the number of *individuals* being carried open to interpretation.

Allowing for the inconsistent nature of our evidence, the number of people from Ireland who set out for a port in Maritime Canada between 1749 and 1852 may have been a quarter million souls, a quite credible figure. Another feature of this large-scale emigration into this region is the fact that many, probably most, of these Irish people did not remain in the Maritimes, but moved on, mainly to the eastern seaboard ports of the United States. A pattern of emigrating in stages played a prominent part in the migration history of Atlantic Canada.

Even considering the problem presented to cartographers of having to represent the round surface of the earth on a flat surface such as a chart or printed page, a glance at a map of North America shows that Atlantic Canada is the nearest part of the continent to Europe. As such, it offered a funnel through which emigrants could reach destinations further along in Canada and the United States. An emigrant who traveled in one vessel from his homeland to a port in north-eastern North America, remained for a few days or several years, then continued onward in a second boat to Boston, New York, Québec or Philadelphia, is termed a "two boater".

The prevalent historic migrations of European people have been from east to west. Atlantic Canada followed that pattern, since people have departed the region for destinations west and south-west for centuries. The mass deportation of the French Acadians was a sorry chapter in the history of North America in the mid-eighteenth century. During the same period several hundred "Foreign Protestants", brought to colonize Nova Scotia, betook themselves to more settled locations in Pennsylvania, New York, and Massachusetts.[6] They were not alone, as several hundred of the people brought out at government expense to found Halifax in 1749 deserted the struggling town for better opportunities in the towns and cities of the Thirteen Colonies.[7]

When the American Revolutionary War broke out in 1775 "a number of the principal inhabitants left for the older colonies." Some New England Planters abandoned the Maritimes and went home. Historians have noted that many Congregational clergy departed to New England leaving a religious void that was filled, first by New Light preachers such as Henry Alline, and later by Methodists and Baptists.[8] A similar story was enacted when the Loyalists came north-east at the end of the Revolutionary War. Finding the prospects unappealing, many turned around after a few years and left what they called "Nova Scarcity".

---

[6] Lunenburg, the principal settlement of the "Foreign Protestants", was founded in spring 1753 by a party numbering 1,453. By January 1758 the population had fallen to 1,374, despite the fact that there were 502 babies born and baptised within that time, compared to 152 reported as dead - Mather Byles DesBrisay, *History of the County of Lunenburg*, 2nd edition (Toronto, 1895), p. 49.

[7] George T. Bates, "The Great Exodus of 1749 or the Cornwallis Settlers Who Didn't," *Collections of the Nova Scotia Historical Society*, Vol. 38, pp. 27 - 62, details the wholesale desertion of settlers from Halifax in its first year or so. See Appendix I for the names of over 200 Irish among the 1749 settlers.

[8] Gordon Stewart and George Rawlyk, *A People Highly Favoured of God* (Toronto: Macmillan of Canada, 1972), pp. 138 -9, 178. Ian F. MacKinnon, *Settlements and Churches in Nova Scotia 1749 - 1776* (Halifax: T. C. Allen, 1930), pp. 96 - 97, named five congregational ministers whose loyalty to the Crown came into issue, concluding that "all the other Congregational clergymen left the province at the commencement of the war; and none are known to have had any sympathies with the British Government." Rev. Samuel Wood of Barrington, in fact, served as a chaplain with the Continental Army, while Rev. Noble of Maugerville [New Brunswick] fled to New England in 1777 after inciting his congregation to sign a local declaration of independence. Beniah Phelps of Cornwallis was so outspoken he was denied permission to leave the colony for a year. Frost of Argyle and Seccombe of Chester were brought before the council to answer charges.

When Scots and Irish emigrants began their transatlantic journey to the Maritimes, not all intended to remain there. The Maritimes, being closer to the British Isles, could be reached for a lower fare than that for direct passage to New York or Philadelphia. For others the critical question was the availability of work in a town or suitable land upon which to farm. Most who remained had been fortunate enough to find a job or acquire a plot of arable soil to support themselves and their families. Among those who did make a living many were blessed with more children than there was farmland, creating a surplus population which sought work in the towns or out-migrated to seek opportunity further afield. In Ireland there were too many people and not enough land. Within two or three generations the situation was essentially replicated in the Maritime Provinces.

The trend to out-migration never stopped. In the Maritimes so many people went to the east coast of the United States for work that scarcely a family was without its son or daughter who had gone to what people called "the Boston states". Later the auto plants of Detroit, the fields of Minnesota and, more recently, the tar sands of Alberta, became the beacons calling out to young Maritimers of all ethnic persuasions. In that sense, Maritime Canada has served as America's Irish doorstep. This region is truly the funnel, the narrow end through which thousands have spread across a continent. This book will try to show features of that funnel at work and connect the tale with the Ireland from which came so many of those people, the ancestors of millions of Canadians and Americans who have never lived here.

An author is not the proverbial "first tiger". Without the diligent research and interest of many others, we would work in a vacuum. Thomas Miller, a retired farmer who wrote a history of Colchester County, archivist James Martell, and professor A. A. MacKenzie eased my path in Nova Scotia. Thanks to Miller the eighteenth century Ulstermen have been studied, while Martell's work on immigration in the province between 1815 and 1838 was invaluable. MacKenzie told much about Cape Breton's Irish. Brendan O'Grady of UPEI and Peter McGuigan opened doors to my research in Prince Edward Island through their detailed study of the Irish there. The writings of the late Daniel Johnson and of professors Peter Toner and William Spray not only published records about the Irish, but served to provide me with several insights. It is not Danny's fault that only the ships from Ulster recorded the home towns of their passengers. From overseas there is the prolific output of Brian Mitchell in Ireland and of David Dobson in Scotland. My frequent recourse to all of these gentlemen is attested in the many footnotes throughout this work.

Thanks to my late friend, Cyril Byrne, I have not continued to sit on the information about the Irish that had been growing in my office for years. He urged me to take the plunge. My sister, Carolyn Smedley, and my wife Pam have read the text, and saved me from sins of omission and commission, and asked the intelligent questions that an author needs to have. My thanks to all.

Terrence M. Punch, CM, FIGRS, FRSAI, St. Columba's Day, 2012

II - IRELAND'S MOUNTING DEMOGRAPHIC CRISIS

Eighty years ago, William Forbes Adams wrote of Ireland that "the scourges of disease, famine, and civil disorder descended with pitiless regularity upon the land, and in the half century that followed [1815], three million of the citizens left the country . . . and it was to America that the victims looked as to a promised land. . . . Other factors – familiarity with the attractions of America, and an established interest in the carrying of passengers – played their part, but it is in the state of Ireland that we must look first for the causes of emigration . . ."[1]

A good introduction to the concept of immigrant agencies may be found in Marianne S. Wokeck, *Trade in Strangers* . . .[2] One type of agent collected emigrant parties and hired vessels to transport them to America, while other agents represented shippers in search of passengers to fill their hulls on return voyages to North America from which they imported cargoes to Britain and the European continent. During the years of the Great Famine, some landlords chartered vessels to carry away surplus tenants who would otherwise have starved to death, or whose maintenance the landowner could not or would not accept. What really determined the course of the emigrant trade was the business interests of the merchants who owned the vessels. A westbound shipment of emigrants would be taken to where the vessel had the best chance of picking up an eastbound cargo. The timber trade brought vessels to Miramichi, Pictou, and Saint John in particular, and to a lesser extent to Halifax, St. Andrews, and Prince Edward Island.

The Great Famine of the late 1840s and Irish political nationalism have long attracted more ink than the more basic issues of infrastructure besetting Ireland and its people in the century before the mass emigrations of the mid-nineteenth century. The more pervasive underlying factors influencing emigration from Ireland have not received the attention they deserve. These may be grouped together under two headings: rapid population growth, and the capacity of Ireland to support the burgeoning multitudes of what was predominantly a peasant population.

"Between sixty and seventy years before the famine the population of Ireland began and continued to increase at a rate previously unknown in the history of Europe. . . . It is . . . agreed by all authorities that about the year 1780 the population of Ireland began to take an extraordinary upward leap. The increase between 1779 and 1841 has been placed at the almost incredible figure of 172 per cent."[3] The population growth can be demonstrated by listing some estimates and census figures over the period in question, as per Table 1 on the next page:[4]

---

[1] William Forbes Adams, *Ireland and Irish Emigration to the New World From 1815 to the Famine*. (New Haven: Yale University Press, 1932), p. 2.

[2] Marianne S. Wokeck, *Trade in Strangers; The Beginnings of Mass Migration to North America* (University Park, PA: The Pennsylvania State University Press, 1999), pp. 32 - 34, 196.

[3] Cecil Woodham-Smith, *The Great Hunger; Ireland 1845 - 1849* (New York: Harper & Row, Publishers, 1962), p. 29.

[4] The 1788 and 1813 figures are from Adams, p. 4. 1821 and 1831 are census figures quoted by Samuel Lewis in his description of Ireland, published in 1837. The census returns for 1841 and 1851 are taken from Terry Coleman, *Passage to America*. (Harmondsworth: Penguin Books, 1974), p. 160. The 1841 census is considered the most accurate of the figures cited. Since the population of Ireland in 1712 has been estimated as 2,800,000, this rapid growth may have begun well before 1788. Historians "are not in total agreement as to why this growth came about." - Robert L. Grace, *The Irish in Quebec; An Introduction to the Historiography* (Québec: Institut québécois de recherche sur la culture, 1993), p. 27.

Table 1 - Irish Population, 1788 - 1841

1788 estimate	4,040,000
1813 unofficial census	5,937,856 (47% increase in 25 years)
1821 census	6,350,420 (7% increase in 8 years)
1831 census	7,282,613 (15% increase in 10 years)
1841 census	8,175,124 (12% increase in 10 years)

These statistics indicate a probable population growth of 4,135,124 people within 53 years. That is to say that the number of inhabitants of Ireland had more than doubled within two generations. Nor can it be claimed that this is the full picture. This was a predominantly rural population. In 1700, 7 per cent of the Irish people lived in a community having as many as 1,500 inhabitants, a proportion that reached 14 per cent only by 1841, In the latter year, only one Irish person in five lived in a community of 20 houses or more.[5]

The great majority were dependent upon what they could grow to feed themselves. In short, a peasant subsistence economy confronted a pattern of land ownership by landlords who, with their agents, were intent on turning a profit from their productions in a market economy. In one generation between 1813/1821 and 1841 the number of people per square mile of arable land, i.e., suitable for crops or grazing, rose considerably, and the growth was most serious in the poorest areas for food production, as Table 2 indicates.

Table 2 - People per Square Mile of Arable Land[6]

1813/1821	Province	1841	Increase
368	Ulster	434	+ 66 (18%)
320	Connaught	411	+ 91 (29%)
320	Munster	396	+ 76 (24%)
255	Leinster	281	+ 26 (10%)

A square mile consists of 640 acres. In a good year 1½ acres could grow sufficient potatoes to feed a family of five or six people. There were drawbacks to this tidy arithmetic. Every year was not a good year, and potatoes could only be kept from one harvest until the next summer at a time when cold storage and refrigeration of food were realities far in the future. Moreover, as the population grew, the subdivisions of the land shrank in extent, so much so that a system of land use known as *conacre* came into widespread use.[7]

---

[5] Kerby A. Miller, p. 35. The most rural counties in Ireland were Leitrim, Cavan, Donegal, Mayo, Monaghan, Roscommon, Longford and Fermanagh, located towards the north-western corner of Ireland.

[6] Figures derived from Adams, p. 5. The proportions of arable land to population were best in County Kildare, where 85% of the land was arable and 187 people were supported by one square mile of land. At the opposite end of the scale, the worst conditions prevailed in County Mayo, where just 36% of the area was arable, and each square mile had to support 475 people in 1841. - Ruth Dudley Edwards, *An Atlas of Irish History*, 2nd ed. (London: Methuen & Co. Ltd., 1981), p. 179. County Mayo shared with counties Kerry, Galway and Donegal the dubious distinction of having less than half of its area suitable for either crops or the grazing of livestock. Yet, these were among the counties in which population growth was greatest in the first third of the nineteenth century.

[7] *Atlas of the Irish Rural Landscape, F. H. A.* Aalen, Kevin Whelan and Matthew Stout, eds. (Toronto: University of Toronto Press, 1997), pp. 85 - 86, offers an excellent discussion of the increasing dependence in Ireland's poorest people on the potato, three million by 1830.

"Conacre was a contract by which the use of a portion of land was let, to grow one crop. Conacre was not a lease but a licence to occupy. . . Very small portions of land were let in conacre; in Tipperary, a quarter-acre was more common than half an acre; in Queen's County [Leix], it was reckoned that half an acre would support a labourer's family."[8] This picture must be modified by considering that rents on good ground were from £6 to £ 7 an acre, but perhaps half of that for poor ground. Even that was high when we realize that "every year the nearly two and a half million labourers . . . had no regular employment."[9] Most of those adult "labourers" had children. Even at a modest estimate of two children per couple, about five million Irish people lived precariously on a small plot of land dependent upon the success of the potato crop. That population was growing rapidly, but the amount of land available for crops was virtually stationary.

The carrying capacity of Erin to feed its children had been reached and surpassed. The classic remedies for over-population were war, epidemic disease and migration of some of the extra people to another area offering resources upon which they could subsist. Sometimes, new land could be rendered arable through clearing of forest or drainage of marshland, neither of which was a viable option for the Irish peasantry. Even had Ireland been free of outside domination, the surplus population would have had to emigrate or perish.

Until the 1840s Ireland had been spared the spectre of island-wide starvation, as the crop failures did not run along end-to-end for several years across the country. In 1807 half the crop was lost through frost. In 1821 and 1822 the southern and western areas of Ireland had crop failures. Counties Mayo, Galway and Donegal lost their potato crops in 1830 and 1831. In many districts dry rot and curl[10] destroyed crops in the years between 1832 and 1837, notably in Ulster in 1835. Other poor harvests followed in 1839, 1841 and 1844. By late 1845 it was apparent that Ireland was about to experience the worst potato harvest in memory. The potato blight from North America had reached the British Isles. In Ireland, where dependence upon the monoculture of potatoes was all that stood between the mass of the rural people and famine, disaster loomed, and death and chaotic emigration took charge by 1846.[11]

The population of Ireland fell from 8,175,124 in 1841 to 6,552,385 in 1851, thanks almost entirely to the disaster of the Great Famine. The "Census Commissioners calculated that, at the normal rate of increase, the total should have been 9,018,799, so that a loss of at least 2½ million persons had taken place. Between 1846 and 1851, nearly a million persons emigrated, and it appears that, roughly, about a million and a half perished during the famine, of hunger, diseases brought on by hunger, and fever."[12] As if that were not enough, a further 822,000 Irish emigrated

---

[8] Woodham-Smith, p. 34.

[9] Woodham-Smith, p. 35.

[10] Curl is a plant disease, one symptom of which is the curling of the leaves of the plant, after which they frequently turn colour and rot. By comparison, blight means that the tubers may rot below ground while the visible part of the plant appears to be normal. The blight that destroyed Ireland's potatoes was *phytophthora infestans*, a parasitic fungus.

[11] Woodham-Smith, pp. 38 - 43, provides a good description of the onset of the potato blight.

[12] Woodham-Smith, p. 411.

between 1851 and 1854.[13] The population had not recovered to a figure above that of 1788 even a century and half afterwards, while a return to the numbers of 1841 remained unattainable. In fact, there were just 5,529,438 in all of Ireland in 1998/2001, not yet up to the estimated population in 1813. North America, including the Maritime Provinces, counts millions with Irish origins, probably more than the number today residing in the Irish homeland.

Table 3 presents the population figures from the censuses of Ireland taken in 1821 and 1831, a time during which considerable emigration to and through the Maritime Provinces was occurring. The figures are presented on a county-by-county basis, and arranged within the four historic provinces of Ireland. The growth over the decade 1821 - 1831 is presented both in numbers and as a percentage. The 1936/1937 census figures of these areas are given. These reveal that only two of the thirty-two counties could claim a population in the 1930s as great as that of a century before. The exceptions owe entirely to the fact that Belfast in County Antrim developed as an industrial hub and, after 1922, as the capital of Northern Ireland. Dublin in the Irish Republic likewise grew as the capital of the country and as its administrative, economic and social centre.

City status did not guarantee population growth. Cork, for example, fell from 107,007 in 1831 to 80,765 (21 %) a century later, while Limerick declined from 66,554 to 41,061 (38 %) in the same period. Even more markedly, Galway shrank from 33,120 in 1831 to just 18,294 in 1936, a loss of 14,826 (44. 5%). More drastic still was Kilkenny which plummeted from 23,741 to 10,237 (57%) during that time. The conclusion has to be drawn that the famine and emigration of the 1840s inflicted a demographic scar on Ireland from which it is still recovering. Meanwhile, populations of Irish descent have grown up across North America, not least of all in the Maritime Provinces of Canada, one of the funnels into the continent for tens of thousands of Ireland's children, Catholic and Protestant, northern and southern. Their millions of descendants search back to find the path, which is a reason why books such as this one are written to try to help.

The search for this path into the past is frequently an uncertain journey. No one can know how many Patrick Murphys or Mary Dohertys left Ireland in search of a future in North America. Their trail is probably cold. They may be a name on one of the relatively few passenger lists or in the records of a customs house or immigration agent. Since they often do not figure in such documents, the researcher must begin the toilsome task of narrowing down the possibilities of time and place.

It has been observed by historians that the past was a foreign country; they did things differently there. Human nature has not altered much through the centuries, but the means of doing things have. Modern armies do not rely on archers carrying bow and arrows, nor ride into action astride a destrier. The foods we have available for our table seldom, if ever, nourished Irish folk two centuries ago. Similarly, travel meant using the muscle power of man or beast, or the use of sails to carry people and their goods across waters too wide and too deep to ford. Until the middle of the nineteenth century most emigration was by sailing vessel. Steamships and railways were beginning to assume the burden of wind-and muscle-power, but down to the 1850s Irish people followed traditional means of getting about. For intending emigrants, most of them poor, many of them malnourished, emigration involved reaching the nearest seaport. The area served by each port was its hinterland, or catchment area.

---

[13] Coleman, p. 160.

Table 3 - Irish Population by Counties, 1821 - 1831

County	1821	1831	Change	+ %	1936/37
Antrim	262,860	316,909	+ 54,049	+ 20.56	635,535
Armagh	197,427	220,134	+ 22,707	+ 11.50	108,815
Cavan	195,076	228,050	+ 32,974	+ 16.90	76,670
Donegal	248,270	291,014	+ 42,834	+ 17.25	142,310
Down	325,410	352,012	+ 26,602	+ 8.17	210,687
Fermanagh	130,997	149,555	+ 18,558	+ 14.17	54,569
Londonderry	193,869	222,012	+ 28,143	+ 14.52	142,736
Monaghan	174,697	195,536	+ 20,839	+ 11.93	61,289
Tyrone	261,865	302,943	+ 41,078	+ 15.70	127,586
ULSTER	**1,990,471**	**2,278,255**	**+ 281,784**	**+ 14.16%**	**1,560,034**
Galway	309,599	381,564	+ 71,965	+ 23.24	168,198
Leitrim	124,785	141,303	+ 16,518	+ 13.28	50,908
Mayo	293,112	367,956	+ 74,844	+ 25.53	161,349
Roscommon	208,729	249,613	+ 40,884	+ 19.59	77,566
Sligo	146,229	171,508	+ 25,279	+ 17.29	67,447
CONNAUGHT	**1,082,456**	**1,311,944**	**+ 229,488**	**+ 21.20%**	**525,468**
Clare	208,089	258,262	+ 50,173	+ 24.11	89,879
Cork	629,786	700,359	+ 70,573	+ 11.21	355,957
Kerry	216,185	263,126	+ 46,573	+ 21.71	139,834
Limerick	218,432	248,201	+ 29,769	+ 13.63	141,153
Tipperary	346,896	402,363	+ 55,467	+ 16.00	137,835
Waterford	127,842	148,233	+ 20,381	+ 15.94	77,614
MUNSTER	**1,747,230**	**1,671,770**	**+ 273,414**	**+ 15.65%**	**924,272**
Carlow	78,952	81,988	+ 3,036	+ 3.85	34,452
Dublin	150,011	183,042	+ 33,031	+ 22.02	586,925
Kildare	99,065	108,424	+ 9,359	+ 9.45	57,892
Kilkenny	158,716	169,945	+ 11,229	+ 7.07	68,614
Leix (Queen's)	134,275	145,851	+ 11,576	+ 8.62	50,109
Longford	107,570	112,558	+ 4,988	+ 4.64	37,847
Louth	101,011	107,481	+ 6,470	+ 6.41	64,339
Meath	159,183	176,926	+ 19,643	+ 12.34	61,405
Offaly (King's)	131,088	144,225	+ 13,137	+ 10.02	51,308
Westmeath	128,819	136,872	+ 8,053	+ 6.25	54,706
Wexford	170,806	182,991	+ 12,185	+ 7.13	94,245
Wicklow	110,767	121,557	+ 10,790	+ 9.74	58,569
LEINSTER	**1,530,263**	**1,670,770**	**+ 141,507**	**+ 9.25%**	**1,220,411**
IRELAND	**6,350,420**	**7,282,613**	**+ 932,193**	**+ 14.68%**	**4,248,185**

III- THE CONCEPT OF CATCHMENT AREAS

Before a system of railways connected major ports with the countryside of Ireland, people were obliged to walk or travel by cart to an emigration port as the first stage of their journey.[1] Many of those emigrants had rarely, if ever, traveled more than eight or ten miles from their birthplace. Accordingly, their geographical knowledge was sketchy at best. Few had any idea of the precise location of Halifax, Saint John, Boston or Philadelphia, which is not surprising. The modern researcher must realize that many emigrants of two centuries ago were little better informed of how to get from their home village to a port such as Londonderry or Waterford. In some instances it was possible to follow on foot down a stream to a river where some type of water craft was available to transport them to a seaport at or near the river mouth. The two classic examples of a harbour reached from a hinterland or catchment area were Waterford and Londonderry.

Waterford had been for many years an important harbour with connections to the ports of North America. Waterford Harbour was known as the *Confluence* because it was the meeting place of the major river system of south-eastern Ireland. The Barrow and the Nore rivers met above New Ross in County Wexford, having drained large parts of counties Kilkenny, Carlow and Leix (formerly Queens County). Together they flowed south towards the Confluence where they joined the River Suir which skirted much of County Tipperary and formed the southern border of that and County Kilkenny. Map 1 shows the many towns which were located beside, or were very close to, those rivers. Somewhere in the neighbourhood of 500 people from those towns settled in Halifax, Nova Scotia, before 1845. This figure does not include those emigrants who passed through Halifax after a stay of one to several years, nor does it count the dozens of Irish from small villages and townlands within the catchment area.

In Halifax, 4,185 of the 7,440 Irish-born Catholics married or buried between 1825 and 1903 hailed from Waterford's riparian hinterland. That accounts for more than half of Halifax's Irish immigrants during the nineteenth century.[2] This pattern of origin owes something to the fact that many emigrants were two-boaters; they came out first from that part of Ireland to Newfoundland and, finding insufficient economic opportunities there, they moved on to Nova Scotia and, to a lesser extent, Prince Edward Island.

The emigrants to Prince Edward Island who came out directly from Ireland did not, as a rule, come from areas served by the two major river systems of Ireland, but from counties Monaghan and Cork, the first of which was served by the ports of Newry and Warrenpoint, and the latter by the ports of Cork, Kinsale and Youghal.

These logistical facts of emigrant life go a fair way towards explaining why the several host communities within the Maritime Provinces acquired populations derived from different home districts in Ireland. The areas served by shipping from ports in the southern parts of Ireland received a higher proportion of Catholic emigrants. Once this is realized, the preponderance of vessels reaching Saint John, New Brunswick, from Londonderry and Belfast in the north of Ireland suggests that the Irish landing from those ports will include a Protestant majority, whether or not they remained in New Brunswick or proceeded to the United States as many did.

---

[1] No integrated program of road building existed in Ireland before 1820. Railways in Ireland developed after 1834, but much of the west was without track as late as 1860 - Aalen, F. H. A., *et al.*, *Atlas of the Irish Rural Landscape.* (Toronto: University of Toronto Press, 1997), pp. 206 - 213.

[2] Terrence M. Punch, *Irish Halifax: The Immigrant Generation, 1815 - 1859* (Halifax: International Education Centre, Saint Mary's University, 1981), pp. 10 - 13.

Maps 1 and 2 show the hinterland or riparian catchment areas of those two major Irish ports of Waterford in the south-east and Londonderry in the north-west. A third map was prepared to illustrate the influence of a river system on the path taken by Irish emigrants during the late 1840s.

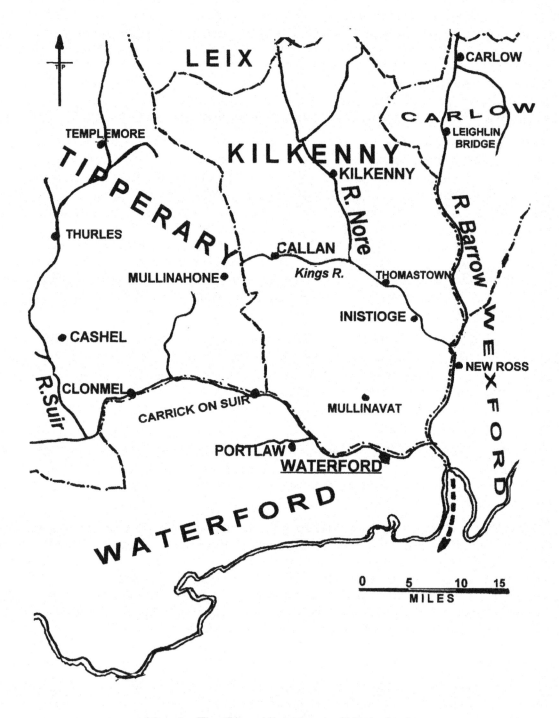

Map 1 - The River Hinterland of Waterford

The city of Londonderry (anciently Derry: place of the oak) is situated near the mouth of the River Foyle which is formed by the confluence near Strabane of the rivers Finn from the west, and the Mourne from the south-east. Another stream, the River Faughan, meets the Foyle just as it enters Lough Foyle, an arm of the Atlantic Ocean. This circumstance determined that Londonderry would become the major port for a considerable area of hinterland south, east and west of itself.

Londonderry served as the seaport for counties Tyrone and Fermanagh, and for much of the counties Donegal and Londonderry. Before the development of a system of large-scale public transportation, people and goods bound out of north-western Ireland converged on the city to take a ship from that harbour.

Thanks to this geographic fact, genealogists who learn that a ship departed Londonderry for a North American port – Québec, Saint John, Philadelphia or New York – may consider the most likely places of origins of the passengers in those vessels to have been counties Donegal, Fermanagh, Londonderry or Tyrone. Some major contributors of emigrants in the 1840s were parishes such as Templemore (Londonderry), Castlederg/Urney and Clogherny (Tyrone), Clonmany, Donaghmore and Fahan Lower/Buncrana (Donegal), Enniskillen and Magheracolmoney (Fermanagh).

HINTERLAND OF THE PORT OF LONDONDERRY

Map 2

In the three seasons, 1847-48-49 – Famine years – thirteen vessels carried 3,328 Irish emigrants between Londonderry and Saint John, New Brunswick. Of these 242 (7.2%) cannot be linked to a home community within the four county catchment area, 74 of them (2.2%) being drawn from Leitrim, Antrim, Down, Belfast, Sligo, Leix or Scotland. In 168 cases no origin was stated or there were several places of the same name and it is not known from which the people came. County Donegal supplied 1,354 of the passengers, while County Londonderry was home to 758, Tyrone to 655, and Fermanagh to 320. Collectively, the four-county catchment area supplied 3,087 (92.8%) of the emigrant traffic from the port of Londonderry. Map 3 shows the geographic pattern of the emigration to New Brunswick from Londonderry.

It is worth noting that in 1831 Buncrana, County Donegal, was home to 1,059 people, and in the three years 1847-1849 sent 94 people to Saint John. That was about 9% of its population. A more dramatic illustration of how deep-reaching the emigration was can be seen by looking at the figures concerning Castlederg in County Tyrone. In 1831 it had a population of 575, and in 1847 - 1849, 127 people from Castlederg emigrated to Saint John, that is, about 22% of everyone in the community.[3]

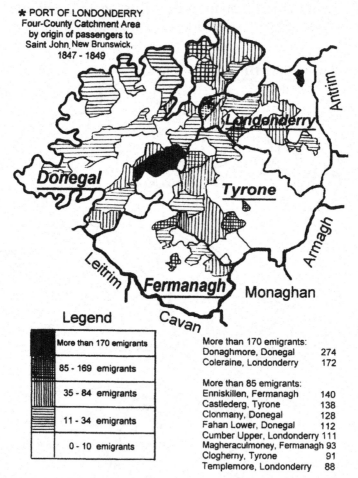

Map 3 - Emigration from Londonderry to Saint John, New Brunswick, 1847 - 1849

---

[3] The 1831 census figures are taken from Samuel Lewis, *A Topographical Dictionary of Ireland* (London: 1837), Volume I, pp. 229, 295.

IV - THE IRISH PORTS IN 1837

Despite the importance of Waterford and Londonderry to the story of Irish emigration to Maritime Canada, they were perhaps involved in only about one-quarter of all the movement. Cork, which had no system of navigable rivers to compare with those ports, sent more ships to the region than either of those other harbours. Before presenting a numerical breakdown of the voyages by point and date of departure, it is helpful to note their location on Map 4, and read what a contemporary publication says about those ports.

Samuel Lewis published his two-volume work, *A Topographical Dictionary of Ireland*, in London in 1837.[1] A brief extract from the entries for the several ports mentioned in Table 4a (pp. 18 - 19) is intended to locate them geographically in Ireland and to indicate the civil parish(es) within which each was situated. Since many Irish records were created by civil parish, this can help focus genealogical research. In the extracts that follow, the reference to Lewis is presented in parentheses, e.g. (Lewis I, p. 1). Note the many references to North America.

Map 4 - Emigration Ports, Ireland to Maritime Canada

---

[1] In the fashion of the time, the full title was a combination of advertising blurb and introductory description. It reads, *A Topographical Dictionary of Ireland, comprising the several counties, cities, boroughs, corporate, market, and post towns, parishes, and villages, with Historical and Statistical Descriptions, embellished with engravings of the arms of the cities, bishopricks, corporate towns and boroughs, and the seals of the several municipal corporations.* The work forms part of a CD available at www.genealogical.com

BALLINA, a sea-port, market, and post-town, in the parish of Kilmoremoy, barony of Tyrawley, county of Mayo . . . 5,510 inhabitants . . . The town is beautifully situated on the river Moy, by which it is separated from the county of Sligo; it . . . contains about 1200 houses . . . The river Moy . . . is navigable from the sea, about six miles distant, for vessels not drawing more than 11 feet of water, to within a mile and a half of the town. (Lewis I, pp. 104 - 105)

BALLYSHANNON, a sea-port, market, and post-town, partly in the parish of Innismacsaint, but chiefly in that of Kilbarron, barony of Tyrhugh, county of Donegal . . . 3,775 inhabitants . . . The town is situated at the . . . the mouth of the river Erne, . . . and in 1831 contained 689 houses, of which 287 are in the parish of Innismacsaint . . . Here is a small custom-house . . . The town is favourably situated for commerce and manufactures, having a large population and a fertile country around it; it is within four miles of Lough Erne, which embraces an inland navigation of more than fifty miles through the richest part of Ireland. . . . The harbour . . . has been rendered accessible to vessels of 250 tons' burden. This great improvement . . . will probably render this place a respectable port. (Lewis I, pp. 165 - 166)

BALTIMORE, a village and sea-port . . . in the parish of Tullagh, Eastern Division of the barony of West Carbery, county of Cork . . . 7 miles from Skibbereen; . . . 459 inhabitants. . . In 1835, nine vessels entered inwards, and the same number cleared outwards either with passengers or ballast . . . The jurisdiction of the port . . . includes the creeks or harbours of Bearhaven, Bantry, Crookhaven, Baltimore, and Castle-Townsend. (Lewis I, pp. 172 - 173)

BANTRY, a sea-port, market, and post-town, in the parish of Kilmocomogue, barony of Bantry, county of Cork . . . 4,275 inhabitants . . . The approaches, with the exception of the new mail coach road along the margin of the bay, are steep and incommodious . . . A new . . . line of road is in progress from Kenmare to Bantry, through Glengariff. (Lewis I, pp. 185 - 187)

BELFAST, a sea-port, borough, market-town, and parish, partly in the barony of Lower [Belfast], but chiefly in that of Upper Belfast, county of Antrim . . . containing in 1821, 44,177, and in 1831, 60,388 inhabitants, . . . and within three years after the latter census the population of the parish had increased nearly 7,000 more . . . The town is advantageously situated on the western bank of the river Lagan . . .the total number of houses 8,022 . . . The trade with the United States and with British North America is also very considerable . . . the imports are timbers and staves . . . In 1835, the [port] cleared 76 [vessels], the latter taking out 2,675 emigrants, of whom 1,824 were destined for the British American colonies, and 851 for the United States. (Lewis I, pp. 191 - 201)

CASTLETOWN-BEARHAVEN, a post-town in the parish of Kilaconenagh, barony of Bere, county of Cork . . 1,468 inhabitants . . . The town has grown up since the discovery of the Allhais copper mines in 1812, as, prior to that time, it consisted of only a few fishermen's cabins, but now it contains more than 300 houses . . . and is rapidly increasing. (Lewis I, pp. 307 - 308)

COLERAINE, a sea-port, borough, market, and post-town, and a parish, in the barony or district called the town and liberties of Coleraine, county of Londonderry . . . 7,646 inhabitants, of which . . . 1978 are in the parish of Killowen, and 5,668 in the town [which] is situated on the east bank of the river Bann, about three miles from its influx into the sea . . . Its chief imports are timber. . . the entrance to the river is obstructed by a bar of shifting sand . . . To remedy this inconvenience, a new harbour was constructed at Portrush, about 4½ miles from the town . . . vessels drawing 17 feet can enter and ride in perfect safety. (Lewis I, pp. 384 - 388)

CORK, a sea-port, city, and a county of itself, and the head of a diocese, locally in the county of Cork, of which it is the capital . . . 107,007 inhabitants . . . on the island formed by the [river] Lee . . . 8,212 dwelling houses . . . The Baltic trade in timber was gradually declining until the practice of bringing it in through Halifax at the colonial duty of 10 s[hillings] per load was resorted to . . . Large quantities of timber are brought from Canada, the trade to which is flourishing; the staves and potashes formerly brought from New York and Baltimore now come mostly from Quebec. . . though several cargoes . . . have been recently imported from the United States via St. John's (New Brunswick) and Nova Scotia. (Lewis I, pp. 408 - 420)

DINGLE, an incorporated sea-port, market, and post-town . . . and a parish, in the barony of Corkaguiney, county of Kerry . . . 6,719 inhabitants . . . Dingle is situated , , , on the northen coast of the bay of the same name, an inlet of which forms the harbour [which] . . . is well adapted for vessels of moderate burden, but not being discoverable from the sea, is what is nautically termed a 'blind' one; it is, however, extremely difficult of access during a strong west wind, and vessels . . . running to the eastward are in danger of being lost on Castlemaine bar. (Lewis I, pp. 460 - 462)

DONAGHADEE, a sea-port and post-town, and a parish, in the barony of Ardes, county of Down . . . 7,627 inhabitants, of which 2,986 are in the town. (Lewis I, pp. 465 - 466)

DONEGAL, a sea-port, market, and post-town, and parish in the barony of Tyrhugh, county of Donegal . . . 6,260 inhabitants, of which number, 830 are in the town . . . [which] is pleasantly situated at the mouth of the river Esk . . . The harbour is formed by a pool on the east side of the peninsula of Durin, where, at the distance of two miles below the town, small vessels may ride in two or three fathoms of water, about half a cable's length from the shore.[2] (Lewis I, pp. 476 - 477)

DROGHEDA, a sea-port, borough, and market-town, and a county of itself, locally in the county of Louth . . . 57 miles from Belfast, and 23 from Dublin; containing 17,365 inhabitants, of which number, 15,138 are in the town . . . [which] is advantageously situated on the great road from Dublin to Belfast, and on the river Boyne, which discharges into the Irish Sea about three miles below, and by which it is divided into two unequal portions . . . The port carries on a very extensive trade chiefly with Canada, Nova Scotia, and New Brunswick. [a railway from Dublin is in prospect] (Lewis I, pp. 498 - 502)

DUBLIN, . . . a city and county of itself, containing in 1831, 265,316 inhabitants, of which number, 204,155 are within the [city proper] . . . It is situated at the . . . mouth of the [river] Liffey, which passes nearly through the middle of it . . . With British America the trade is very great in timber, as a return cargo of vessels sailing thither from Dublin with emigrants. With Newfoundland there is no direct trade, the cod and seal oil are imported from Liverpool or brought by canal from Waterford, which has a direct trade with Newfoundland; dried cod and ling [herring] being much used in the southern counties, but not much in the northern or middle. (Lewis I, pp. 525 - 538)

DUNGARVAN, a sea-port, borough, market, and post-town, and a parish, in the barony of Decies-without-Drum, county of Waterford . . . 12,450 inhabitants, of which number, 8,386 are in the town and borough . . . The town, which contains 1,570 houses, is situated at the head of a spacious bay . . . on a peninsula formed by two arms of the bay . . . The harbour affords good shelter for vessels drawing from 14 or 15 feet of water at any time of the tide. (Lewis I, pp. 577 - 579)

---

[2] A cable's length was about 100 fathoms. A fathom is six feet, so half a cable's length would be approximately 300 feet.

GALWAY, a sea-port, borough, and market-town, and a county of itself, locally between the baronies of Clare, Dunkellin, and Moycullen, county of Galway . . . 33,120 inhabitants . . . The town is most advantageously situated at the head of the spacious bay to which it gives name, and at the mouth of a river coming from Lough Corrib . . . The total number of houses in 1831 was 2,683. (Lewis I, pp. 645 - 649)

KILLALA, a sea-port, market, and post-town, and parish, and the seat of a diocese, in the barony of Tyrawley, county of Mayo . . . 3,875 inhabitants, of which number, 1,125 are in the town . . . The town is situated on a bay of the same name, and on the west bank of the river Moy; it contains about 200 houses . . . From the improvements of the port of Ballina, what formerly came into this port for the supply of that town is conveyed thither direct by the river Moy . . . The harbour affords good and safe anchorage for vessels drawing eight or nine feet of water, and . . . 12 feet . . . in high water.   (Lewis II, pp. 119 - 120)

KILLYBEGS, a sea-port, market, and post-town, and a parish . . . in the barony of Boylagh, but chiefly in that of Bannagh, county of Donegal . . . 4,287 inhabitants, of which number, 724 are in the town . . . [which] is situated at the head of a beautiful and safe harbour . . . and at the base of a most mountainous tract extending northward, and consists of 126 houses . . . The harbour is nearly circular in form, well sheltered, and accessible to ships of considerable burden . . . the best anchorage is in 8½ fathoms [51 feet] near the west side.   (Lewis II, pp. 158 - 159)

KINSALE, a sea-port, borough, and market-town, in the barony of Kinsale, county of Cork . . . 7,823 inhabitants, of which number, 6,897 are in the town . . . [which] is pleasantly and advantageously situated near the mouth of the river Bandon . . . which here forms a capacious and secure harbour . . . The total number of houses . . . was, in 1831, 1,266 . . . The trade of the port . . . consists chiefly in the export of agricultural produce, and the import of timber from British America . . . the river Bandon is navigable for vessels of 200 tons to Colliere's quay, 12 miles above the town.   (Lewis II, pp. 230 - 234)

LARNE, a sea-port, market, and post-town, and a parish, in the barony of Upper Glenarm, county of Antrim . . . 3,182 inhabitants, of which number, 2,616 are in the town . . . [which] is beautifully situated on the shore of Lough Larne . . . and is divided into the old and new towns, consisting together of 482 houses . . . About the middle of the last century [i.e. 1750] this was the only port from which emigrant vessels sailed. The present trade consists . . . in the importation of North American timber.   (Lewis II, pp. 245 - 246)

LIMERICK, a city . . . situated on the river Shannon, locally in the county of Limerick (of which it is the capital) . . . containing in 1821, 59,045, and in 1831, 66, 554 inhabitants, of which number, 44,100 are in the city and suburbs . . . The situation of Limerick, about sixty Irish miles from the sea, and its extent of river navigation, render the port an object of peculiar importance; but . . . it is too high up the river . . . with insufficient water for large vessels in the higher parts of the channel . . . [in 1833 planning for port improvements began].   (Lewis II, pp. 265 - 277)

LONDONDERRY, a city and port, in the parish of Templemore, and county of Londonderry . . . 10,130 inhabitants . . . the city is advantageously situated on the western or Donegal side of the river Foyle, about five statutory miles above the point where it spreads into Lough Foyle . . . Imports tobacco from the United States, from which ships come chiefly to take out emigrants, who resort to this part from the inland districts in great numbers.   (Lewis II, pp. 297 - 303)

NEW ROSS, an inland port, borough and market-town, and a parish, partly in the barony of Shelburne, but chiefly in that of Bantry, county of Wexford . . . 7,523 inhabitants, of which number, 5,011 are in the town and borough . . . The town is beautifully situated on the side of a hill declining to the Ross river (formed hy the Nore and Barrow, which unite about one mile to the north of it) . . . The total number of houses, in 1831, was 1,040 . . . The town is well situated for trade, the river being navigable up to it at high tides for vessels of 500 or 600 tons' burden . . . The principal export trade is in grain, flour, livestock, bacon, and butter. Porter, ale and beer are sent to Newfoundland, whence fish and oil are received in return; a considerable trade in timber is carried on with the Baltic and with North America, the latter resulting from the system of emigration from this port, which for several years has been very considerable. (Lewis II, pp. 530 - 533)

NEWRY, a sea-port, borough, market and post-town, and a parish, partly in the barony of Oneilland West, and partly in that of Upper Orior, county of Armagh . . . 30 miles from Belfast, and 50 from Dublin . . . 24,557 inhabitants, of which number, 13,134 are in the town . . . A new line of road has been opened, and an excellent approach formed from Warrenpoint, where the river extends into the bay . . . [36 miles of dredging and canals from the coast to Lough Neagh] . . . Vessels of the greatest draught can come up to Warrenpoint, within five miles of the town, where they can ride in from 6 to 8 fathoms of water in all states of the tide in perfect security . . . The chief . . . trade is with the United States and British North America . . . [in] timber and staves. (Lewis II, p. 430 - 434)

SLIGO, a sea-port, assize, borough, market and post-town, in the barony of Upper Carbery, county of Sligo . . . 15,152 inhabitants . . . It is advantageously situated on the . . . [navigable] river Garvogue, which connects Lough Gill with the bay of Sligo . . . The greater part of the town is in the parish of St. John, . . . the smaller portion in the parish of Calry. . . The maritime trade of the port is the chief source of prosperity of the town. (Lewis II, pp. 568 - 570)

STRANGFORD, a small sea-port and post-town, in the parish of Ballyculter, county of Down . . . 583 inhabitants . . . only 119 houses . . . Strangford Lough is a safe and deep harbour, admitting vessels of the largest draught. (Lewis II, pp. 579 - 580)

TRALEE, a borough, assize, sea-port, market and post-town, in the barony of Trughanacmy, county of Kerry . . . 11,021 inhabitants, of which number, 9,568 are in the town . . . [which] contained in 1831, 1,354 houses . . . [The extreme shallowness of river Leigh] prevents the approach of vessels exceeding 50 or 60 tons nearer than Blennerville, about 1½ miles distant, and obliges larger vessels to lie . . . off Fenit Point, a distance of about five miles. To remedy this defect [an act passed in 1829 created] a corporate board for the purpose of constructing a navigable canal adequate to bring up large vessels to the town. When finished, vessels of 300 tons' burden will be enabled to discharge at the quay. (Lewis II, pp. 640 - 642)

WARRENPOINT, a sea-port, post-town, and district parish, in the barony of Upper Iveagh, county of Down . . . 5 miles from Newry . . . 2,428 inhabitants . . . In 1780 it consisted only of two houses . . . it now contains 462 houses . . . Large vessels trading to Newry are obliged to lie here, where there is deep water, good anchorage, and perfect shelter, as the further passage up the channel is intricate and dangerous . . . Plans are underway for improving . . . navigation. (Lewis II, p. 675)

WATERFORD, a sea-port, city and county of itself, and the seat of a diocese, locally in the county of Waterford, of which it is the capital . . . 28,821 inhabitants, of which number, 26,377 are in the city and suburbs . . . The city if beautifully situated on the southern bank of the [river] Suir, about 16 miles from its influx into the sea; it extends principally along the margin of the river. [much trade with Newfoundland] (Lewis II, pp. 687 - 695)

WESTPORT, a sea-port, market and post-town, in the parish of Aughaval, barony of Murrisk, county of Mayo . . .; 4,448 inhabitants. The town is situated at the south-eastern extremity of Clew Bay, and at the mouth of a small river . . . The total number of houses is 617 . . . The trade of the port . . . consists in the . . . importation of timber from America.   (Lewis II, pp. 699 - 700)

WEXFORD, a sea-port, borough, market, post and assize town, in the barony of Forth, county of Wexford . . . 10,673 inhabitants . . . The town is situated on the lower part of a hill, close to the shore of the estuary of the [river] Slaney, where it opens into the broad shallow expansion of Wexford haven. [The port was at Rosslare]   (Lewis II, pp. 707 - 711)

YOUGHAL, a sea-port, borough, and market-town . . . 11,327 inhabitants, of which number, 9,608 are in the town . . . [which] is pleasantly situated on the western shore of the harbour . . .[at the confluence of the river] Toragh and the Blackwater. The harbour is safe and commodious . . . and accessible to vessels of 500 tons' burden.   (Lewis II, pp. 725 - 730)

Table 4a - Irish Ports of Departure to the Maritime Provinces, 1749 - 1852

Irish Port	To 1816	1817-1820	1821-1832	1833-1838	1839-1844	1845-1849	1850-1852	Total
Cork	12	10	14	32	48	101	10	227
Londonderry	12	22	10	46	24	39	8	161
Waterford	2	5	26	20	17	16	1	87
Belfast	6	17	14	22	21	5	1	86
Sligo			10	18	17	29	1	75
Dublin	6	12	14	15	12	12		71
Galway			1	4	7	35	1	48
Limerick		5	3	3	8	17	1	37
Newry/Warrenpoint		3	1	9	5	8	1	27
Donegal				3	6	13	1	23
Kinsale			1	1	4	16		22
Ballyshannon		1	2	8	4	4		19
Baltimore				8	3	5		16
Castletown-Berehaven						13	1	14
Bantry				1	3	6		10
New Ross/Wexford			2	1	1	5		9
Westport					2	5		7
Youghal					1	5		6

Dingle/Tralee					2	2		4
Drogheda					1	3		4
Killala/Ballina						3	1	4
Coleraine/Ballymoney		2		1				3
Donaghadee						1		1
Dungarvan					1			1
Killybegs						1		1
Larne	1							1
Strangford				1				1

Table 4b - No specific Port of Origin in Ireland in 84 instances

Route Taken Ireland . . .	To 1816	1817-1820	1821-1832	1833-1838	1839-1844	1845-1849	1850-1852	Total
Via Newfoundland**	6	9	15	13	1			44
Ireland, no port stated	2		7		1	7		17
Via Liverpool, England					1	11		12
Via London, England	9							9
Via Glasgow, Scotland			1					1
Via the Azores		1						1
Total of tables 4a & 4b	56	87	121	206	190	363	27	1050

** Of those, 2 had originated at Waterford, 1 each in Dublin, New Ross and Cork.

See page 101 for a year-by-year tally of the voyages between Ireland and the Maritime Provinces between 1749 and 1852. Information before 1816 is sporadic, rendering it impractical to seek patterns beyond generalities, e.g., emigration diminished in wartime. A discernable boom in emigration occurred in the immediate post-war years 1817 - 1820, then movement leveled until after 1830, hitting a high in the mid-1830s. Migration ebbed into the early 1840s, and soared during the famine years 1845 - 1849. Immigration into the Maritimes directly from Ireland diminished thereafter.

Comparison of Tables 4a and 4 b (above) with Table 6 on page 109 will enable a reader to see when traffic rose and fell at either end of the transatlantic emigration path. Halifax was the leading port of entry from 1749 until about 1832, when Saint John took the lead and retained it. The areas hardest hit by the famine of the 1840s were reflected in the rise of traffic sailing from ports in County Cork (e.g., Cork, Kinsale, Castletown) and western Ireland (e.g., Sligo, Galway).

V - SHIPS FROM IRELAND TO THE MARITIMES, 1749-1852

BIBLIOGRAPHY

The bibliography serves as a key to the reference in the following lengthy listing of ships from Irish ports which came to Maritime Canada between 1749 and 1852. In order to follow the references in the tabulation, this list should be consulted. The opening date was chosen due to the fact that British settlement in the Maritimes began with the founding of Halifax in 1749. By 1852, mass migration from Ireland into most of the region had become a trickle. As steamships superseded sailing vessels, more Irish emigrants to North America were able to cross directly to the United States, and the phenomenon of the "two-boater" receded in significance.

Primary Sources

CO = Colonial Office Papers, series and volumes as shown.

NSA = Nova Scotia Archives (MG are manuscript groups; papers created by non-governmental agencies, and RG are record groups created by government departments)

PANB = Public Archives of New Brunswick. PANB/RS 555 contains the Provincial Secretary's Immigration Administration Records. Refer for some material to archives.gnb.ca/Irish/Databases/ImmigrationRecords/Documents.aspx?culture=en-CA&F=16225&S=0527&E=0748

PANS = Public Archives of Nova Scotia; now called NSA, above.

PANS Report = The annual report of the Public Archives of Nova Scotia for the year 1936.

Newspaper Sources

AR = *Acadian Recorder*, a weekly newspaper in Halifax, Nova Scotia, which regularly published a column "Shipping News"

CG = City Gazette, a newspaper in Saint John, New Brunswick

CorkC = *Cork Chronicle*, newspaper in Cork, Ireland

CP = *Colonial Patriot*, a weekly newspaper in Pictou, Nova Scotia, which often published shipping news

DE = *Daily Examiner*, a newspaper in Charlottetown, Prince Edward Island

HibC = Hibernian Chronicle, Irish newspaper

MH = *Morning Herald*, a newspaper in Halifax, Nova Scotia

NBC = *New Brunswick Courier,* a weekly newspaper in Saint John, New Brunswick, which regularly reported the arrival and departure of vessels

NBRG = New Brunswick Royal Gazette, the official newspaper of the province

NS = *The Novascotian*, a weekly newspaper in Halifax, Nova Scotia, which published shipping news

Patriot = *The Patriot*, a newspaper in Charlottetown, Prince Edward Island

PEIR = *Prince Edward Island Register*, a Charlottetown newspaper

Rgaz. = *Royal Gazette*, the official government paper at Halifax, Nova Scotia

Times = *The Times*, a newspaper at Halifax, Nova Scotia

WC = *Weekly Chronicle*, a weekly newspaper at Halifax, Nova Scotia

WO = *Weekly Observer*, a newspaper at Saint John, New Brunswick

Periodicals

Abegweit Review, an occasional journal published in Charlottetown, PEI. Specific articles cited below
Island Magazine, an occasional magazine published in Charlottetown, PEI. Vols. 16-20, 26 consulted
[Referred to as **Island Magazine, issue number**]

Books

Aalen, F. H. A., Kevin Whelan and Matthew Stout, eds. *Atlas of the Irish Rural Landscape.* Toronto: University of Toronto Press, 1997.

Adams, William Forbes. *Ireland and Irish Emigration to the New World From 1815 to the Famine.* New Haven: Yale University Press, 1932. [Referred to as **Adams/page number**]

Campey, Lucille H. *Planters, Paupers, and Pioneers; English Settlers in Atlantic Canada.* Toronto: Natural Heritage Books, 2010.

Coleman, Terry. *Passage to America.* Harmondsworth: Penguin Books, 1974.

Cowan, Helen I. *British Emigration to British North America.* Toronto: University of Toronto Press, 1928.

Cushing, J. Elizabeth, Teresa Casey, and Monica Robertson. *A Chronicle of Irish Emigration to Saint John, New Brunswick, 1847.* Saint John, NB: The New Brunswick Museum, 1979. [Referred to as **Cushing/page number**]

DesBrisay, Mather Byles, *History of the County of Lunenburg,* 2nd edition. Toronto: William Briggs, 1895.

DCB V = *The Dictionary of Canadian Biography,* Vol. V. Toronto: University of Toronto Press, 1983, page 555, entry for Alexander McNutt.

Dobson, David. *Ships from Ireland to Early America 1628-1850,* Volume I. Baltimore: Clearfield Company, Inc., 1999. [Referred to as **Dobson I/page number**].

Dobson, David. *Ships from Ireland to Early America 1628-1850,* Volume II. Baltimore: Clearfield Company, Inc., 2004. [Referred to as **Dobson II/page number**].

Dobson, David. *Ships from Ireland to Early America 1628-1850,* Volume III. Baltimore: Clearfield Company, Inc., 2010. [Referred to as **Dobson III/page number**].

Dobson, David. *Ships from Scotland to America 1628 - 1828,* Vol. IV. Baltimore: Genealogical Publishing Company, 2011.

Edwards, Ruth Dudley. *An Atlas of Irish History,* 2nd edition. London: Methuen & Co. Ltd., 1981.

Grace, Robert L. *The Irish in Quebec; An Introduction to the Historiography.* Québec: Institut québécois de recherche sur la culture, 1993.

Guillet, Edwin C. *The Great Migration; the Atlantic Crossing by Sailing Ship 1770 - 1860,* 2nd edition. Toronto: University of Toronto Press, 1963.

Houston, Cecil J., and William J. Smyth, *Irish Emigration and Canadian Settlement; Patterns, Links, & Letters.* Toronto: University of Toronto Press, 1990. [Referred to as **Houston & Smyth/page number**]

Johnson, D. F. *The St. John County Alms and Work House Records.* Saint John, NB: D. F. Johnson, 1985. [Referred to as **Alms House**]

Johnson, Daniel F. *Irish Emigration to New England Through the Port of Saint John, New Brunswick, Canada 1841 to 1849.* Clearfield Company, Inc., 1996. [Referred to as **Johnson/page number**]

Johnston, A. A. *History of the Catholic Church in Eastern Nova Scotia.* Antigonish, NS: St. Francis Xavier University Press, 1960.

Lewis, Samuel. *A Topographical Dictionary of Ireland,* 2 volumes. London, 1837.

McGregor, John. *British America,* 2 volumes. Edinburgh, 1832.

MacKenzie, A. A. *The Irish in Cape Breton.* Antigonish, NS: Formac Publishing Co. Ltd., 1979. [Referred to as **MacKenzie/page number**]

MacKinnon, Ian F. *Settlements and Churches in Nova Scotia 1749 - 1776.* Halifax: T. C. Allen, 1930.

Mannion, John J. *Irish Settlements in Eastern Canada; A Study of Cultural Transfer and Adaptation.* Toronto: University of Toronto Press, 1974.

Martell, J. S. *Immigration to and Emigration from Nova Scotia 1815-1838.* Halifax: Public Archives of Nova Scotia, 1942. [Referred to as **Martell/page number**]

Miller, Kerby A. *Emigrants and Exiles; Ireland and the Irish Exodus to North America.* New York: Oxford University Press, 1985.

Miller, Thomas. *Historical and Genealogical Record of the First Settlers of Colchester County.* Halifax: A. & W. MacKinlay, 1873 [Referred to as **Miller/page number**].

Mitchell, Brian. *Irish Passenger Lists 1847-1871.* Baltimore: Genealogical Publishing Co., Inc., 1988. [Referred to as **Mitchell/page number**]

Moyles, R. G. *"Complaints is many and various, but the odd Divil likes it".* Toronto: Peter Martin Associates Limited, 1975.

O'Grady, Brendan. *Exiles & Islanders; the Irish Settlers of Prince Edward Island*. Montréal: McGill-Queen's University Press, 2004. [Referred to as **O'Grady/page number**]

Passengers to New Brunswick: The Customs House Records – 1833, 34, 37 & 38. Saint John: The New Brunswick Genealogical Society, 1987. [Referred to as **Customs/page number**]

Power, Thomas P., ed. *The Irish in Atlantic Canada 1780-1900*. Fredericton, NB: New Ireland Press, 1991. [Referred to as **Power/page number**].

Punch, Terrence M. *Erin's Sons: Irish Arrivals in Atlantic Canada 1761 - 1853*, Vol. I. Baltimore: Genealogical Publishing Company, 2008.

Punch, Terrence M. *Erin's Sons: Irish Arrivals in Atlantic Canada 1761 - 1853*, Vol. II. Baltimore: Genealogical Publishing Company, 2009.

Punch, Terrence M. *Erin's Sons: Irish Arrivals in Atlantic Canada 1751 - 1858*, Vol. III. Baltimore: Genealogical Publishing Company, 2009.

Punch, Terrence M. *Erin's Sons: Irish Arrivals in Atlantic Canada to 1863*, Vol. IV. Baltimore: Genealogical Publishing Company, 2010.

Punch, Terrence M. *Irish Halifax: The Immigrant Generation, 1815 - 1859*. Halifax: International Education Centre, 1981.

Stewart, Gordon, and George Rawlyk. *A People Highly Favoured of God*. Toronto: Macmillan of Canada, 1972.

Taylor, Maureen A. *Rhode Island Passenger Lists*. Baltimore: Genealogical Publishing Co., Inc., 1995.

Toner, P. M., ed. *New Ireland Remembered: Historical Essays on the Irish in New Brunswick*. Fredericton: New Ireland Press, 1988

Wokeck, Marianne S. *Trade in Strangers; The Beginnings of Mass Migration to North America*. University Park, PA: The Pennsylvania State University Press, 1999.

Woodham-Smith, Cecil. *The Great Hunger; Ireland 1845 - 1849*. New York: Harper & Row, Publishers, 1962.

Articles

Acheson, T. W., "The Irish Community in Saint John 1815 - 1850," *New Ireland Remembered*. Fredericton: New Ireland Press (1988), pp. 27 - 54.

Addington, Charles, *Some Passengers from Ireland to New Brunswick, 1846* (London, ON, 1985).

Allison, D.,"Notes on the Census of 1767," *Collections of the Nova Scotia Historical Society*, Vol. VII (1891), pp. 45 - 71.

Barnett, Cleadie B., "List of the Passengers embarked in the Barque *Robert Watt* of Saint Andrew, Ralph Salliman, Master, and Who Have Contracted to be Landed at Saint Andrews, New Brunswick . . . 1837," in *We Lived: A Genealogical Newsletter of New Brunswick Sources*, No. 14 (June 1982), pp. 173 - 174.

Bates, George T., "The Great Exodus of 1749 or the Cornwallis Settlers Who Didn't," *Collections of the Nova Scotia Historical Society*, Vol. 38 (1973), pp. 27 - 62.

Clohossey, Edward A., "Excerpts from a Family History," *The Abegweit Review*, 6:1 (Spring 1988), pp. 128 - 147.

Cousins, John, "The Irish of Lot Seven," *The Abegweit Review*, Vol. 4:1 (Spring 1983), pp. 27 - 33.

Delicaet, Paul, "Passengers aboard the *Thetis*, Cork to Bathurst, New Brunswick, in April 1837," *The Irish Ancestor*, Vol. XII, Nos. 1 and 2 (1980), pp. 65 - 66.

Farmer, G. Kevin, "Making a Community in Kinkora," *The Abegweit Review*, Vol. 5:1 (Winter 1985), pp. 51 - 58.

Flewwelling, Mrs. R. G., "Immigration to and Emigration from Nova Scotia, 1839-51," *Collections of the Nova Scotia Historical Society*, Vol. 28 (1949), pp. 75 - 105. [Referred to as **Flewwelling**]

Jones, Orlo, and Douglas Fraser, "Those Elusive Immigrants," *The Island Magazine*, No. 16 (Fall-Winter 1984), pp. 36 - 41. [Referred to as **Island Magazine, 16**]

Jones, Orlo, and Douglas Fraser, "Those Elusive Immigrants," *The Island Magazine*, No. 17 (Summer 1985), pp. 33 - 37. [Referred to as **Island Magazine, 17**]

Jones, Orlo, and Douglas Fraser, "Those Elusive Immigrants," *The Island Magazine*, No. 18 (Fall-Winter 1985), pp. 29 - 35. [Referred to as **Island Magazine, 18**]

McGuigan, Peter, "From Wexford and Monaghan: the Lot 22 Irish," *The Abegweit Review*, Vol. 5:1 (Winter 1985), pp. 61 - 96.

McGuigan, Peter, " The Lot 61 Irish: settlement and stabilization," *The Abegweit Review*, Vol. 6:1 (Spring 1988), pp. 33 - 63.

O'Grady, Brendan, "The Monaghan Settlers," *The Abegweit Review*, Vol. 4:1 (Spring 1983), pp. 51 - 79. [Referred to as **Monaghan/page number**]

O'Shea, Arthur, "The Iona Parish," *The Abegweit Review*, Vol. 6:1 (Spring 1988), pp. 87 - 106.

Porter, Reginald, "The First Irish Settlers of Tignish," *The Abegweit Review*, Vol. 4:1 (Spring 1983), pp. 27 - 33.

Power, T. P., "Sources for Irish Immigration and Settlement in the Public Archives of New Brunswick, Fredericton," *The Irish in Atlantic Canada 1780 - 1900*, Thomas P. Power, ed. Fredericton: New Ireland Press, 1985, pp. 151 - 183.

Punch, Terrence M., "Finding Our Irish," *Nova Scotia Historical Review*, Vol. 6:1 (1986), pp. 41 - 63.

Punch, Terrence M.," 'Gentle as the snow on a rooftop': The Irish in Nova Scotia to 1830," *The Untold Story: The Irish in Canada*, Robert O'Driscoll & Lorna Reynolds, eds. Toronto: Celtic Arts of Canada, 1988.

Punch, Terrence M., "The Irish in Nova Scotia, before 1830," *Canadian Genealogist*, Vol. 1:3 (1979), pp. 173 - 180.

Punch Terrence M., "Newfoundland's Links with Nova Scotia," *Family History Seminar 1987*, Elsa Hochwald, ed. St. John's, NL: Newfoundland and Labrador Genealogical Society, 1988, pp. 19 - 35.

Punch, Terrence M., "Ships from Ireland to Nova Scotia, 1765-1850," *An Nasc*, Vol. 13 (Spring 2001), pp. 3 - 10. [Referred to as **An Nasc/page number**]

Spray, William A., " 'The Difficulties Came Upon Us Like a Thunderbolt': Immigrants and Fever in New Brunswick in 1847," *The Irish in Atlantic Canada 1780 - 1900*, Thomas P. Power, ed. Fredericton: New Ireland Press, 1985, pp. 107 - 126.

Spray, William A., "The Irish in Miramichi," *New Ireland Remembered*, P. M. Toner, ed. Fredericton: New Ireland Press, 1985, pp. 55 - 62.

Toner, P. M., "The Irish of New Brunswick at Mid Century: The 1851 Census," *New Ireland Remembered*, P. M. Toner, ed. Fredericton: New Ireland Press, 1988, pp. 106 - 132.

Wright, Harold E., "Partridge Island: Rediscovering the Irish Connection," *The Irish in Atlantic Canada 1780 - 1900*, Thomas P. Power, ed. Fredericton: New Ireland Press, 1985, pp. 127 - 149 [Referred to as **Wright/page number**]

SHIPS FROM IRELAND TO THE MARITIMES, 1749-1852

Month	Vessel	Port from	Port to	Passengers	Reference
			1749		
June	Alexander	London	Halifax	Yes	These ships brought
June	Baltimore	London	Halifax	Yes	the founding settlers
June	Beaufort	London	Halifax	Yes	to Halifax, N.S. There
June	Canning	London	Halifax	Yes	were 210 identifiably
June	Everley	London	Halifax	Yes	Irish people in the
June	London	London	Halifax	Yes	nine vessels. Names
June	Merry Jacks	London	Halifax	Yes	listed in *Nova Scotia*
June	Wilmington	London	Halifax	Yes	*Archives* published in
June	Winchelsea	London	Halifax	Yes	1859, pp. 506 - 557.[1]
			1750		
-	Britannia	Dublin	Halifax	Yes; servants	CO 221/28-31
-	George	Dublin	Halifax	Yes; transport	CO 221/28-31
-	Jane & Bridget	Dublin	Halifax	Yes; transport	CO 221/28-31
-	Jenny & Sally	Dublin	Halifax	troop transport	CO 221/28-31
			1761		
-	Charming Molly[2]	Cork	Halifax	-	Dobson II/24
Oct	Hopewell[3]	Londonderry	Halifax	about 300	Miller/184, 190, 199
			1762		
June	Catherine	Cork	Halifax	-	Dobson II/22
Oct	Hopewell[4]	Londonderry	Halifax	Yes	DCB V/555
Oct	Nancy	Londonderry	Halifax	170	DCB V/555

---

[1] Irish identified in *Alexander* (13), *Baltimore* (21), *Beaufort* (15), *Canning* (16), *Everley* (2), *London* (46), *Merry Jacks* (47), *Wilmington* (17), and *Winchelsea* (33). Others may have been Irish but cannot be identified as such. See Appendix I for the names of those who were definitely or probably Irish.

[2] The *Charming Molly* was captured by the French and taken to Martinique in the West Indies.

[3] Several passengers in the *Hopewell* may be identified in Thomas Miller's history of Colchester County. Specifics of where some of them came from may be found in Terrence M. Punch, *Erin's Sons: Irish Arrivals in Atlantic Canada 1761-1853* (Baltimore: Genealogical Publishing Company, 2008), Vol. I, p. 11. While the ebullient Alexander McNutt claimed 300 passengers, his detractors said that he had more like 250, perhaps 70 short of his proposed complement - CO 217, Vol. 21, folio 325. See Appendix II for the names of many of the Ulster arrivals directly from Ireland between 1761 and 1773. Mentions of a voyage to Nova Scotia by the ship *Jupiter* seem to be erroneous. Perhaps a vessel of that name went elsewhere in British North America in 1761.

[4] Although this ship was advertised to be making a voyage in 1762, it is probable that it did not do so, when McNutt, the emigration promoter, could find only 170 to go in the *Nancy*. I consider this voyage of the *Hopewell* was probably aborted. Ian F. MacKinnon, pp. 28, 31, believed that most of the 1762 group went to New Dublin, on the south shore of the province. Most of those who settled in Londonderry Township, NS, "were brought directly from Ulster."

Month	Vessel	Port from	Port to	Passengers	Reference
			1765		
May	Admiral Hawke	Londonderry	Halifax	about 50	Dobson I/2
			1766		
June	Hopewell	Londonderry	Halifax	Yes	Dobson I/72
Oct	Falls	Londonderry	Halifax	Yes	Dobson III/38
			1769		
June	Nancy	Londonderry	Halifax	-	Dobson I/106
Nov	Admiral Hawke	Londonderry	Halifax	111	MacKinnon[5]
			1771		
Aug	Hopewell	Londonderry	Halifax	Yes	Dobson I/72
–	John and James	Belfast	PEI	9 families	O'Grady/16
			1772		
July	John and James	Belfast	PEI	190	Dobson I/82
July	William and John	Belfast	PEI	106	Dobson I/151
Aug	Nancy	Londonderry	Halifax	Yes	Dobson II/94
			1773		
July	Yaward	Belfast	PEI	50 families[6]	Dobson I/153
			1774		
June	James and Mary	Larne	Ft. Cumberland	Yes	Dobson I/77
			1775		
Nov	Elizabeth[7]	Cork	PEI	Yes	Island Magazine, 18

---

[5] MacKinnon, pp. 28 - 30, lists several economic, religious and civic reasons for the Ulster emigrations of the eighteenth century, among them oppressive landlordism, English protectionism, enforced tithing to support the Anglican Church of Ireland, exclusion of Presbyterians from civil and military office until 1779, and denial of legal recognition of Presbyterian marriages until 1782. Lord Egmont had a large grant on Stewiacke River, NS, and offered 160 acres per family to the northern Irish settlers. Joseph Woodmass sent Lord Egmont a list of those who accepted the offer and this amounts to a partial passenger list for the *Admiral Hawke* in 1769 - British library, Add. MSS 47054A, folio 25.

[6] The number of passengers is as given in Brendan O'Grady, *Exiles & Islanders; the Irish Settlers of Prince Edward Island* (Montréal: McGill-Queen's University Press, 2004), p. 16.

[7] The *Elizabeth* was wrecked off Lot 11, Prince Edward Island, on 5 November 1775. She was carrying 14 passengers from London, England, and an unknown number taken on at Cork, Ireland.

Month	Vessel	Port from	Port to	Passengers	Reference
			1778		
Sep	William	Cork	Halifax	6	PANS Report 1936[8]
Oct	Fame	Waterford	Halifax	11	PANS Report 1936
Nov	Susannah	Cork	Halifax	6	PANS Report 1936
Dec	Commerce	Cork	Halifax	15	PANS Report 1936
			1779		
Jan	Sally and Mary	Cork	Halifax	7	PANS Report 1936
July	Elizabeth and Nancy	Cork	Halifax	5	PANS Report 1936
			1780		
Oct	Lyon	[Ireland]	Halifax	22	PANS Report 1936
-	Neptune[9]	Cork	Halifax	-	Dobson II/96
			1789		
June	Prince	Cork	Halifax	Yes	*HibC*, 23 Mar 1789
			1790		
June	Irish Volunteer	Waterford	Halifax	Yes	*HibC*, 4 Mar 1790
			1793		
June	Union	Cork	PEI	-	Dobson I/144
			1799		
May	Polly[10]	Belfast	Halifax	9	*Rgaz*, 7 May 1798
			1801[11]		

---

[8] The information in the Public Archives of Nova Scotia Report for 1936 was based on primary sources contained in NSA, RG 1, Vol. 178. Those in the seven ships reported between 1778 and 1780 are named in Terrence M. Punch, *Erin's Sons: Irish Arrivals in Atlantic Canada, 1751 - 1858* (Baltimore: Genealogical Publishing Company, 2009), Vol. III, pp. 77 - 78. Whether any of these crewmen remained in Halifax as immigrants is not known.

[9] The *Neptune* was captured by the French and taken to Santa Cruz.

[10] The story of this voyage touches on the Irish rebellion of 1798. Cf., Terrence M. Punch, "The Passengers on the 'Polly'," *The Irish Ancestor,* Vol. VIII:2 (1976), pp. 82 - 84. The men were taken to Québec and did not remain in the Maritimes.

[11] Colonel Thomas **DAWSON** from County Monaghan and his wife Elizabeth Frances **TAIT**, came to PEI in 1801 with their family. No vessel is named - Brendan O'Grady, "The Monaghan Irish," *The Abegweit Review*, Vol. 4:1 (Spring 1983), pp. 52 - 53.

Month	Vessel	Port from	Port to	Passengers	Reference
			1806[12]		
			1811		
July	Aeolus [13]	Dublin	PEI	43	O'Grady/100-103
			1812		
Aug	Margaret[14]	[Londonderry]	Halifax	Yes	NSA, RG 20 "A"
Aug	Prudence[15]	Dublin	Halifax	-	Dobson 1/122
–	Elizabeth[16]	Cork	PEI	Yes	O'Grady/63

---

[12] While we have no record of the ships that brought them, there was a flow of Irish into Nova Scotia, as witness the observation made by the governor, Sir John Wentworth to Lord Castlereagh on 3 February 1806, that a "more numerous emigration of useless Irishmen pass annually from Newfoundland through this Province, where some of them remain one, two, or perhaps three years, and then proceed to the United States, – This class of men are not disposed to industry, obedience or temperance, nor is their departure to be regretted, except only as they might be serviceable, if they could be engaged in His Majesty's Army and Navy." - NSA, RG 1, Vol. 54, p. 81.

[13] There is quite a story here. The *Belisarius* departed from Dublin with 62 passengers bound for New York where it arrived about 5 July 1811. She was intercepted on George's Bank off Newfoundland on 24 June by HMS *Atlanta*. Alleging a violation of the customs rules, the captain of the *Atlanta* removed 62 Irishmen and brought them to Halifax, where two of the men (Patrick and William **PHELAN**) remained. After impressing 17 men into the Royal Navy, the remaining 43 were taken to PEI in the *Aeolus*, arriving there by 18 July - O'Grady, *Exiles & Islanders*, pp.100 - 103. Two of those people were the brothers Edward and Michael **REILLY** - Reginald Porter, "The First Irish Settlers of Tignish," *The Abegweit Review*, Vol. 4:1 (Spring 1983), p. 29. Once we add in the 31 people named by O'Grady, p. 102, three wives and 4 families, we can see that there were 6 children among those families, to reach the total 43 souls. O'Grady states that 20 were definitely in the *Aeolus*: Thomas and Mary **BIRD**, John and Eliza **BIRK**, Ally **BURTON**, John, Joseph and Ann **GILBERT**, Richard, Jane, James, Mary and Jane **KING**, Lawrence **CURRENT**, Michael **MURPHY**, Valentine, Catherine and Eliza **NEEDHAM**, Thomas **NEWMAN** and Thomas **WALSH**. The probable passengers were Jane **CONNOR** and family, Mary Ann Gilbert, William **HARDING** and wife, Robert **HUGHES** and family, William **MacDONALD**, Stephen **MATTHEWS** and wife, Denis **MENTEUR** or **MENIEUR**, William **NAILOR** and family, Rev. Mr. **RYAN**, Henry **STANHOPE** and wife, Benjamin **TUCKERBURY** and family. O'Grady, *ibid*., p. 83, adds John **READY** and his wife Elizabeth, dau of Michael **REILLY**, County Kerry. It looks as if rather more than 43 people were brought to PEI from the *Belisarius* via the *Aeolus*.

[14] John **RIDDLE** and his sister, together with Thomas **McKAY**, all of County Derry, sailed on 27 June 1812 for New York. The War of 1812 having broken out, the *Margaret*, Timothy **DRUE**, master, was captured by H. M. brig *Ring Cove* and brought into Halifax as a prize. Riddle in 1812 and McKay in 1815 petitioned for land grants in Cumberland County, NS - NSA, RG 20, Series "A", post 1800.

[15] The *Prudence* was bound for New York, but the War of 1812 broke out and she was captured by the Royal Navy on 10 Aug 1812 and taken to Halifax, NS.

[16] This ship may have come out in 1813, as one author states that Peter, Joseph and James **AHEARN** from County Wexford arrived in PEI in 1813 - Porter, pp. 27 - 33   p. 32. Since both are secondary sources, the dating of the *Elizabeth's* voyage must be treated as *circa* 1812/1813.

Month	Vessel	Port from	Port to	Passengers	Reference
			1815[17]		
Nov	Two Friends[18]	[Belfast]	Halifax	3	An Nasc/5
			1816[19]		
July	Montague[20]	Ireland	Halifax	Yes	An Nasc /5
Oct	Hibernia[21]	Cork	Halifax	105	*AR*, 2 Nov 1816
Dec	Haron	Ireland/NL	Halifax	Yes	*AR*, 21 Dec 1816
Dec	Industry	Ireland/NL	Halifax	150	*AR*, 14 Dec 1816
Dec	Shamrock[22]	Ireland/NL	Halifax	49	*AR*, 25 Jan 1817
Dec	Susan	Ireland/NL	Halifax	Yes	Martell/40
Dec	Union	Ireland/NL	Halifax	Yes	*AR*, 21 Dec 1816
Dec	William and Jane	Ireland/NL	Halifax	51	*AR*, 21 Dec 1816

---

[17] A. A. MacKenzie, *The Irish in Cape Breton* (Antigonish: Formac Publishing Co. Ltd., 1979), p. 31, states that 25 Irish immigrants landed at Sydney, Cape Breton, in 1815. No vessel is named. Adams, p. 422, states that a ship from Belfast came to Saint John with passengers. O'Grady writes in *Exiles & Islanders*, p. 56, that "the victims of Newfoundland's post-1815 economic collapse fled into the Maritime colonies by the thousand. In that movement Prince Edward Island received hundreds of families . . . as well as hundreds of families who were transients on their trek toward New Brunswick and New England." Given that half the population of Newfoundland was Irish, and a greater proportion of them worked in the depressed fishery, this represents a fairly large share of the Irish immigration into the Maritimes. The Irish in the Newfoundland fishery were primarily drawn from the southern counties of Wexford, Waterford, Kilkenny and Cork, and that pattern would be represented in the exodus of several thousand people from that colony in the 1815 - 1820 period.

[18] The vessel left three passengers in Halifax, then proceeded to New York.

[19] In addition to the Irish arriving in the listed vessels, there was an official report that "about 500 fine young men chiefly Irish" had arrived at Halifax "lately", but were "totally destitute of bread or means of subsistence". Governor Lord Dalhousie, writing to Lord Bathurst on 2 January 1817, considered that they were the overflow of "an immense emigration to Newfoundland last summer." - J. S. Martell, *Immigration to and Emigration from Nova Scotia 1815-1838* (Halifax: Public Archives of Nova Scotia, 1942), p. 40. Adams, pp. 422 - 425, reckoned that five vessels reached New Brunswick ports with Irish emigrants in 1816: two from Waterford and one each from Belfast, Dublin and Limerick. The names of these vessels has not been found. Five vessels reached Halifax that year, two from Waterford and one each from Belfast, Dublin and Limerick. Insofar as the same number of ships from each port reached each destination, we must consider that the same five vessels called at both Maritime ports. Lord Dalhousie's letter uses the term "lately" to separate those arrivals from earlier passengers who were landed during the summer. If we discount the *Shamrock*, "believed lost", we have five vessels from Ireland via Newfoundland, which are probably the same vessels of which Adams found traces. A. A. MacKenzie, p. 31, states that 47 Irish immigrants landed at Sydney, Cape Breton, in 1816, but names no vessels.

[20] From Halifax the vessel proceeded to New York.

[21] The *Hibernia*'s passengers were described as farmers and mechanics.

[22] The *Shamrock* sailed from the south coast of Ireland and left St. John's, NL, on 1 Dec 1816 with 49 Irish passengers, but was believed lost en route to Halifax.

Month	Vessel	Port from	Port to	Passengers	Reference
			1817[23]		
Jan	Isabella	Ireland/NL	Halifax	55	*AR*, 4 Jan 1817
Jan	Consolation[24]	Ireland/NL	Halifax	30	*AR*, 25 Jan 1817
Feb	Lively[25]	Ireland/NL	Halifax	20	*AR*, 8 Feb 1817.
June	Union	Belfast	St. Andrews	Yes	Dobson II/131
July	Angelique	Ireland/NL	Halifax	30	*AR*, 12 July 1817
July	Brunswick[26]	Londonderry	Halifax	Yes	*AR*, 19 July 1817
July	Halifax Packet[27]	Londonderry	Halifax	171	*AR*, 26 July 1817
July	Kitty[28]	Dublin/NL	Halifax	44	An Nasc/5
July	New Brunswick Packet	Londonderry	Halifax & PEI	Yes	Dobson I/109[29]
July	Sarah	Limerick	PEI	18	Dobson I/132
Aug	Marcus Hill	Londonderry	Halifax	250	*AR*, 2 Aug 1817

---

[23] Adams, p. 95, states that "the Nova Scotian ports to the east [Pictou, Sydney] received only a trickle. Halifax practically dropped from the picture in 1818, and never reappeared as an important destination. This was due partly to the hostile policy of the Nova Scotian government, which discouraged settlers, . . . and partly to the inconvenience of Halifax as a stopping place for the United States. The New Brunswick ports were much better situated for emigrant traffic." The *Limerick General Advertiser*, 30 June 1818, informed "tradesmen and others, who cannot go to the States" [due to a British law prohibiting the emigration of artisans beyond British realms], that "St. Andrews is within a mile of" the United States. Adams, pp. 422-425, noted that 16 Irish vessels brought passengers to Nova Scotia in 1817, and another 20 reached New Brunswick. Only one vessel, the *Union*, has been found as being on its way to New Brunswick, but several of those coming to Nova Scotian ports may have continued thither, but even so, the 20 Adams cites cannot be accounted for by name.

[24] Forced by winter storms into Popes Harbour, on the eastern shore of Nova Scotia. The passengers were mainly mechanics, i.e., tradesmen - Martell, p. 42. The *Consolation* landed in Newfoundland in May 1816 and was in Halifax the following January. One passenger was Michael **CASEY** who was committed to the Halifax Bridewell, 11 Feb 1818 - NSA, RG 1, Vol. 411, doc. 87.

[25] Forced by adverse weather into Beaver Harbour, on the eastern shore of Nova Scotia. Three men from the *Lively* were committed to the Halifax Bridewell in 1817/18: Stephen **HABERLAND**, Patrick **McCLACKLIN**, and John **O'BRIEN** - NSA, RG 1, Vol. 411, doc. 87.

[26] The *Brunswick* called at Pictou before going to Halifax. Two passengers were in jail in Halifax a few months after arrival: Patrick **RYAN** and John **WALSH** - NSA, RG 1, Vol. 411, doc. 87.

[27] William **KING**, a Presbyterian from the north of Ireland, petitioned for a land grant in Annapolis County, NS, in 1817 and mentions arriving "4 months ago" in the *Halifax Packet* - NSA, RG 20, Series "A", post 1800.

[28] The passengers in the *Kitty* were called "Dublin tradesmen". Seventy-seven went to St. John's, NL, in the *Concord* in 1815. Two years later 44 went to Halifax - Punch, *Erin's Sons: Irish Arrivals in Atlantic Canada*, Vol. I, p. 70, gives the names of 42 men and 2 wives.

[29] The *New Brunswick Packet* seems to have got around a bit. It left Londonderry in May, landed in Newfoundland on 1 June 1817, then visited PEI before reaching Halifax on 9 Aug 1817. On 24 Dec 1817 one passenger – Thomas **SMITH** – was committed to the Halifax Bridewell - NSA, RG 1, Vol. 411, doc. 87.

Month	Vessel	Port from	Port to	Passengers	Reference
Aug	Critic	Ireland/NL	Halifax	36	*AR*, 30 Aug 1817
Aug	Harriet[30]	Dublin	PEI	Yes	Dobson I/67
Sep	Amelia[31]	Coleraine	Halifax	84	*AR*, 13 Sep 1817
Sep	Hibernia	Londonderry	Halifax	17	*AR*, 13 Sep 1817
Sep	Mary	Dublin	Halifax	88	*AR*, 13 Sep 1817
Oct	Angelique[32]	Ireland/NL	Halifax	50	*AR*, 1 Nov 1817
Oct	Union	Dublin/NL	Halifax	65	*AR*, 18 Oct 1817
Nov	Sisters	Ireland/NL	Halifax	46	*AR*, 29 Nov 1817
Dec	Comet	Cork	Halifax	30	*AR*, 13 Dec 1817
Dec	Lord Nelson[33]	Londonderry	Shelburne	Yes	Dobson I/92

1818[34]

---

[30] The *Harriet* seems to have been the vessel in which James **PHEE** of County Louth emigrated. It is possible that John **READY** and his wife, Elizabeth, daughter of Michael **REILLY**, were fellow passengers - Porter, pp. 29-30. O'Grady, *Exiles & Islanders*, p. 83, says the couple came in the *Aeolus* in 1811. To these we may add John **LARGE** from either County Leix or County Offaly - O'Grady, *Exiles & Islanders*, p. 32.

[31] Robert **BLACK**, 26, with a wife and child, of Coleraine, County Londonderry, petitioned for a land grant at Douglas Township, Hants County, NS, in 1818, having come out to Halifax the previous year - NSA, GR 20, Series "A", post 1800.

[32] The passengers in the *Angelique* in the October trip were referred to as "mostly labourers". One passenger was Morice **TINOLLY** who was landed in PEI and proceeded to Halifax on 1 Nov 1817 where he ended up in jail - NSA, RG 1, Vol. 411, doc. 87. Another probable passenger was Michael **BURKE**, a single man whose petition for a land grant at Paradise Bridge, Annapolis County, NS, in 1819 states that he arrived in Halifax about 1 November 1817 - NSA, GR 20, Series "A", post 1800.

[33] The *Lord Nelson*, en route to Saint John, New Brunswick, was wrecked near Shelburne, Nova Scotia. Michael Tobin and Samuel Cunard reported to Governor Dalhousie of Nova Scotia, 6 Feb 1818 that during "December last we were visited by above 300 Men, Women & Children from Newfoundland . . . many of them being shipwrecked on their way here & had lost the Remains of what they may have saved from the fires of 7th & 21 November." - Martell, p. 43.

[34] If Adams, p. 89, is correct, Londonderry sent 10 ships to Halifax, Saint John and St. Andrews, with 5 each having sailed from Belfast and Dublin. The former are accounted for here, but just 3 from Dublin appear, although possibly the vessel from the Azores had embarked its passengers at Dublin. Adams, p. 97. reported the number of Irish emigrants in 1818 from Belfast to ports in the Maritimes as: Pictou 246, PEI 22, Saint John 43 [the *Ganges*, apparently], and St. Andrews 1,939, for a total of 2,250. We have no vessels named as going to Pictou or PEI from Belfast in 1818, yet another instance that reveals the incomplete nature of shipping records. Perhaps the *Fame* was refloated and able to reach St. Andrews with its 114 passengers. We know that the *Martin* and the *Neptune* [p. 32] went to "Saint John", but St Andrews was at the time an outport of Saint John, so the passengers in the two ships should probably be credited as landing Irish at St. Andrews, rather than at Saint John. Even so, there must be two to four other ships of which we find no record.

We have not to hand the months in which many ships arrived in 1818 and several later years. It is worth quoting Adams, p. 74, on this point, where he writes that "April, May, and June were the recognized emigrant months . . ." With that in mind, and allowing from five to eight weeks for the Atlantic crossing, any vessel for which we lack date of arrival was more likely to have reached port between late May and the end of August. Halifax and Sydney in Nova Scotia, Saint John and St. Andrews in New Brunswick enjoyed one advantage over ports in the Gulf of St. Lawrence or Québec in that they remained ice-free most winters.

Month	Vessel	Port from	Port to	Passengers	Reference
May	Alexander	Londonderry	Saint John	150	Houston & Smyth/82
May	Halifax Packet	Londonderry	Saint John	213	Dobson II/53
May	Prince of Coburg[35]	Cork	Halifax	Yes	*AR*, 30 May 1818
June	Fame[36]	Waterford	Halifax	183	*AR*, 13 June 1818
June	Industry[37]	Newry	Halifax, etc.	92	*AR*, 13 June 1818
June	Nelson[38]	Cork	PEI	3	Dobson I/108
July	Alexander Buchanan[39]	Londonderry	Yarmouth	Yes	Dobson I/6; II/5
July	Four Brothers	Waterford	Halifax	50	*AR*, 11 July 1818
July	Swift[40]	Azores	Halifax	51	Dobson I/139
Aug	Amelia	Coleraine	Halifax	Yes	An Nasc/6
Aug	Harp	Limerick	St. Andrews	Yes	Dobson III/45
Sep	Amicus[41]	Cork	Halifax	Yes	CO 221/33
Sep	Clyde	Dublin	Halifax	85	*AR*, 5 Sep 1818
Sep	Ganges	Belfast	Saint John	43	Dobson II/47
Sep	Ocean[42]	Dublin	PEI	Yes	O'Grady/65
Oct	Fame[43]	Belfast	Halifax	114	*AR*, 10 Oct 1818

---

[35] The *Prince of Coburg* proceeded to Québec from Halifax.

[36] Peter **BYRN** petitioned for a land grant at Parrsboro, NS, in 1820. He mentioned that he landed at Halifax in June 1818. The *Fame* arrived between 6 and 12 June 1818 - NSA, GR 20, Series "A", post 1800.

[37] The *Industry* carried 157 passengers, of whom 92 left the vessel at Halifax, while another 65 continued to Philadelphia. Among the passengers were John, William and Nathaniel **ANGUS** from County Down, who arrived in Nova Scotia in June 1818 and sought land grants at Shinimicas River, Cumberland County in 1821 - NSA, GR 20, Series "A", post 1800.

[38] It is probable that Richard **AYLWARD** of County Waterford emigrated in the *Nelson* - Porter, p. 32. Another passenger was Michael **BRENNAN** from County Kerry - O'Grady, *Exiles & Islanders*, p. 83.

[39] The *Alexander Buchanan* was wrecked at Cape Sable, NS, in July 1818. The crew and passengers were rescued. The Overseers of the Poor at Yarmouth, Nova Scotia, still had eight of those passengers in their care on 11 February 1819 - NSA, RG 5, Series "P", Vol. 80, doc. #19. The passengers named were Christopher, Mary and Elizabeth **BROWNLEIGH**, Robert and Jane **RUTLEDGE**, John and Jane **ARMSTRONG**, and William **IRVINE**. They were "all sick of Typhus Fever whereof Irvine died."

[40] The *Swift* brought 51 Irish emigrants who had been shipwrecked near the Azores. W. H. Reed, British consul for the Azores reported their departure for Halifax in a letter dated 30 May 1818. - Martell, p. 46.

[41] In a petition for land at Harmony, Queens County, NS, in 1827 Joseph **ARMSTRONG**, 38, stated that he "had free passage from Cork to Halifax" in 1818. Only the *Amicus* or possibly the *Adeline* made that connection in 1818 - NSA, GR 20, Series "A", post 1800.

[42] As Patrick **McHUGH** from County Monaghan came out to settle at Tignish, PEI, in 1818, the likely ship which brought him was the *Ocean* - Brendan O'Grady, "The Monaghan Settlers," *The Abegweit Review*, Vol. 4:1 (Spring 1983), p. 52.

[43] The *Fame* went ashore at Cole Harbour, just east of the entrance to Halifax Harbour. No lives were lost.

Month	Vessel	Port from	Port to	Passengers	Reference
Nov	Marinhull[44]	Ireland/NL	Halifax	22	*AR*, 10 Oct 1818
-	Martha[45]	Newry	Halifax	84	*AR*, 24 Oct 1818
-	Adeline	Cork	Halifax	Yes	CO 221/33
-	Industry	Warrenpoint	Miramichi	Yes	Dobson II/63
-	Bartley[46]	Londonderry	Saint John	130	Dobson II/14
-	Draper	Londonderry	Saint John	114	Houston & Smyth/82
-	General Brock	Londonderry	Saint John	186	Dobson II/48
-	George	Belfast	Saint John	90	Houston & Smyth/82
-	Lord Whitworth	Londonderry	Saint John	235	Houston & Smyth/82
-	Martin	Belfast	Saint John	Yes	Dobson II/85
-	Neptune	Belfast	Saint John	Yes	Dobson II/97
-	Prompt	Londonderry	Saint John	251	Houston & Smyth/82
-	Sarah	Londonderry	Saint John	156	Houston & Smyth/82
-	Thomas	Limerick	New Brunswick	Yes	O'Grady/58
-	Thomas Henry	Londonderry	Saint John	335	Houston & Smyth/82
-	Young Halliday	Dublin	Saint John	67	Dobson II/141

1819[47]

Month	Vessel	Port from	Port to	Passengers	Reference
Feb	Constellation[48]	[Belfast]	Saint John	Yes	Dobson I/35
May	Ben Lomond[49]	Londonderry	Saint John	Yes	Dobson II/15
May	John[50]	Dublin	PEI	Yes	Dobson I/82

---

[44] The passengers in the *Marinhull* were called settlers, meaning that they were destined to take up land, rather than ply a trade in town. One of them was William **MURPHY** who petitioned for a land grant at Roman Valley, Sydney [this part is now Guysborough] County, in 1829. He states that he arrived in NS in 1818 from Newfoundland in the brig *Marinhull* - NSA, RG 20, Series "A", post 1800.

[45] The passengers in the *Martha* were called settlers, intending to take up land in the country.

[46] The *Bartley* and the eleven ships listed after it arrived in Saint John during 1818. The cited authors gathered their information from miscellaneous issues of the *City Gazette* (Saint John, NB).

[47] Adams, p. 420, reports that 2,297 Irish emigrants went from the port of Belfast to the Maritimes in 1819 down to 5 July. The known ships cannot account for so many passengers. I have attributed the *Constellation* and the *Lord Gardner* to Belfast, although available records merely mention "Ireland" as their port of origin. Adams, pp. 422 - 425, shows 63 vessels from Ireland to New Brunswick and 12 to Nova Scotia in 1819. As only 14 vessels have been found and identified, there were evidently many voyages by ships whose names we do not know. John **GILBERT** of Wicklow and his wife Frances **FIFE** came to Parrsboro, NS, in 1819, with six children: Dorcas, Elizabeth, Thomas, David R., Frances Suzanne, and John.

[48] The *Constellation* was wrecked off the coast of Nova Scotia, but its passengers and crew were saved and taken to Saint John.

[49] Since the *Ben Lomond* sailed from Greenock, Scotland, via Londonderry, it is probable that some of its passengers were Scottish rather than Irish.

[50] Some of those in the *John* were Quakers from Mountmellick, County Leix. Among them were Samuel **HALL** and his wife Sarah; James A. **MOORE**; John **PLEADWELL**, his wife Margaret **PIGOTT** and their daughter Ellen; John **LANE**, his wife Joyce **LESTER** and their children Sarah and William; John Lane II; Samuel Lane; Edward Lane and his wife Ann Pleadwell from Mountrath; Philip Lane and his wife Lydia **LYSTER**; Joseph Lane and his wife Elizabeth Pleadwell - O'Grady, *Exiles & Islanders*, p. 37.

Month	Vessel	Port from	Port to	Passengers	Reference
June	Enterprise	Dublin	Halifax	103	*AR*, 12 June 1819
June	Halifax Packet[51]	Londonderry	Halifax	113	*AR*, 12 June 1819
June	Hope	Dublin	Saint John	Yes	Adams/155
June	Johns	Kinsale	Halifax	130	*AR*, 26 June 1819
June	Lord Gardner	[Belfast]	Halifax & NB	Yes	*AR*, 12 June 1819
June	Sir John Cameron	Waterford	Halifax	112	*AR*, 26 June 1819
July	Frances Ann	Londonderry	Halifax	120	*AR*, 31 July 1819
July	Mary	Ireland/NL	Halifax	Yes	*AR*, 10 July 1819
July	Mermaid[52]	Dublin	Cape Negro	73	*AR*, 31 July 1819
Sep	Chatty	Dublin	Halifax	113	*AR*, 11 Sep 1819
-	Chesterfield[53]	Cork	Saint John	53	Dobson I/31
-	Fawcett	Limerick	PEI	-	O'Grady/64

1820[54]

Month	Vessel	Port from	Port to	Passengers	Reference
Mar	Clyde	Belfast	Saint John	Yes	Dobson II/26
May	Carron	Cork	PEI	11	Island Magazine, 16
May	Dykes[55]	Belfast	St. Andrews	Yes	Dobson II/35
May	Jane[56]	Waterford	PEI	57	Island Magazine, 16
May	Rubicon[57]	Waterford	Halifax	150	*AR*, 20 May 1820
June	Alexander	Limerick	PEI	93	Island Magazine, 16
June	Eclipse	Belfast	Saint John	Yes	Dobson II/36
June	Isabella	Londonderry	Saint John	Yes	Dobson I/76
June	Jess and Flora	Londonderry	Saint John	Yes	Dobson I/81

---

[51] William **ROBINSON**, 21, single man from Ulster, Ireland, sailed in May 1819. Later that year he petitioned for a land grant in Douglas Township, Hants County. The details suggest that the vessel in which he came was the *Halifax Packet* - NSA, RG 20, Series "A", post 1800.

[52] The *Mermaid* went ashore near Cape Negro, Nova Scotia, on 16 July 1819. The passengers and crew were saved.

[53] Some of the *Chesterfield*'s passengers went on to Virginia.

[54] Adams, p. 422, states that 3,025 Irish passengers landed in New Brunswick in 1820, of whom 2,592 came to Saint John, and 433 elsewhere in the province. Given that St. Andrews came under the authority of the port of Saint John, we find eight ships by name that reached New Brunswick from Ireland.

[55] The *Dykes* sailed about 10 March, and the *Martha* about 1 May. It was reported before 10 June 1820, that two vessels from Ireland had left "upwards of 600 passengers" at St. Andrews - *The Island Magazine*, 16, p. 38. These may have been the vessels referred to.

[56] Patrick **MORRISSEY** of County Waterford arrived in PEI in 1820. This is the most likely ship in which he arrived. Mr. and Mrs. **ROBERTS**, she being the former Catherine **CLOHOSEY** from County Kilkenny, came on this ship - Edward A. Clohossey, "Excerpts from a Family History," *The Abegweit Review*, 6:1 (Spring 1988), p. 129.

[57] A probable passenger was Michael **DONALLY** of County Waterford, who petitioned for a land grant at Tracadie, NS, in 1821. He mentioned arriving in Halifax from Waterford about 18 months before - NSA, GR 20, Series "A", post 1800. The *Rubicon* from Waterford docked at Halifax between 13 and 19 May 1820.

Month	Vessel	Port from	Port to	Passengers	Reference
June	Kent	Belfast	Halifax, Pictou	Yes	Dobson II/74
June	Martha	Belfast	St. Andrews	Yes	Dobson II/85
June	Oliphit[58]	Belfast	Halifax	43	AR, 3 June 1820
July	Union	Belfast	St. Andrews	Yes	Dobson II/131
July	Vittoria	Belfast	St. Andrews	Yes	Dobson II/134
Sep	Fame	Belfast	Saint John	Yes	Dobson II/43
Sep	Frances and Lucy[59]	Londonderry	Halifax	Yes	AR, 16 Sep 1820
-	Endeavour	Cork	PEI	-	O'Grady/63
-	Martin[60]	Cork	PEI	Yes	O'Grady/67
-	Saltern's Rock	Cork	PEI	Yes	O'Grady/63
			1821[61]		
May	Amicus[62]	Cork	Halifax	98	AR, 26 May 1821

[58] One passenger was William **THOMAS** from Ireland, who petitioned for a land grant at Pictou, NS, and mentions his arrival in June 1820. Another was William **WORK**, 28, from Ireland, who petitioned for land in Halifax County. He states that he sailed to Nova Scotia in May 1820. A third was Alexander **ROBB** of County Down, who sailed in the brig *Oliphit* with his wife and four children in 1820. In 1821 he petitioned for land in Amherst Township, NS - NSA, RG 20, Series "A", post 1800. The Robb family remained in that area.

[59] One passenger, Michael **McNAMEE** of Tyrone, was drowned - *Weekly Chronicle*, 15 Sep 1820.

[60] The claim by a passenger, Maurice **O'HALLORAN,** that the guns were being fired in the port of Cork to announce the coronation of George IV in 1820 (O'Grady, *Exiles & Islanders*, p. 276, n. 14) is not accurate. The king's *accession* occurred on 29 January, but word of that would have taken several days to reach Cork, so this celebration must be dated to February 1820. If the coronation was the occasion, that occurred on 19 July 1821, which puts O'Halloran's emigration to 1821 and probably means he came out in the *Endeavour* that year. This is a good example of how oral traditions can have the basic fact correct, but the details wrong. O'Halloran and his wife, née **REILLY**, came from Tralee, County Kerry, as did others.

[61] James **WALSH**, 26, a single man from Ireland, petitioned for a land grant at Tracadie, NS, in 1822, and mentions arriving in the previous autumn [1821]. James **MURRAY** from Ireland, with a wife and child, petitioned for a land grant on the Antigonish-Guysborough Road. He states that he had been in that area for 5 months - NSA, RG 20, Series "A", post 1800. Adams, p. 422, states that 2,067 Irish passengers landed in New Brunswick in 1821, of whom 1,985 came to Saint John, and 82 elsewhere. Perhaps the latter were passengers in the *Mars*, the one ship with a destination in New Brunswick of which notice was found. Evidently, many voyages left no known record. Sometimes we learn of Irish arrivals for whom no passenger list survives, but who turn up in records years afterwards. For example, John R. **HERRON**, a native of County Cork, emigrated about 1812 to Newfoundland where he remained for "8 or 9 years". Then he removed to Nova Scotia and worked for "4 or 5 years" at Halifax before moving about 1826 to Horton, and again in 1829 to Cornwallis Township, where he worked for about 17 years. He sought relief from the government in a petition dated 31 Aug 1846, probably 25 years after he entered the province - NSA, RG 5, Series "P", Vol. 83 #118.

[62] Luke **GARDNER** and Bryan **KAVANAGH**, single men from Ireland, and James **CAMPBELL**, 29, with a wife and two children, from County Down, petitioned for land grants at Amherst Township, Cumberland County, in 1821, having arrived in the *Amicus* - NSA, RG 20, Series "A", post 1800. Another, Robert **FULLER**, 50, with wife and five children (the eldest, William, age 20) sought a land grant at Ohio, Sydney [this part is now Antigonish] County, in 1821. Either the *Rob Roy* or the *Amicus* brought out three men who petitioned for land grants at Hammonds Plains on the road between Annapolis and Halifax in 1821, as recent arrivals at Halifax. They were Michael **CARNEY**, County Wexford, Samuel **GRAHAM**, County Armagh, and William **DONAGHY**, from Ireland - NSA, RG 20, Series "A", post 1800.

Month	Vessel	Port from	Port to	Passengers	Reference
May	Rob Roy[63]	Belfast	Halifax	139	*AR*, 19 May 1821
Aug	Mars	Belfast	St. Andrews	210	Dobson II/85
-	Endeavour[64]	Cork	PEI	Yes	O'Grady/63
-	Sarah[65]	Dublin	PEI	Yes	O'Grady/65

1822[66]

Month	Vessel	Port from	Port to	Passengers	Reference
June	San Domingo[67]	New Ross	PEI	87	Island Magazine, 16
July	Devonshire	Waterford	PEI	42	Island Magazine, 16

---

[63] Three probable arrivals in the *Rob Roy* petitioned for land grants in Nova Scotia: Lowry **ELLIS**, 31, single man from Ireland, at Upper Stewiacke, Colchester District; John **McGREGOR**, 28, with wife and 2 children, at Preston Road, Halifax County. A third man, Thomas **LOGAN**, Sr., from Ulster, but lately arrived, petitioned for a land grant on the Halifax-Truro Road. With him were his 5 sons: William, 33, Henry, 26, Thomas, 23, George, 18, and Alexander, 16. William **HENNICY**, 27, at Tracadie, NS, mentioned arriving in "Summer 1821", and he might be indicating he had emigrated in either the *Rob Roy* or the *Amicus*. Another such instance was William **JOHNSTON** from Ireland, 21, unmarried, who arrived in June 1821, and sought a land grant at Dorchester Township, Antigonish - NSA, RG 20, Series "A", post 1800.

[64] Passengers included Morris **GRIFFIN** and his wife, née **REILLY** and daughter from Tralee, County Kerry; Patrick Griffin and his wife; Richard **HOWARD** and his wife; Patrick **(O)REILLY** and his wife; and Gerrard (O)Reilly - O'Grady, *Exiles & Islanders*, pp. 75 - 76.

[65] In a petition for a land grant at Knoydart, Antigonish area, in 1828 John **KICKHAM** and Michael **MURPHY** state that they came out from Ireland in the autumn of 1821 - NSA, RG 20, Series "A", post 1800. Given the tendency for new settlers to move about in search of land, and given that many landlords in PEI would not sell farmland to immigrants, this man's experience may well be a case in point. The *Sarah* came about the right time to PEI. James **MAGUIRE**, 23, asked for a grant at South River, Antigonish, in 1829, and also mentions coming out from Ireland in the autumn of 1821.

[66] According to a Customs Return of Immigrants at Halifax, 1822, 74 Irish were landed there in 1822 - NSA, RG 1, Vol. 238, doc. 27. Adams, p. 422, states that 5,226 Irish passengers landed in New Brunswick in 1822, of whom 4,684 came to Saint John, and 542 elsewhere in the province. We do not have the names of the 12 to 15 vessels on which they sailed. According to a letter written to the author by John R. MacQuarrie, a local historical expert at Pugwash, Nova Scotia, 20 Jan 1980, the *Pandora* of Waterford brought passengers there in 1822, and in 1826 there was an unsuccessful proposal to rename Pugwash as Waterford - NSA, MG 100, Vol. 23, item. 35. MacQuarrie mentions Irish settlers circa 1818 from County Clare: Patrick **MACKIE**, James **HICKEY**, and William **SMYTH**.

[67] The *San Domingo* arrived at Charlottetown, PEI, on 20 June 1822, and discharged some passengers. Some Irish immigrants remained on board on their way to Newfoundland. On 23 June the ships struck a reef at Beaton Point, the northeastern tip of PEI. Some survivors stayed in PEI and settled at Elmira. They had family names **CAMPION**, **DRUMMOND**, **HARRIS**, **HUGHES**, **PIERCE**, **PRICE**, and **TIERNEY** - O'Grady, *Exiles & Islanders*, pp. 107 - 108. One passenger who stayed in PEI was Moses **HARRIS** with his daughter, age 3 - *Daily Examiner* (Charlottetown), 26 June 1913.

Month	Vessel	Port from	Port to	Passengers	Reference
			1823[68]		
June	General Elliot	Cork	PEI	113	Island Magazine, 16
-	Benjamin Shaw	Waterford	PEI	Yes	O'Grady/60
-	Flash[69]	Dublin	PEI	Yes	*Patriot,* 31 Dec 1910
-	Mayflower[70]	Ireland	[Pictou]	Yes	NSA, RG 20 "A"
-	Proud Ardent[71]	Belfast	Barrington, NS	Yes	An Nasc/6
			1824[72]		
July	Brothers	Ireland/NL	Halifax	3	AR, 24 July 1824
Aug	Elizabeth[73]	Sligo	Saint John	112	Dobson I/48
			1825		
June	Brothers	Ireland/NL	Halifax	16	AR, 4 June 1825
July	Resolution	Dublin	Halifax	34	AR, 23 July 1825
			1826		
June	Maria	Cork	Halifax	27	AR, 24 June 1826
June	Nassau[74]	Ireland	Halifax	95	AR, 17 June 1826
June	Thomas	Waterford	Halifax	91	AR, 3 June 1826

---

[68] Adams, p. 422, states that 4,761 Irish passengers landed in New Brunswick in 1823, of whom 3,224 came to Saint John, 1,095 to St. Andrews, and 442 elsewhere in the province. We do not have the names of the several vessels on which they sailed.

[69] Two of the passengers in the *Flash* were James **DOUGAN** and his son Thomas Anthony.

[70] Michael **ROCHE**, 26, single man from Ireland, stated in his petition for land at Manchester, NS, that he was 4 months in the province, having arrived in the *Mayflower* - NSA, RG 20, Series "A", post 1800.

[71] The *Proud Ardent* went aground on the Half Moons near Barrington, Nova Scotia, while en route to Saint John, New Brunswick. Several of the passengers remained in Nova Scotia. James and Letty **LAMROCK** and their son James, 1 year old, were among those passengers. They came from "Oforney" [I think Donaghedy, County Tyrone, was intended] and the family remained in Nova Scotia - NSA, MG 4, mfm. of Barrington Township Book.

[72] Adams, p. 422, states that 2,049 Irish passengers landed in New Brunswick in 1824, of whom 1,175 came to Saint John, 275 to St. Andrews, and 599 elsewhere in the province. We do not have the names of the several vessels on which they sailed.

[73] The *Elizabeth* struck a ledge at Cape Sable Island and had to be towed in to Barrington, Nova Scotia. There was no loss of life.

[74] The *Nassau* was wrecked on Sable Island, The *Two Brothers* brought 95 survivors to Halifax, while a further 20 or 30 remained on Sable Island. The schooner *Mary* brought "the remainder of the crew and passengers" of the *Nassau* to Halifax - AR, 17 June 1826.

Month	Vessel	Port from	Port to	Passengers	Reference
June	Acadia[75]	Ireland/NL	Halifax	Yes	*AR*, 24 June 1826
July	Albion	Dublin	Halifax	47	*AR*, 22 July 1826
July	Hopewell	Belfast	Pictou	50	*AR*, 15 July 1826
Oct	Mary	Ireland/NL	Halifax	31	*AR*, 21 Oct 1826
Oct	Nancy	Dublin	Halifax	116	*AR*, 21 Oct 1826
Nov	Admiral Lake	Ireland/NL	Halifax	13	*AR*, 25 Nov 1826
Nov	Caledonia	Ireland/NL	Liverpool, NS	84	*AR*, 25 Nov 1826
Nov	William Hunter	Ireland/NL	Halifax	53	*AR*, 25 Nov 1826
-	James & Henry Cumming	Londonderry	Saint John	Yes	Dobson I/77
-	Martin[76]	Limerick	PEI	40	O'Grady/65
-	Nicholas	Belfast	Miramichi	90	On line[77]

1827[78]

Month	Vessel	Port from	Port to	Passengers	Reference
May	Liberty	Waterford	Halifax	127	*NS*, 3 May 1827
June	Bolivar	Waterford	Halifax	350	*NS*, 14 June 1827
June	Cherub[79]	Waterford	Halifax	200	*NS*, 7 June 1827
June	James Bailey	Belfast	St. Andrews	Yes	Dobson I/77
June	Letitia	Dublin	Halifax	210	*NS*, 21 June 1827
July	Cumberland[80]	Waterford	Halifax	350	*NS*, 5 July 1827
July	Hannah	New Ross	PEI	43	Island Magazine, 16
Sep	Forte[81]	Ireland/NL	Halifax	40 families	Dobson I/55

---

[75] The *Acadia* struck on a rock near Canso Light, Nova Scotia, and was towed to safety. "Some of the passengers" were brought to Halifax in the *Eliza* - *AR*, 24 June 1826.

[76] The *Martin* was probably the vessel which brought out John **CARROLL** of County Tipperary, with his wife Ann **HORAN**, and daughters Johanna, Margaret, Hanora and Mary - Porter, p. 31. The ship also called at Miramichi, NB - irishfamine.ca/quarantine-coastal-areas/accounts-from-miramichi/page-6.

[77] See irishfamine.ca/quarantine-coastal-areas/accounts-from-miramichi/page-6

[78] A Halifax newspaper, the *Novascotian*, 28 June 1827, carried a report of another immigrant vessel which is not named: "A brig from Derry, Ireland, bound to St. John, N.B., with Passengers, put into Shelburne last week, and landed a number there, some of whom arrived here [Halifax] on Sunday night last, – others we understand are on their way." A. A. MacKenzie, p. 31, states that several vessels landed immigrants at Sydney, Cape Breton, in 1827, but names no ships.

[79] Pierce **BOWE**, 63, and Pierce **BOWE**, 17, from Comeragh, County Waterford, were passengers in the *Cherub*, as was probably the family of John and Mary **BUGGY** - Punch, *Erin's Sons: Irish Arrivals in Atlantic Canada*, Vol. I, pp. 14, 15.

[80] A partial list of 58 passengers who traveled to Nova Scotia in the *Cumberland* in 1827 appeared in Punch, *Erin's Sons: Irish Arrivals in Atlantic Canada*, Vol. I, pp. 97 - 99. To these may be added Daniel, son of Nicholas and Catherine (Brennan) **KENNY** from County Kilkenny.

[81] The *Forte* brought out 40 masons and their families. The men were to work on building the Shubenacadie Canal through central Nova Scotia.

Month	Vessel	Port from	Port to	Passengers	Reference
Sep	James[82]	Belfast	Halifax	130	NS, 13 Sep 1827
-	Eleanor	Ireland	Miramichi	200	On line[83]
-	Foveran	Ireland	Miramichi	250	On line[84]
-	Mountaineer[85]	Waterford [?]	Miramichi	Yes	Dobson I/106

1828[86]

Month	Vessel	Port from	Port to	Passengers	Reference
May	Benjamin Shaw[87]	Waterford	PEI	189	PEIR, 20 May 1828
May	Saltern's Rock[88]	Cork	Halifax	80	AR, 31 May 1828
June	Dale	Dublin	Halifax	100 '	AR, 7 June 1828
June	Hannah	Wexford/NL	PEI	45	Dobson I/65
June	Huskisson[89]	Ballyshannon	Saint John	Yes	NBC, 28 June 1828

---

[82] Sir James Kempt reported, 7 September 1827, that the James came from Waterford and that all the crew and passengers "are labouring under Typhus Fever. One hundred and sixty embarked in Ireland – five died at Sea, – and the Vessel being obliged to put into St. John[s] Newfoundland for Medical Assistance and Provisions, thirty-five were left behind there too ill to proceed." - NSA, RG 1, Vol. 307, doc. 124.

[83] See irishfamine.ca/quarantine-coastal-areas/accounts-from-miramichi/page-6 Its probable embarkation port was Dublin.

[84] See irishfamine.ca/quarantine-coastal-areas/accounts-from-miramichi/page-6 Its probable embarkation port was Dublin. Could the ship's proper name have been Favourite?

[85] The vessel continued on to Gaspé Bay, Québec. It probably sailed from Waterford. See also irishfamine.ca/quarantine-coastal-areas/accounts-from-miramichi/page-6

[86] The Customs Return of Immigrants at Sydney, 1828, mentions the arrival of 90 Irish - CO 217/143, cited by Martell, p. 62. It also appears that 233 Irish passengers arrived at Saint John, NB, that summer in the brig Henry Arnot. They had wound up in Brazil, presumably having survived either a storm or a shipwreck, and were being brought from Rio de Janeiro to New Brunswick - Novascotian, 18 Sep 1828. One passenger was Mary HOCTOR, 30 - Punch, Erin's Sons: Irish Arrivals in Atlantic Canada, Vol. I, p. 25.

[87] It appears that the passengers from this vessel became the focus of a legal wrangle. A Halifax newspaper, The Acadian, reported on 6 June 1828: "EMIGRANTS – On Monday a schr. arr. from P. E. Island, with 30 passengers; her captain was regularly warned not to allow them to land, and the conditions of the act passed last season were complied with, but in the course of the day they acquired boats and succeeded in getting on shore. The captain stated that COOK, the person to whom we were indebted for several cargoes of distress last summer, had brought the passengers out from Ireland; and, as he supposed, being aware that a law had passed which would amount to a prohibition – hired his vessel to bring them to Halifax. The poor man was thrown into Jail – but His Majesty's Council having been called, and having taken into consideration, the peculiarly hard nature of the case, directed him to be set at liberty." - NSA, mfm. reel 5191.

[88] The Novascotian, 29 May 1828, reports the number of passengers as being 70.

[89] Six passengers put a notice of thanks to the captain of the Huskisson in NBC, 28 June 1828. Their names were Owen CASSIDY, Richard CASSIDY, John GALLAGHER, John INGRAM, Hugh McIVER, and James O'NEIL. James BRITTON, late captain of the brig Huskisson died 13 May 1828 on the passage from Ballyshannon - NBC, 14 June 1828, so that the notice appeared posthumously.

Month	Vessel	Port from	Port to	Passengers	Reference
Aug	Dispatch[90]	Londonderry	Halifax	181	Dobson III/28
Aug	Hero	Sligo	Saint John	Yes	Dobson I/69
-	Cadmus	Sligo	Saint John	Yes	Dobson I/25
-	Catherine MacDonald	Sligo	Saint John	Yes	Dobson I28

1829

Month	Vessel	Port from	Port to	Passengers	Reference
May	Benjamin Shaw	Waterford	PEI	Yes	Island Magazine, 16
May	Marchioness of Donegal	Belfast	Pictou, NS	42	*CP*, 20 May 1829
May	Pandora[91]	Waterford	PEI	[61]	Island Magazine, 16
Oct	Marchioness of Donegal[92]	Belfast	PEI	Yes	O'Grady/107
Nov	Collina[93]	Dublin	PEI	Yes	Island Magazine, 16
Dec	Gleaner	Ireland/NL	Halifax	Yes	*AR*, 5 Dec 1829
-	Beaver	Londonderry	Saint John	Yes	Dobson I/16

1830[94]

Month	Vessel	Port from	Port to	Passengers	Reference
May	Benjamin Shaw	Waterford	Pictou, NS	300	*CP*, 29 May 1830
May	Britannia	Sligo	Saint John	Yes	Dobson I/23

---

[90] The *Dispatch* was bound for Québec, but was wrecked at the Ile-aux-Morts, NL. Of the 181 passengers, 152 survived and were taken to Halifax in H.M.S. *Tyne* - AR, 2 Aug 1828. The newspaper account makes clear that there were Scots among the passengers.

[91] O'Grady, *Exiles & Islanders*, p. 60, states that the *Pandora* carried 582 Irish immigrants in eleven voyages. Since the subsequent ten voyages conveyed a total of 521 passengers, the 1829 sailing must have brought 61. Either this ship or the *Benjamin Shaw* brought out Patrick **DALTON** from County Kerry, his wife Margaret **McCARTHY**, and their children: Patrick, Catherine, Margaret, John, Thomas, Michael, and Hanora - Porter, p. 31. James **FITZGERALD** of County Kilkenny is another immigrant who seems to have come out in one of the two vessels that year - *Ibid.*, p. 33.

[92] The *Marchioness of Donegal* was wrecked in October 1829 on reefs off East Point, PEI, with the loss of five lives - O'Grady, *Exiles & Islanders*, 107. He does not mention the fate of the survivors.

[93] One passenger in the *Collina* was Henry **COWLEY** - *Island Magazine/16*, p. 41.

[94] Clement Hubert, J.P., of Arichat, NS, reported to Lt.-Gov. Maitland, 15 Oct 1830, that the "peaceable inhabitants of this community are threatened with instant destruction of their lives and property by a lawless and merciless mob of Irishmen, many of them just arrived from Newfoundland, and a great number yet expected – This feeling has been caused by the Election which terminated here yesterday. Many have been wounded and one of the Irishmen killed, by the Scotch party, when attacked by the Irish – the Scotch remaining peaceable when left alone – The Scotch have all gone home, and the Irish left to act as they please . . ." – NSA, RG 1, Vol. 337, doc. 20. Adams, p. 415, estimated that 6,103 Irish emigrants reached the Maritimes in 1830. We can account for about 900 such arrivals in eight of the listed ships. Nine other ships might have conveyed a further thousand or so. Given the disparity between the six thousand figure of Adams and the possible two thousand found or postulated, there must be at least another 20 - 25 voyages which we have not found in records examined. In October 1830 the *Bittern* out of Wick, Scotland, arrived at Pictou with Irish passengers - www.rootsweb.amcestry.com/pictou/passlist

Month	Vessel	Port from	Port to	Passengers	Reference
May	Corsair[95]	Glasgow	PEI	206	O'Grady/147-8
June	Charlotte Keen [Kerr]	Belfast	Pugwash, NS	Yes	NS, 15 July 1830
June	Favourite[96]	Dublin	PEI	3	Island Magazine, 17
June	Feronia	Ireland	Saint John	Yes	Wright/134
June	Hannah[97]	New Ross/NL	PEI	30	Island Magazine, 17
June	Kelton[98]	Cork	Saint John	175	NS, 10 June 1830
June	Leslie Gault	Londonderry	Saint John	Yes	Wright/134
June	Solon	Waterford	Halifax	150	NS, 3 June 1830
July	Don[99]	Waterford	Orwell Bay, PEI	Yes	Island Magazine, 17
July	Saltern's Rock[100]	Cork	PEI	Yes	Island Magazine, 17
July	William Booth[101]	[Belfast]	Saint John	Yes	NBC, 26 June 1830

---

[95] The *Corsair*'s passengers were Irish people, mainly from northern counties, who had lived in Glasgow for varying lengths of time. They sailed on 2 April, reaching Charlottetown, PEI, on 19 May 1830. O'Grady, *Exiles & Islanders*, pp. 147 - 153, states that this voyage brought out 32 families from County Monaghan, and names 38 people who were, or may have been, passengers. The 1841 census enables us to suggest 64 passengers with varying degrees of assurance. Thirteen may be named as certainly passengers in the *Corsair*: James **BROGAN** [and his wife], Peter **DUFFY** [and his wife and 3 children], James **GILLAN** [and his wife and 3 children from County Londonderry], John **HAGGARTY**, Bernard **HERON**, Edward and William **KELLY**, John **KELLY** [and his wife from County Londonderry], Thomas **LOGAN**, Peter **McGILL** [and his wife and daughter], Peter **MURPHY**, Peter **O'HARE**, and Bernard **SWEENEY** - 25 people in all. Fifteen people were "probably" in the vessel: Ann **BRADY**, widow of John **FLINN**, William **CROZIER**, Robert **DEAN**, Mrs. Mary Ann **HEGGS** and James **HERON** from Donegal, Arthur **McGILL**, age 34, his wife Sarah **CURRAN** and his mother, all from County Antrim, James **McLAUGHLIN** and his wife Mary **PHILLIPS**, James **MOYNAGH**, his wife Mary **McQUAID** and her sister Elizabeth **McQUAID** [sisters of Francis McQuaid], John **MOONEY** and Henry Mooney [with his wife and 8 children] - 24 people in all. Two were possibly aboard: James **O'HARE** and Samuel **WILSON** [age 45, from County Armagh]. "Believed to have been aboard" were the brothers Bernard **JENNINGS** [weaver] and his wife Catherine **O'ROURKE** [with a daughter] and Peter Jennings and his wife Catherine [with 4 children] - 9 people in all. Finally there were four "who might have sailed" in the *Corsair*, namely, Thomas **FRIZZELL** from County Antrim, Daniel **HUGHES** from Tyholland, County Monaghan, and Patrick and Jane **O'DONNELL** from County Mayo.

[96] One known passenger in the *Favourite* was Mr. **CONNERY** - *Island Magazine/17*, p. 33.

[97] Thomas **HACKETT** from County Kilkenny probably emigrated in the *Hannah* - Porter, p. 31.

[98] The *Kelton* was wrecked at Little Port Hebert, NS, 1 June 1830, and 12 passengers drowned.

[99] It seems probable that Thomas **MORRISSEY**, a 20-year-old from County Kilkenny, came out in the *Don*.

[100] John **KENNEDY** from County Kerry appears to have emigrated in the *Saltern's Rock* in 1830 - Porter, p. 32. Also aboard were Kennedy's wife, Mary **PHEE**, and John **DORGAN** and his wife Margaret **LANE** of Capaclough [Cappaclogh, in Kilgobban Parish] - O'Grady. *Exiles & Islanders*, p. 83.

[101] One recent arrival from Ireland in the *William Booth* was James, son of James **WOODS** of Banbridge, County Down, who drowned at Saint John on 8 July 1830 - *NBC*, 10 July 1830. Another was Gregory **CASSIDY**, 21, from Mullaghdun, Fermanagh, who was buried on 22 June 1830, having died in a fall - *NBC*, 26 June 1830. A third was Terence **MONTAGUE**, a Catholic priest, 30, from Errigal, Tyrone, who died on 23 June 1830 - *City Gazette*, 30 June 1830.

Month	Vessel	Port from	Port to	Passengers	Reference
Aug	John and Mary[102]	Belfast	Halifax	[24]	*NS*, 5 Aug 1830
Aug	Peggy	Sligo	Saint John	Yes	Dobson I/114
Aug	Trafalgar	Sligo	Saint John	Yes	Dobson I/142
Nov	Quebec Trader	Dublin	PEI	2	Island Magazine, 17
-	Jane	Cork	Miramichi	Yes	On line[103]
-	Spy	Limerick	PEI	-	O'Grady/65

1831

Month	Vessel	Port from	Port to	Passengers	Reference
Apr	Adelphi	Cork	Halifax	241	*NS*, 21 Apr 1831
May	Argyle	Waterford	Halifax	240	*AR*, 21 May 1831
May	Britannia	Sligo	Saint John	97	Dobson I/23
May	Don	Waterford	Halifax	135 or 153	*NS*, 26 May 1831
May	Pandora[104]	Waterford	Pictou	130	*CP*, 28 May 1831
May	President[105]	Londonderry	Saint John	Yes	Dobson I/118
May	Quebec Trader[106]	Waterford	PEI	19	O'Grady/65
June	Archibald	Belfast	Halifax	31	*NS*, 16 June 1831
June	Aurora	Waterford	Halifax	101	*NS*, 9 June 1831
June	Charlotte Kerr	Sligo	Halifax	93	Dobson I/31
June	Hannah	Wexford/NL	PEI	22	Island Magazine, 17
June	Hibernia[107]	Kinsale	Halifax	180	*NS*, 30 June 1831
July	Adelaide	Galway	Granville, NS	60	Dobson I/1
July	Carleton	Ireland/NL	Halifax	4	*NS*, 14 July 1831
July	Duncan[108]	Dublin	Halifax	250	Dobson I/43

---

[102] The Customs Return of Immigrants at Halifax, 1830, reported the arrival of 174 Irish at that port. – NSA, RG 1, Vol. 238, doc. 27. Since the *Solon* [p. 40] reportedly carried 150 passengers, the remaining 24 appear to have arrived in the *John and Mary*.

[103] See irishfamine.ca/quarantine-coastal-areas/accounts-from-miramichi/page-6

[104] Six of the *Pandora*'s passengers were named in the *Colonial Patriot* (Pictou, NS), 4 June 1831. The three couples were married soon after their arrival at New Glasgow, NS: Robert **DOYLE** to Ann **MULLIGAN**, Thomas **HUGGAN** to Catherine **DUNN**, and Richard **DALY** to Mary **DOLLARD**. The last-named was from County Kilkenny, as was most likely Daly.

[105] The brig *President*, built in 1824, probably in Québec, "displaced 105 tons, and was wrecked off the Wicklow coast of Ireland in 1833. . . . Passenger journeys to Saint John took up a great deal of the outbound journeys." - Cecil J. Houston and William J. Smyth, *Irish Emigration and Canadian Settlement; Patterns, Links, & Letters*. Toronto: University of Toronto Press, 1990, p. 86.

[106] The names of three passengers were Mr. **CONNERY**, Richard and Miss **GOFF** - *The Island Magazine*/17, p. 34.

[107] The brig *Hibernia*, "with 200 passengers, hove to off the mouth of the harbour . . . and landed about 50 of them in boats, and then proceeded on her passage." - *NS*, 30 June 1831.

[108] The *Duncan* carried 250 passengers and landed 100 of them at Mary Joseph, on the eastern shore of Nova Scotia, and of these 70 went on to Halifax. The remainder of the passengers proceeded to Saint John, NB - *Novascotian*, 4 Aug 1831. The numbers were reported differently later , and that almost 200 were on their way to Halifax, and about 60 were proceeding to Saint John - *Novascotian*, 11 Aug 1831.

Month	Vessel	Port from	Port to	Passengers	Reference
July	Powels	Ireland/NL	Sydney	Yes	Martell/69
Aug	Lady Sherbrooke[109]	Londonderry	Halifax	300	*NS*, 17 Aug 1831
Aug	Success	Ireland/NL	Halifax	Yes	*NS*, 25 Aug 1831
Aug	Venus[110]	Dublin	PEI	40	Island Magazine, 17
Aug	William Harrington	Limerick	Pictou	115	*CP*, 20 Aug 1831
Oct	Eleanor Gordon[111]	Londonderry	Saint John	56	Customs/110-111
Nov	Leslie Gault	Londonderry	Saint John	Yes	Dobson II/77
Nov	Quebec Trader	Dublin	PEI	19	Island Magazine, 17
-	Billow	Newry	Saint John	Yes	Dobson I/20

1832

Month	Vessel	Port from	Port to	Passengers	Reference
Apr	Pallas[112]	Cork	Halifax	120	*NS*, 12 Apr 1832
Apr	Sarah	Londonderry	Saint John	220	Dobson III/94
Apr	Wellington	Cork	Halifax	128	*NS*, 26 Apr 1832
May	Betock	Waterford	Halifax	126	*NS*, 31 May 1832
May	Jane	Waterford	Halifax	111	*NS*, 7 June 1832
May	Jane	Cork	Halifax	101	*NS*, 7 June 1832
May	Pandora[113]	Waterford	PEI	108	Dobson I/113
May	President	Londonderry	Saint John	Yes	Dobson I/118
May	William[114]	Ireland	Saint John	Yes	*NBRG*, 13 June 1832
June	Friends	Waterford	Halifax	181	*AR*, 9 June 1832
June	Highlander	Waterford	Halifax	Yes	*AR*, 9 June 1832
July	John and Mary	Belfast	Wallace, NS	68	*CP*, 4 Aug 1832
July	Susannah	Cork	Halifax	30	*NS*, 12 Apr 1832
Aug	Britannia	Sligo	Saint John	Yes	Dobson I/23
Aug	Hippo	Waterford	Halifax	Yes	*AR*, 9 Sep 1832.
Aug	Independence[115]	Kinsale	Saint John	15	Dobson III/51
Aug	Minstrel	Cork	Halifax	145	*NS*, 23 Aug 1832

---

[109] The *Lady Sherbrooke* was wrecked at Cape Bay, NL, 31 July 1831. The 27 passengers who were rescued were brought to Halifax in the *Pomona*.

[110] The *Venus* carried 190 passengers, dropping off 40 at Three Rivers, PEI, and taking the remainder on to Québec. O'Grady, *Exiles & Islanders*, p. 65, calls the vessel the *Venus II*.

[111] The passenger list was published in *Passengers to New Brunswick: The Custom House Records – 1833, 34, 37 & 38* (Saint John: New Brunswick Genealogical Society, 1987), pp. 110 - 111.

[112] The *Pallas* discharged 120 passengers at Halifax. - *Halifax Journal*, 11 June 1832. The ship probably went on to New Brunswick with another 80, since Dobson II, p. 101, credits the vessel with 200 passengers.

[113] Among the passengers brought out in the *Pandora*'s voyages in 1832 were Patrick **NELLIGAN** from County Kerry, with his wife and sons John, Patrick, and Michael - Porter, p. 30.

[114] One passenger from the brig *William* was William **FARMER**, who died, 31 May 1832, in the Alms House at Saint John, having "lately arrived" - *New Brunswick Royal Gazette*, 13 June 1832.

[115] The passenger list was published in *Passengers to New Brunswick: The Custom House Records*, pp. 150 - 151.

Month	Vessel	Port from	Port to	Passengers	Reference
Sep	Pandora[116]	Waterford	PEI	19	Island Magazine, 17
Nov	George and Henry	Dublin	PEI	Yes	Island Magazine, 17
Dec	Betsy and Nancy	Ireland/NL	Halifax	14	AR, 8 Dec 1832

1833[117]

Month	Vessel	Port from	Port to	Passengers	Reference
Jan	Symmetry[118]	Londonderry	Saint John	40	Customs/324 - 325
May	Albion[119]	Newry	Saint John	130	Dobson II/4
May	Bartley[120]	Londonderry	Saint John	111	Dobson III/13
May	Billow[121]	Londonderry	Saint John	109	Dobson III/14
May	Dorcas Savage[122]	Belfast	Saint John	155	Dobson II/32; III/28
May	Duncan Gibbs[123]	Dublin	St. Andrews	384	Dobson I/43
May	Emerald	Dublin	St. Andrews	160	Dobson I/50
May	Gilbert Henderson	Dublin	St. Andrews	140	Dobson I/61
May	Hannah[124]	Belfast	Cape Breton	Yes	Dobson I/65
May	Independence[125]	Kinsale	Saint John	61	Dobson III/51

[116] Maurice **SOMERS**, his wife Mary **KENNY**, and one child, who settled at Kinkora, PEI, seem to have crossed in the *Pandora* in 1832. The couple had seven more children born by the time of the 1841 census of PEI.

[117] Between 1833 and 1836, with occasional reference to 1839, the Ordnance Survey Memoirs name 244 emigrants from Ulster to the Maritimes. See Appendix III for their names.

[118] The passenger list was published in *Passengers to New Brunswick: The Custom House Records*, pp. 324 - 325. The list gives the precise place of origin. The vessel seems to have sailed in September 1832 and arrived in January 1833.

[119] The *Albion* sank, 2 May 1833 and most passengers were lost. The *Neptune* rescued 15 people.

[120] The passenger list was published in *Passengers to New Brunswick: The Custom House Records,* pp. 21 - 23. The list gives specific place of origin.

[121] The passenger list was published in *Passengers to New Brunswick: The Custom House Records,* pp. 32 - 34. The list gives county of origin, in all cases county Donegal, Londonderry or Tyrone.

[122] The passenger list was published in *Passengers to New Brunswick: The Custom House Records ,* pp. 89 - 93.

[123] Some of the passengers in the *Duncan Gibbs* went on to Québec.

[124] The *Hannah* sank near St. Ann, Cape Breton, on 31 May 1833. The passengers were saved, but did not remain in Cape Breton.

[125] The passenger list was published in *Passengers to New Brunswick: The Custom House Records,* pp. 141 - 143.

Month	Vessel	Port from	Port to	Passengers	Reference
May	Neptune[126]	Newry	Saint John	71	Dobson II/97; III/79
May	New Felix	Dublin	St. Andrews	36	Dobson I/109
May	Pallas[127]	Cork	Saint John	130	Dobson III/82
May	Pandora	Waterford	PEI	34	Island Magazine, 17
May	Pomona	Dublin	St. Andrews	167	Dobson I/117
May	St. Catherine	Waterford	Halifax	138	NS, 2 May 1833
May	Stephen Wright	Dublin	St. Andrews	326	Dobson I/137
May	Sydney	Ireland/NL	Halifax	30	NS, 6 June 1833
May	Volunteer[128]	Cork	Cape Breton	200	Dobson II/134
May	Ward[129]	Limerick	Saint John	74	Customs/355-359
June	Active	Londonderry	Saint John	273	Customs House/1
June	Dolphin	Ireland/NL	Halifax	10	NS, 20 June 1833
June	Elizabeth[130]	Galway	Saint John	94	Dobson III/35
June	Ellergill	Londonderry	Saint John	321	Customs/115
June	John and Mary[131]	Belfast	Saint John	148	Customs/162-165
June	Madawaska[132]	Londonderry	Saint John	179	Customs/196-199
June	Maria[133]	Belfast	Saint John	13	Customs/203-204

---

[126] The passenger list was published in *Passengers to New Brunswick: The Custom House Records*, pp. 226 - 227. The list gives precise place of origin in Armagh, Down and Monaghan. The *Neptune* rescued 15 passengers from the sunken *Albion*.

[127] The passenger list was published in *Passengers to New Brunswick: The Custom House Records*, pp. 237 - 240. This list is undated, so it could possibly belong in 1834.

[128] The *Volunteer* was wrecked off Cape Breton Island, 30 May 1833. All passengers were saved.

[129] The passenger list was published in *Passengers to New Brunswick: The Custom House Records*, pp. 355 - 359. The list gives passengers' places of origin in west Munster.

[130] The passenger list was published in *Passengers to New Brunswick: The Custom House Records*, pp. 112 - 114. One passenger, Patrick **McDONOUGH**, 30, a carpenter, was sought by his brother Michael, of Boston, who advertised in the *Boston Pilot*, 18 July 1840.

[131] The passenger list was published in *Passengers to New Brunswick: The Custom House Records*, pp. 162 - 165.

[132] The passenger list was published in *Passengers to New Brunswick: The Custom House Records*, pp. 196 - 199. The list gives place of origin in western Ulster.

[133] The passenger list was published in *Passengers to New Brunswick: The Custom House Records*, p. 203 - 204. The thirteen named were Richard, 21, stone cutter, Margaret, 25, spinster, Eliza, 23, spinster, Jane, 2, and Joseph, ¼, **CRANGLEY**; James, 26, labourer, Jane, 28, spinster, Hugh, 30, labourer, Mary, 5, and Samuel,1, **CROTHERS**; William **McCAUDRY**, 28, stone cutter, Samuel **McCUTCHEON**, 19, labourer, and Elizabeth **ROCKLA**, 66, spinster. Given the configuration of the two family groups, it appears "spinster" was used in an occupational sense, and that two of those women were also wives. At Belfast on 19 April that appeared to be the passenger list. However, upon reaching Saint John it turned out that the vessel took on six additional passengers at the port of Irvine, Scotland, two of whom – John **GIBB,** 23, and Thomas **GIBB**, 19 – were labourers from the Parish of St. Andrew's in Dublin, probably brothers. The total passenger bill was therefore 19 persons, 15 Irish and 4 Scots.

Month	Vessel	Port from	Port to	Passengers	Reference
June	Salus[134]	Londonderry	Saint John	176	Dobson III/93
June	Sea Horse[135]	Dublin	St. Andrews	59	Dobson I/134
June	Thomas Hanford[136]	Cork	Saint John	158	Customs/329-333
June	Trafalgar[137]	Limerick	Saint John	5	Dobson III/103
June	Trial[138]	Londonderry	Saint John	101	Dobson III/103
June	Union	Cork	Halifax	30	Martell/75
June	Zephyr[139]	Ballyshannon	Saint John	89	Customs/374-375
July	Charity[140]	Kinsale	Saint John	68	Dobson III/21
July	Edward Reid[141]	Londonderry	Saint John	154	Customs/96-98
July	Jane Vilet	Londonderry	Saint John	255	Customs/158
July	Latonia	Dublin	Pugwash, NS	176	Dobson I/88
July	Reward[142]	Cork	Saint John	83	Dobson III/88
July	Susan Jane[143]	Ballyshannon	Saint John	54	Dobson III/99

---

[134] The passenger list was published in *Passengers to New Brunswick: The Custom House Records*, pp. 293 - 297. The list gives the precise place of origin in Ulster.

[135] The passenger list was published in *Passengers to New Brunswick: The Custom House Records*, pp. 308 - 309. The vessel proceeded on to Québec. The passenger list gives the county of origin in various counties of Leinster province: 20 from Dublin, 14 from Kildare, 13 from Leix, 8 from Longford, and 4 from Meath.

[136] The passenger list was published in *Passengers to New Brunswick: The Custom House Records*, pp. 329 - 333. The ship is called the *Thomas Hansforth* in Dobson/1.

[137] The passenger list was published in *Passengers to New Brunswick: The Custom House Records*, p. 343. Their names were James **HARRAGAN**, 23, farmer from Adare, Francis **LAUGHLAN**, 22, gentleman, Limerick, Dennis **O'DAY** from Adare, Ellen **O'MEALY**, 22, spinster from Limerick, Joseph O'Mely, 19, gentleman, Limerick.

[138] The passenger list was published in *Passengers to New Brunswick: The Custom House Records*, pp. 344 - 346. The list gives the precise place of origin in western Ulster.

[139] The passenger list was published in *Passengers to New Brunswick: The Custom House Records*, pp. 374 - 375.

[140] The passenger list was published in *Passengers to New Brunswick: The Custom House Records*, pp. 64 - 67.

[141] The passenger list was published in *Passengers to New Brunswick: The Custom House Records*, pp. 96 - 100. The list gives county of origin: Donegal, Fermanagh, Londonderry or Tyrone.

[142] The passenger list was published in *Passengers to New Brunswick: The Custom House Records*, pp. 277 - 279.

[143] The passenger list was published in *Passengers to New Brunswick: The Custom House Records*, pp. 318 - 319.

Month	Vessel	Port from	Port to	Passengers	Reference
July	Ugoni[144]	Belfast	Saint John	174	Customs /348-352
Aug	Creole	Ireland/NL	Halifax	Yes	*NS*, 22 Aug 1833
Aug	Forth[145]	Londonderry	Saint John	104	Customs/124-126
Aug	Molly Moore	Waterford	Pictou	38	*CP*, 27 Aug 1833
Aug	Silestria[146]	Belfast	Saint John	66	Customs/310-312
Aug	William[147]	Cork	Saint John	14	Customs/361-362
Aug	William of Fishguard[148]	Kinsale	Saint John	80	Customs/358-360
Sep	Billow[149]	Londonderry	Saint John	39	Customs/35-36
Sep	Leslie Gault[150]	Londonderry	Saint John	70	Customs/185-187
Sep	Mary Ann[151]	Belfast	Saint John	4	Customs/211
Sep	Providence[152]	Cork	Saint John	32	Customs/263-264
Sep	Quintin Leitch[153]	Newry	Saint John	10	Customs/270-271

---

[144] The passenger list was published in *Passengers to New Brunswick: The Custom House Records*, pp.345 - 352.

[145] The passenger list was published in *Passengers to New Brunswick: The Custom House Records*, pp. 124 - 126. The list gives precise place of origin.

[146] The passenger list was published in *Passengers to New Brunswick: The Custom House Records*, pp. 310 - 312.

[147] The passenger list was published in *Passengers to New Brunswick: The Custom House Records* pp. 361 - 362. The passengers were Mary, 30, wife, Ann, 10, and Thomas, 7, **BURNS**; Mary , 30, wife, and Thomas, 6, **DESMOND**; Thomas **HANSON**, 22, labourer; Catherine **HAYES**, 15; Jeremiah **LONG**, 25, labourer; Thomas **NEAL**, 18, seaman; William **RING**, 22, labourer; Edward **SAXTY**, 23, seaman; James, 23, labourer, and Mary **SULLIVAN**, 22, wife; James **WOOD**, 23, labourer.

[148] The passenger list was published in *Passengers to New Brunswick: The Custom House Records*, pp. 358 - 360.

[149] The passenger list was published in *Passengers to New Brunswick: The Custom House Records*, pp. 35 - 36. The list gives origin: Tyrone, 17, Donegal, 16, Fermanagh, 5, Londonderry, 1.

[150] The passenger list was published in *Passengers to New Brunswick: The Custom House Records*, pp. 185 - 187. The list gives precise place of origin.

[151] The passenger list was published in *Passengers to New Brunswick: The Custom House Records*, p. 211. The passengers were John **CLARK**, 30, labourer, William **CLARKE**, 28, labourer, Patrick **HAGAN**, 25, labourer, and Charles **LISON**, 23, farmer.

[152] The passenger list was published in *Passengers to New Brunswick: The Custom House Records*, pp. 263 - 264.

[153] The passenger list was published in *Passengers to New Brunswick: The Custom House Records*, pp. 270 - 271. The passengers were Matthew, 28, farmer and shoemaker, Susan, 24, spinster, and Catherine, 17, spinster, **COLLINS** from Louth, County Louth; Margaret, 23, spinster, John, 3, and Patrick, 1, **DONAHY** from Armagh, County Armagh; Nancy, 51, spinster, and Catherine, 18, spinster, from Armagh, County Armagh; John **LOCKHEART**, 28, farmer from Maney Glass, County Armagh [perhaps Moneyglass, County Antrim], and John **McCONNELL**, 24, shoemaker from Rostrevor, County Down.

Month	Vessel	Port from	Port to	Passengers	Reference
Sep	Thomas Hanford[154]	Cork	Saint John	10	Dobson III/102
Oct	Sarah[155]	Belfast	Saint John	40	Customs/300-301
Oct	Triton[156]	Newry	Saint John	13	Customs/347
Oct	Zephyr[157]	Ballyshannon	Saint John	71	Customs/371-373
-	Ann and Mary[158]	Cork	Saint John	37	Customs/13-14
-	Britannia[159]	Sligo	Saint John	106	Customs/43-45
-	Everetta[160]	Londonderry	Saint John	42	Dobson I/52
-	Hibernia[161]	Kinsale	Saint John	85	Dobson III/48
-	Jane[162]	Galway	Saint John	58	Customs/156-157

[154] The passenger list was published in *Passengers to New Brunswick: The Custom House Records*, p. 328. The passengers were Michael, 22, labourer, and Patrick, 32, labourer, **CONNOLY**; Robert, 25, farmer, Mary, 25, wife, and Robert, 3, **HALL**; Lillis **MILLS**, 22, spinster; Mary, 30, spinster, and Patrick, 32, labourer, **MURRAY**; Mary **PRATT**, 33, spinster; and Fanny **ROYNAN**, 21, spinster.

[155] The passenger list was published in *Passengers to New Brunswick: The Custom House Records*, pp. 300 - 301.

[156] The passenger list was published in *Passengers to New Brunswick: The Custom House Records*, p. 347. The passengers were Margaret, 40, spinster [clearly an instance where 'spinster' was used in an occupational sense], William, 6, son, Mary Jane, 4, daughter, Eliza, 2, daughter, and Jane, 24, spinster, **OSBURN**, from Castleblaney, County Monaghan; Jo. **KEMPSTON**, 30, bleacher from Keady, County Armagh; Eliza, 25, and Jane, 20, spinsters from Mourne, County Down; Jane, 40, spinster, Jane, 8, Mary Ann, 6, and Alexander, 2, **DOUGLASS** from Mourne, County Down.

[157] The passenger list was published in *Passengers to New Brunswick: The Custom House Records*, pp. 371 - 373. There are two lists, with 43 and 28 people, respectively, giving the total of 71. Over half the names in the shorter list appear to repeat those in the longer list, so that the actual number of passengers is uncertain.

[158] The passenger list was published in *Passengers to New Brunswick: The Custom House Records*, pp. 13 - 14.

[159] This is a good example of how variable are the numbers of passengers reported. Dobson III/16 found 94 passengers, the Customs count claims 101. My name-by-name count found 106 passengers. Such discrepancies appear in several other instances. While one could attribute a drop between the number reported to embarked and the number who safely arrived at the destination to deaths on the voyage, to have an increase without any births being reported on the passage suggests either poor bookkeeping or that the ship picked up passengers after clearing customs in Sligo.

[160] The passenger list was published in *Passengers to New Brunswick: The Custom House Records*, pp. 105 - 106. The list gives precise place of origin in Tyrone, Fermanagh and Londonderry.

[161] The passenger list was published in *Passengers to New Brunswick: The Custom House Records*, pp. 132 - 133.

[162] The passenger list was published in *Passengers to New Brunswick: The Custom House Records*, pp. 156 - 157. The year is not stated, but circumstantial evidence suggests the year was 1833.

Month	Vessel	Port from	Port to	Passengers	Reference
-	Lune	Dublin	Saint John	1	Power/178
-	Matilda[163]	Cork	Saint John	163	Customs/214-217
-	Morning Star	Belfast	Saint John	Yes	Power/178
-	Protector[164]	Londonderry	Saint John	325	Customs/256-262

1834

Month	Vessel	Port from	Port to	Passengers	Reference
Apr	Thomas Hanford	Cork	Saint John	3	Customs/338
Apr	William[165]	Londonderry	Saint John	80	Customs/363-365
May	Ceres[166]	Sligo	Halifax	172	AR, 24 May 1834
May	Charity[167]	Kinsale	Saint John	152	Customs/64-67
May	Edwin[168]	Dublin	Saint John	160	Customs/101-104
May	Fidelity[169]	Dublin	Cape Breton	Yes	Dobson I/55
May	Hannah	Cork	Saint John	278	Customs/130
May	Henrietta	Ireland/NL	Halifax	30	NS, 29 May 1834
May	Independence[170]	Kinsale	Saint John	235	Customs/144-149
May	King	Waterford	Halifax	159	NS, 22 May 1834
May	Margaret[171]	Belfast	Saint John	10	Dobson I/95; III/68
May	Molly Moore	Waterford	Halifax	119	NS, 8 May 1834
May	Neptune[172]	Newry	Saint John	120	Customs/222-225
May	Pons Aelii	Cork	Saint John	246	Dobson III/85

---

[163] The year is not stated, but circumstantial evidence suggests the year was 1833.

[164] The passenger list was published in *Passengers to New Brunswick: The Custom House Records*, pp. 256 - 262. The year is not stated, but circumstantial evidence suggests that the year was 1833. The list gives place of origin in Ulster.

[165] The passenger list was published in *Passengers to New Brunswick: The Custom House Records*, pp. 363 - 364. The list gives place of origin: 46 from County Donegal, 27 from Tyrone, 15 from Fermanagh, and 2 from County Londonderry.

[166] The *Ceres* carried 172 people, of whom 47 disembarked at Halifax, and 125 at Saint John.

[167] The passenger list was published in *Passengers to New Brunswick: The Custom House Records*, pp. 64 - 67.

[168] The passenger list was published in *Passengers to New Brunswick: The Custom House Records*, pp. 101 - 104.

[169] The *Fidelity* was wrecked off Scatari Island, Cape Breton, and 29 passengers were lost.

[170] The passenger list was published in *Passengers to New Brunswick: The Custom House Records*, pp. 144 - 149.

[171] The *Margaret* was wrecked near Cape Sable, NS, 8 May 1837. Ten passengers were saved.

[172] The passenger list was published in *Passengers to New Brunswick: The Custom House Records*, pp. 222 - 225. The list gives place of origin.

Month	Vessel	Port from	Port to	Passengers	Reference
May	Proselyte[173]	Limerick	Richibucto, NB	233	Dobson I/120
May	Pandora[174]	Waterford	PEI	76	Island Magazine, 17
June	Ambassador[175]	Londonderry	Saint John	178	Customs/7-11
June	Ann and Mary[176]	Cork	Saint John	110	Customs/15-17
June	Cupid[177]	Warrenpoint	Saint John	151	Customs/76-79
June	Dorothy	Sligo	Saint John	172	Customs/94-95
June	Highlander[178]	Londonderry	Saint John	200	Customs/136-140
June	Jane	Waterford	Halifax	108	NS, 5 June 1834
June	Lady Douglas[179]	New Ross	Saint John	27	Customs/176
June	Leslie Gault[180]	Londonderry	Saint John	128	Customs/181-184
June	Sea Horse[181]	Galway	Saint John	129	Customs/305-307
June	Susanna	Dublin	Saint John	111	Customs/323
June	Trafalgar[182]	Galway	Saint John	162	Customs/339-342

---

[173] The *Proselyte* was wrecked at Flat Islands, NL, 10 May 1834. The *Juno* took 233 survivors to Richibucto, New Brunswick, arriving there on 29 May 1834.

[174] One passenger in the *Pandora* was George **CONROY**. The remaining 75 were "in steerage".

[175] The passenger list was published in *Passengers to New Brunswick: The Custom House Records*, pp. 7 - 11. The list gives county of origin, in all but seven instances Donegal, Londonderry or Tyrone.

[176] The passenger list was published in *Passengers to New Brunswick: The Custom House Records* , pp. 15 - 16.

[177] The passenger list was published in *Passengers to New Brunswick: The Custom House Records*, pp. 76 - 79. The list gives place of origin: 95 from County Louth, 29 from County Down, and 27 from County Armagh, making a total of 151 passengers.

[178] The passenger list was published in *Passengers to New Brunswick: The Custom House Records*, pp. 136 - 140. The list gives precise place of origin in western Ulster.

[179] Some of the passengers were bound for St. John's, Newfoundland.

[180] The passenger list was published in *Passengers to New Brunswick: The Custom House Records*, pp.181 - 184. The list gives precise place of origin in western Ulster.

[181] The passenger list was published in *Passengers to New Brunswick: The Custom House Records*, pp. 305 - 307. One passenger, Mary **CRADDOCK**, Headford, Galway, was sought by her husband John **FORD** of Boston - *Boston Pilot*, 28 July 1838. Also sought was Peter **KILLALAGH**, 25, labourer, who landed at Saint John, then went to Digby, NS. His brother Patrick **KILLALEY** advertised in the *Boston Pilot*, 3 July 1841.

[182] The passenger list was published in *Passengers to New Brunswick: The Custom House Records*, pp. 339 - 342.

Month	Vessel	Port from	Port to	Passengers	Reference
June	Betsy Heron[183]	Belfast	Saint John	220	Power/180
June	Eden[184]	Cork	Bay Chaleur	181	NS, 5 June 1834
June	Eleanor[185]	Londonderry	Saint John	74	Customs/107-109
June	Nancy[186]	Londonderry	Saint John	95	Customs/219-221
June	Perseus[187]	Londonderry	Saint John	307	Customs/242-249
July	Breeze[188]	Dublin	Saint John	115	Customs/40-42
July	Dorcas Savage[189]	Belfast	Saint John	171	Customs/89-93
July	Levant Star[190]	Cork	Saint John	109	Customs/189-191
July	Nicholson	Sligo	Saint John	164	Customs/230
July	Ranger[191]	Londonderry	Saint John	120	Customs/272-274
July	Sarah[192]	Belfast	Saint John	98	Customs/302-304
July	Zephyr[193]	Ballyshannon	Saint John	120	Customs/376-378
Aug	Britannia	Sligo	Saint John	101	Customs/46-49
Aug	Cupid	Newry	Saint John	18	Customs/80

---

[183] The passenger list was published in *Passengers to New Brunswick: The Custom House Records*, pp. 24 - 28.

[184] The *Eden* called at Halifax late in May 1834 and may have left some passengers there.

[185] The passenger list was published in *Passengers to New Brunswick: The Custom House Records*, pp. 107 - 109. The list gives precise place of origin.

[186] The passenger list was published in *Passengers to New Brunswick: The Custom House Records*, pp. 219 - 221. The list gives precise place of origin.

[187] The passenger list was published in *Passengers to New Brunswick: The Custom House Records*, pp. 242 - 249. Although the document claims there were 294 passengers, the roster lists 99 from County Donegal, 81 from Antrim, 72 from Londonderry and 55 from Tyrone, giving a total of 307 passengers, three of whom were not present when the ship embarked.

[188] The passenger list was published in *Passengers to New Brunswick: The Custom House Records*, pp. 40 - 42,

[189] The passenger list was published in *Passengers to New Brunswick: The Custom House Records* , pp. 89 - 93.

[190] The passenger list was published in *Passengers to New Brunswick: The Custom House Records*, pp. 189 - 191.

[191] The passenger list was published in *Passengers to New Brunswick: The Custom House Records*, pp. 272 - 274.The list gives county of origin: Donegal, Londonderry, or Tyrone.

[192] The passenger list was published in *Passengers to New Brunswick: The Custom House Records*, pp. 302 - 304.

[193] The passenger list was published in *Passengers to New Brunswick: The Custom House Records*, pp. 376 - 378.

Month	Vessel	Port from	Port to	Passengers	Reference
Aug	Leslie Gault[194]	Londonderry	Saint John	12	Customs/179
Aug	Maria[195]	Cork	Saint John	125	Customs/205-207
Aug	Molly Moore	Waterford	Pictou	14	Dobson I/105
Aug	Preston[196]	Sligo	Saint John	72	Customs/251-253
Aug	Thomas Hanford[197]	Cork	Saint John	74	Customs/334-336
Sep	Pandora	Waterford	PEI	9	Island Magazine, 17
Sep	Robert Burns[198]	Londonderry	Saint John	243	Customs/280-285
Sep	William	Londonderry	Saint John	21	Customs/366
Oct	Ceres[199]	Sligo	Saint John	9	Dobson III/21
Oct	Independence	Kinsale	Saint John	33	Customs/152
Oct	Orient[200]	Belfast	Saint John	10	Customs/231
Nov	James Lemon[201]	Londonderry	Saint John	5	Customs/154

---

[194] The passenger list was published in *Passengers to New Brunswick: The Custom House Records*, p. 179. The passengers were John, 30, labourer, Mary , 28, spinster [occupational term], James, 15, labourer, and Rebecca, 7, **McCLAIN** from Muff, County Donegal; James, 26, labourer, and Mary, 25, spinster, **DEVLIN** from Derry; Jane **MORRISON**, 25, spinster, from Derry; John **O'HARE**, 27, labourer, from Derry; Thomas **SMITH**, 24, labourer, from Derry; W. **McCONNELL**, 19; Isabella, 30, and Eliza, 14, **HOOD**, spinsters from St. Johnstown, County Donegal.

[195] The passenger list was published in *Passengers to New Brunswick: The Custom House Records*, pp. 205 - 207.

[196] The passenger list was published in *Passengers to New Brunswick: The Custom House Records*, pp. 251 - 253. One passenger was James **MORGAN**, 20, from Boyle, Roscommon, who landed at Saint John on 13 Aug 1834 and then proceeded to Eastport, Maine. He was sought by his father William Morgan - *Boston Pilot*, 5 Oct 1839.

[197] The passenger list was published in *Passengers to New Brunswick: The Custom House Records*, pp. 94 - 96.

[198] The passenger list was published in *Passengers to New Brunswick: The Custom House Records*, pp. 280 - 285. The list gives the exact place of origin.

[199] The passenger list was published in *Passengers to New Brunswick: The Custom House Records*, p. 60.

[200] The passenger list was published in *Passengers to New Brunswick: The Custom House Records*, p. 231. The passengers were James, 24, labourer, and Maria, 18, spinster, **CLAWSON**; Patrick, 50, labourer, Isabella, 45, spinster, James, 28, nailer, Mary, 20, spinster, Catherine, 19, spinster, Louisa, 15, spinster, Isabella, 12, spinster, and William, 10, **DUFFY**.

[201] The passenger list was published in *Passengers to New Brunswick: The Custom House Records*, p. 154. Three of the five passengers were Scots from Glasgow. The two Irish passengers were John **GAMBLE**, 25, labourer from County Tyrone, and Mary **MILLER**, 24, spinster from 'S. Lerty' [south liberty, city of Londonderry].

Month	Vessel	Port from	Port to	Passengers	Reference
Oct	Protector[202]	Ballymoney	Saint John	30	Customs/254-255
Nov	Thomas Hanford[203]	Baltimore	Saint John	5	Dobson III/102
Nov	Katherine	Belfast	Saint John	2	Customs/168
Dec	Anna	Cork	PEI	1	O'Grady/63
-	Charlotte	Cork	Saint John	Yes	Power/180
-	Daniel O'Connell[204]	Londonderry	Saint John	105	Customs/81-83
-	Matilda[205]	Cork	Saint John	163	Power/180
-	Triton	Newry	Saint John	Yes	Power/179

1835[206]

Month	Vessel	Port from	Port to	Passengers	Reference
May	Grace[207]	Belfast	PEI	221	Island Magazine, 17
May	Pandora[208]	Waterford	PEI	35	Island Magazine, 17
June	Britannia	Sligo	Saint John	Yes	Dobson I/23
June	Molly Moore	Waterford	Crapaud, PEI	12	Island Magazine, 17
June	Susan Crane [Jane?]	Sligo	Saint John	Yes	Dobson I/138

[202] The passenger list was published in *Passengers to New Brunswick: The Custom House Records*, pp. 254 - 255. The list gives the precise place of origin. Some records refer to this ship as the *Protection*.

[203] The passenger list was published in *Passengers to New Brunswick: The Custom House Records*, p. 337. The passengers were Thomas **HOLMES**, 50, mariner; Thomas **DONOVAN**, 45, labourer; Johannah, 30, Denis, 3, and Mary, 1 yr. 6 mos., **FALVEY**.

[204] The passenger list was published in *Passengers to New Brunswick: The Custom House Records,* pp. 81 - 83. The list is undated but the source covers only the years 1833, 1834, and 1837, 1838. The list reported 61 passengers from Donegal, 27 from Londonderry, 4 from Tyrone, and 3 from Monaghan.

[205] The passenger list was published in *Passengers to New Brunswick: The Custom House Records*, pp. 214 - 217.

[206] An unnamed ship from Ireland reached PEI via Canso, Nova Scotia, before 15 Dec 1835 - *The Island Magazine*/17, p. 37. Adams, p. 415, found 10,479 arrivals in the Maritimes from Ireland in 1834, a year for which the Saint John Custom House records exist, but just 2,686 in 1835, for which those records are lost. He offered no figures at all for 1836 due to the absence of records upon which to base an estimate.

[207] The *Grace* lost 25 passengers, including one man and 24 children who died en route during a measles outbreak. The remaining 196 people were safely landed. Peter McGuigan, "From Wexford and Monaghan: the Lot 22 Irish," *The Abegweit Review*, Vol. 5:1 (Winter 1985), p. 65, puts the number of passengers in the *Grace* considerably higher, at 340 souls. Patrick and Mary **HUGHES** from the Parish of Tynan, County Armagh, were passengers in the *Grace*. Philip Hughes and his family from the same place may have been, although O'Grady, *Exiles & Islanders*, p. 151, gives their date of emigration as 1834.

[208] Mr. N. and Miss **CONROY** and Mr. **FORAN** were passengers, along with 32 "in the steerage - *The Island Magazine*/17, p. 37. Among the latter were probably William **DILLON** and Patrick **CARRIGAN** from County Tipperary - O'Grady, *Exiles & Islanders*, p. 82. Other passengers may have been John **BRENAN** and his wife Alice **BRENHAM** and family, and John **KEEFE** and his wife Margaret **DAWSON** and their family. Both families lived at Kinkora, PEI, in 1841 when the census of PEI was made. John **LANIGAN** from County Tipperary was another passenger - *The Herald* (Charlottetown), 7 Feb 1887.

Month	Vessel	Port from	Port to	Passengers	Reference
June	Timanda	Waterford	Halifax	66	*NS*, 25 June 1835
June	William Ewing[209]	Belfast	Saint John	300	Dobson I/151
Oct	Ceres	Sligo	Saint John	Yes	Dobson I/29
Oct	Cordelia	Ireland/NL	Halifax	28	*NS*, 8 Oct 1835
-	Margot	Belfast	PEI	80	Dobson III/85

1836

Month	Vessel	Port from	Port to	Passengers	Reference
May	Aimwell	Londonderry	Saint John	Yes	Dobson II/3
May	Bob Logic	Cork	Halifax	86	*NS*, 26 May 1836
May	Eagle[210]	Waterford	Pictou	122	*NS*, 2 June 1836
May	Elizabeth	Cork	Halifax	75	*NS*, 2 June 1836
May	Leslie Gault	Londonderry	Saint John	Yes	Dobson II/77
May	Spruce	Sligo	Saint John	Yes	Dobson I/137
May	Zephyr[211]	Donegal	Saint John	Yes	*NBC*, 21 May 1836
June	Charity	Londonderry	Saint John	Yes	Dobson II/23
June	Intrepid	Londonderry	Saint John	Yes	Dobson II/63
June	Maria[212]	Dublin	Halifax	67	*NS*, 3 July 1836
June	Molly Moore	Waterford	Halifax	70	*NS*, 9 June 1836
June	Pandora[213]	Waterford	PEI	47	Island Magazine, 18
July	Formosa	Londonderry	Saint John	Yes	Dobson II/44
July	Highlander	Londonderry	Saint John	Yes	Dobson II/59
July	Water Witch	Ireland/NL	Halifax	9 or more	*NS*, 28 July 1836
Sep	Aimwell	Londonderry	Saint John	Yes	Dobson II/3
Sep	Leslie Gault	Londonderry	Saint John	Yes	Dobson II/77
Sep	Spruce	Londonderry	Saint John	Yes	Dobson II/122
Sep	Thomas Hanford[214]	Cork	PEI	15	Dobson I/141
Oct	Charity	Londonderry	Saint John	Yes	Dobson II/23

---

[209] The *William Ewing* was wrecked off Scatari Island, Cape Breton, 17 June 1835. All the crew and passengers were rescued. The schooner *Trio* brought 94 passengers to Halifax, but most of the survivors were sent to Québec - Martell, p. 80.

[210] The *Eagle* left 111 passengers at Pictou, then took the remaining 11 to Miramichi, NB.

[211] Ten passengers in the *Zephyr* put a notice of thanks to Captain John **HUGHES** in the *NBC*, 21 May 1836. Their names were: John **BROGAN**, James **COLVIN**, Patrick **DUNBEVIE**, Andrew **HIGARTY**, Benjamin **JOHNSON**, Andrew **LOVE**, Francis **MILLER**, James **MULLIN**, Robert **PATERSON**, and James **ROGLE**.

[212] The brig *Lancaster* sailed from Dublin with 77 passengers bound for New York, on 21 May 1836, but seem to have been cast away at Sable Island where the captain set the vessel on fire! The crew and passengers were saved and 17 of them sent to Halifax in the schooner *Michael Wallace* - *AR*, 11 June 1836. The brig *Maria* conveyed the remaining 67 passengers and crew to Halifax - *AR*, 2 July 1836.

[213] Thomas **CONROY**, Cochrane **DOYLE** and Miss **O'FARREL** were passengers, along with "44 in steerage" - *The Island Magazine*/18, p. 32.

[214] Simon **DODD** was a passenger, along with "14 in steerage" - *The Island Magazine/18*, p. 32.

Month	Vessel	Port from	Port to	Passengers	Reference
			1837[215]		
May	Britannia	Sligo	Saint John	Yes	Dobson I/23
May	Don	Waterford	Halifax	112	*AR*, 3 June 1837
May	Eagle	Waterford	Halifax	106	*AR*, 3 June 1837
May	Hope[216]	Cork	Saint John	Yes	*NBC*, 3 June 1837
May	Lord John Russell	Waterford	Halifax	181	*NS*, 25 May 1837
May	Margaret[217]	Belfast	Halifax	188	*AR*, 3 June 1837
June	Aisthorpe	Sligo	Saint John	130	Dobson I/3
June	Bell	Sligo	Saint John	120	Dobson I/17
June	Emily	Ireland/NL	Halifax	14	*NS*, 15 June 1837
June	James Lemon	Belfast	Saint John	Yes	Dobson II/65
June	Kingston[218]	Bantry	Saint John	Yes	*NBC*, 24 June 1837
June	Pandora	Waterford	PEI	20	Island Magazine, 18
June	Thetis[219]	Cork	Bathurst, NB	78	Dobson III/101
July	Agnes	Sligo	Saint John	130	Dobson I/3
July	Belsey Castle	Sligo	Sydney	18	Dobson I/17
July	Clitus	Cork	Halifax	106	*NS*, 3 Aug 1837
July	Lady Ann[220]	Belfast	Wallace, NS	48	Island Magazine, 18
July	Manly	Sligo	Saint John	160	Dobson I/94
July	Robert Watt[221]	Cork	St. Andrews	288	Customs/286-293

---

[215] Adams, p. 415, estimates that 8,612 Irish passengers landed in the Maritimes in 1837. We have the names of 17 ships which landed 2,060 passengers, an average of 121 souls per voyage. Seven other vessels are on record, but even if we credit each with as many passengers as the *Robert Watt*'s 288, we are at best able to account for half the number that Adams estimated. We do not have the names of the remaining vessels nor from which ports they sailed.

[216] Thomas **KELLY**, "an emigrant passenger landed from the barque *Hope*, which lately arrived from Cork, Ireland" was drowned alongside at Saint John - *New Brunswick Courier*, 3 June 1837.

[217] The *Margaret* was abandoned and 170 of her passengers brought to Restigouche, NB, by the *Carlton*, and 18 to Halifax in the schooner *Adelle*.

[218] Daniel **SAUNDRY**, "a passenger lately arrived in the schooner *Kingston* from Bantry, Ireland" was drowned alongside the previous evening at Saint John - *New Brunswick Courier*, 24 June 1837.

[219] The passenger list was published by Paul Delicaet, "Passengers aboard the *Thetis*, Cork to Bathurst, New Brunswick, in April 1837," *The Irish Ancestor*, Vol. XII, Nos. 1 and 2 (1980), pp. 65 - 66. There are 78 names on the passenger list but 8 were struck off as not embarking. The passengers' surnames point to origins in west Cork and Kerry. The vessel sailed on 12 April and arrived in June.

[220] The *Lady Ann* carried 48 settlers from County Monaghan to Wallace, NS, of whom 35 were taken by sloop to PEI - O'Grady, *Exiles & Islanders*, p. 154.

[221] The passenger list was published by Cleadie B. Barnett, "List of the Passengers embarked in the Barque *Robert Watt* of Saint Andrew, Ralph **SALLIMAN**, Master, and Who Have Contracted to be Landed at Saint Andrews, New Brunswick . . . 1837," in *We Lived: A Genealogical Newsletter of New Brunswick Sources*, No. 14 (June 1982), pp. 173 - 174.

Month	Vessel	Port from	Port to	Passengers	Reference
Sep	William Alexander	Portheawl[222]	PEI	Yes	Island Magazine, 18
Oct	Hibernia	Dublin	Crapaud, PEI	Yes	Island Magazine, 18
-	Ann and Mary	Waterford	Saint John	85	PANB/RS 555
-	Industry	Cork	St. Andrews	Yes	Power/182
-	Protector[223]	Londonderry	Saint John	325	Customs/256-262
-	Royalist	Londonderry	Sydney, NS	136	Dobson I/129

1838[224]

Month	Vessel	Port from	Port to	Passengers	Reference
Apr	Hibernia	Kinsale	Saint John	31	Customs/135
May	Leslie Gault	Londonderry	Saint John	29	Customs/188
May	Pallas[225]	Cork	St. Andrews	98	Customs/233-236
June	Jane per Zephyr[226]	Cork	Halifax	50	AR, 30 June 1838
June	Margaret	Ireland/NL	Halifax	6	AR, 16 June 1838
June	Maria Brooke[227]	Ballyshannon	Saint John	67	Customs/208-209
June	Pictou	Ireland/NL	Halifax	7	AR, 30 June 1838
June	Susan[228]	Londonderry	Saint John	125	Dobson III/99
June	Susan Jane[229]	Ballyshannon	Saint John	41	Customs/320-321
June	Susan Maria Brooke	Ballyshannon	Saint John	68	Dobson III/100
July	Camilla	Belfast	Saint John	57	Customs/54
July	Harmony[230]	Strangford	Saint John	16	Customs/131

---

[222] This would be Porthall, in Clonleigh Parish, near Lifford, in County Donegal.

[223] The undated list was published in *Passengers to New Brunswick: The Custom House Records,* pp. 256 - 262, but circumstantial evidence suggests that it applies to a voyage in 1837.

[224] Adams, p. 415, estimates that 1,061 Irish passengers landed in the Maritimes in 1838. We have the names of 25 ships which landed 1,000 passengers, an average of 40 souls per voyage. For once there seem to have been few, if any, elusive trips by ships that cannot be identified.

[225] The passenger list was published in *Passengers to New Brunswick: The Custom House Records,* pp. 233 - 236.

[226] The *Jane* was cast away near Shelburne, NS. The 50 passengers who were rescued were taken in the *Zephyr* to Halifax.

[227] The passenger list was published in *Passengers to New Brunswick: The Custom House Records,* pp. 208 - 209. The voyage of the *Susan Maria Brooke* is probably that of the same ship.

[228] The passenger list was published in *Passengers to New Brunswick: The Custom House Records,* pp. 315 - 317. The list gives the precise place of origin.

[229] The passenger list was published in *Passengers to New Brunswick: The Custom House Records,* pp. 320 - 321.

[230] The passenger list was published in *Passengers to New Brunswick: The Custom House Records,* p. 131: John, 32, stone mason, Anne, 30, his wife, Catherine, 9, and Mary Ann, 6 mos, **COATS** from Carrycarland [Carrick, Ireland?]; Peter, 33, labourer, Ellen, 33, his wife, Margaret, 11, Catherine, 10, Mary, 8, Richard, 6, John, 4, and Selena, 1, **GREEMAN**; Cecily **McVEY**, 35, spinster; Daniel, 52, labourer, and daughter Mary, 23, **GRACEY**, all from Kilmegan; and John **SMYTH**, 34, farmer from 'Talleyratten' [likely Tullyratty, County Down].

Month	Vessel	Port from	Port to	Passengers	Reference
July	Industry[231]	Cork	St. Andrews	8	Customs/153
July	Mary Caroline	Cork	Saint John	17	Customs/213
July	Prudence[232]	Londonderry	Saint John	180	Dobson III/87
Aug	Britannia[233]	Ballyshannon	Saint John	42	Customs/50-51
Aug	Condor[234]	Londonderry	Saint John	57	Customs/73-75
Aug	Granville[235]	Sligo	Saint John	22	NS, 23 Aug 1838
Aug	Pictou	Ireland/NL	Halifax	3	AR, 11 Aug 1838
Sep	Jane	Ireland/NL	Halifax	6	AR, 8 Sep 1838
Oct	Caronge[236]	Londonderry	Saint John	19	Customs/56
Oct	Hebe	Ireland/NL	Halifax	6	AR, 27 Oct 1838
Oct	Pictou	Ireland/NL	Halifax	9	AR, 6 Oct 1838
Oct	Susan Maria Brooke[237]	Donegal	Saint John	6	Customs/322
-	Mary[238]	Newry	Saint John	30	Dobson III/72

---

[231] The passenger list was published in *Passengers to New Brunswick: The Custom House Records*, p. 153. The passengers were Timothy, labourer, and Bridget **COURTNEY**, John **DRISCOLL**, mariner, Robin **DWYER**, labourer, Garret **FOLEY**, labourer, Robert **HALL**, merchant, John **HENNESSEY**, labourer, and Thomas **O'NEIL**, labourer.

[232] The passenger list was published in *Passengers to New Brunswick: The Custom House Records*, pp. 265 - 268. The list gives the county of origin: Donegal, Fermanagh, Londonderry, or Tyrone. Eleven passengers were Scots from Glasgow.

[233] The passenger list was published in *Passengers to New Brunswick: The Custom House Records* pp. 50 - 51. Supposedly, 35 embarked (Dobson III/16), but a careful count of the list found that 42 arrived at Saint John.

[234] The passenger list was published in *Passengers to New Brunswick: The Custom House Records*, pp. 73 - 75. The list gives place of origin.

[235] The *Granville* was wrecked on Sable Island. The passengers were taken to Halifax in the *Victory*.

[236] The passenger list was published in *Passengers to New Brunswick: The Custom House Records,* p. 56. The passengers were: John J., 17, George, 15, and Catharine, 13, **BLACK**; Billy **BRIDDEN**, 20 ; Jane, 36 , Biddy, 9, John, 7, and Mary, 2, **COLL**; Margaret **DOHERTY**, 18; Alexander **DUDLEY**, 18; William **DUNBAR**, 27; Hugh **KELLY**, 22; James **McFARLANE**, 19; Hugh **McGUIRE**, 17; John **McAUGHLIN**, 24; Margaret, 32, and Rose Ann, 7, **MACKLIN**; Thomas **O'FLAHERTY**, 23; and Rose **SWEENY**, 19.

[237] The passenger list was published in *Passengers to New Brunswick: The Custom House Records*, p. 322. The passengers were Cathleen **DOHER[T]Y**, 17; John **McDONOUGH**, 24; Sarah, 21, and Susan, 19, **QUINN**; Edward **SHERIDAN**, 5; and Mary **THOMAS**, 18.

[238] The passenger list was published in *Passengers to New Brunswick: The Custom House Records,* p. 210. The list gives the precise place of origin. Seven passengers did not embark.

Month	Vessel	Port from	Port to	Passengers	Reference
			1839[239]		
May	Argyle[240]	Waterford	PEI	62	Dobson I/14
May	Britannia	Sligo	Saint John	Yes	Dobson I/23
May	Consbrook[241]	Belfast	PEI	308	Island Magazine, 18
May	Agitator	Belfast	PEI	314	Island Magazine, 18
June	Aide de Camp[242]	Londonderry	Saint John	Yes	Dobson I/3
June	Lavinia	Sligo	Saint John	Yes	Dobson I88
July	Gertrude	Londonderry	Saint John	145	PANB/RS 555
Aug	Grecian	Waterford	PEI	Yes	Island Magazine, 18
-	Londonderry	Londonderry	Saint John	Yes	Dobson I/91
-	Ponsilia [Pons Aelii]	Cork	Miramichi	Yes	Spray[243]
			1840[244]		
May	Argyle	Waterford	PEI	61	Island Magazine, 18
May	Britannia	Sligo	Saint John	Yes	Dobson I/23
May	Lion	Sligo	Saint John	Yes	Dobson I/90
June	Alexander	Sligo	Saint John	Yes	Dobson I/6
June	Isabella	Sligo	Saint John	Yes	Dobson I/76
June	Rosebank[245]	Belfast	PEI	208	Island Magazine, 18

---

[239] Adams, p. 415, estimates that 4,506 Irish passengers landed in the Maritimes in 1839. We have the names of nine ships which landed perhaps two thousand souls. The remainder cannot be accounted for.

[240] The *Argyle* or the *Grecian* brought out John **DORGAN** and Michael **NELLIGAN** from County Kerry in 1839 - Porter, p. 31.

[241] The *Consbrook's* passengers came from County Monaghan.

[242] The *Aide de Camp* was wrecked on Brier Island, NS, and 15 passengers were drowned.

[243] William A. Spray,"The Irish in Miramichi," *New Ireland Remembered*, P. M. Toner, ed., Fredericton: New Ireland Press, 1988, p. 56, names Patrick **NELLIGAN** as a passenger.

[244] Adams, p. 415, estimates that 8,631 Irish passengers landed in the Maritimes in 1840. We have the names of nine ships which landed perhaps twelve hundred souls. The remainder are unknown. Sometimes we learn of Irish arrivals but for whom no passenger list will be found, and who only turn up in records years after the fact. A good example of this is John **GRANVILLE**, a native of County Offaly, born about 1815. When he was 15 years old he emigrated to Newfoundland where he remained for 9 years and was married. Then [1840] he removed to Nova Scotia and worked for 5 years clearing land on the North Mountain, Cornwallis Township. He was driven to seek relief when his wife died shortly after delivering their third child. In his petition dated 16 Oct 1845 at Cornwallis, Granville lists his children as Mary, 6; Michael, 2; and Bridget, 2 months - NSA, RG 5, Series "P", Vol. 83 #118.

[245] It seems probable that one passenger in the *Rosebank* was Ellen **McINNIS**, age 16, from County Monaghan, and who settled in Iona, PEI. - Arthur O'Shea, "The Iona Parish," *The Abegweit Review*, Vol. 6:1 (Spring 1988), p. 93. Other passengers were probably Owen **McKENNA**, age 19, from County Monaghan, and James **MURTAGH** from Armagh - O'Grady, *Exiles & Islanders*, pp. 77, 151.

Month	**Vessel**	**Port from**	**Port to**	**Passengers**	**Reference**
Sep	Ellen Stewart	Limerick	PEI	Yes	Island Magazine, 18
Sep	Lawrence	Waterford	PEI	21	Island Magazine, 18
-	Carrick	Westport	Sydney	32	MacKenzie/31[246]

1841[247]

May	Albion	Cork	Saint John	195	Johnson/190
May	Bolivar	Waterford	Miramichi	235	PANB RS 555[248]
May	Caroline	Ballyshannon	Saint John	Yes	Johnson/190
May	Dealy	Bantry	Saint John	137	Johnson/190
May	Don	Waterford	Miramichi	66	PANB RS 555[249]
May	Eagle	Waterford	Miramichi	51	PANB RS 555[250]
May	Envoy	Londonderry	Saint John	266	Dobson I/51
May	Friends	Westport	Saint John	126	Johnson/190
May	Globe	Belfast	Saint John	82	Johnson/190
May	Gratitude	Cork	Saint John	Yes	Johnson/190
May	Isadore	Kinsale	Saint John	75	Johnson/190
May	Kathleen	Limerick	Saint John	8	Johnson/191
May	Lord Sandon	Kinsale	Saint John	206	Johnson/191
May	Louisa	Cork	Saint John	Yes	Johnson/191
May	Macao	Londonderry	Saint John	Yes	Johnson/191
May	Margaret Pollock[251]	Belfast	PEI	685	Island Magazine, 18
May	Montreal Packet	Dublin	Saint John	Yes	Johnson/191

---

[246] A. A. MacKenzie, p. 31.

[247] A. A. MacKenzie, p. 31, states that 33 or more Irish immigrants landed at Sydney, Cape Breton, in 1841. No vessels named. Adams, p. 415, estimates that 8,778 Irish passengers landed in the Maritimes in 1841. We know the names of nine ships which landed 1,606 souls. The remaining 53 ships in the list could have carried all, or most, of the remainder. The *Elizabeth* and the *Glengarry*, out of Liverpool, England, may have carried some Irish emigrants to Saint John in 1841 - Johnson, p. 190.

[248] No passengers are named in the ship return, but details men, women and children - page 25, archives.gnb.ca/Irish/Databases/ImmigrationRecords/Documents.aspx?culture=en-CA&F=16226&S=0959&E=1005

[249] No passengers are named in the ship return, but details men, women and children - page 21, archives.gnb.ca/Irish/Databases/ImmigrationRecords/Documents.aspx?culture=en-CA&F=16226&S=0959&E=1005

[250] No passengers are named in the ship return, but details men, women and children - page 2. archives.gnb.ca/Irish/Databases/ImmigrationRecords/Documents.aspx?culture=en-CA&F=16226&S=0959&E=1005

[251] On the passage of 31 days, 24 died, and four died after reaching port. All were children under the age of 5 who died of measles. The ship was quarantined because several still had the disease. O'Grady, *Exiles & Islanders*, pp. 69, 170, names nine certain, and six probable, passengers in the *Margaret Pollock*. The former were Patrick **BRADLEY** and Andrew **CAMPBELL** from County Monaghan; Peter **CORR**, Francis **CURRAN** from Drumsnat, County Monaghan; Thomas **HAMMILL**; Mr. **McGYRAL**; John and Peter **McQUAID** from County Monaghan; and Patrick **SMITH**. The six possible passengers were John **DREEHAN** from County Tyrone, and five from County Monaghan: John **CLINTON**; Dennis and Peter **CURRAN**; Dennis **MULLIGAN**; and Bernard **MURPHY**.

Month	Vessel	Port from	Port to	Passengers	Reference
May	Nero	Limerick	Miramichi	97	PANB RS 555[252]
May	Pallas[253]	Cork	Saint John	187	Johnson/191
May	Prudence	Londonderry	Saint John	73	Johnson/191
May	Rowena	Cork	Saint John	199	Johnson/191
May	Royal William[254]	Cork	Saint John	Yes	Johnson/191
May	Thomas Gelston	Belfast	PEI	139	Island Magazine, 18
May	Wilkinson	Belfast	Saint John	Yes	Dobson II/137
June	Agnes	Sligo	Saint John	Yes	Johnson/190
June	Alexander	Sligo	Saint John	Yes	Dobson I/6
June	Amazon	Cork	Saint John	Yes	Johnson/190
June	Brothers	Newry	Saint John	65	Johnson/190
June	Carrywell	Ballyshannon	Saint John	Yes	Johnson/190
June	Cherub	Londonderry	Saint John	Yes	Johnson/190
June	Comet	Cork	Saint John	Yes	Johnson/190
June	Edwin	Sligo	Saint John	Yes	Dobson I/45
June	Emerald	Kinsale	Saint John	Yes	Johnson/190
June	Harmony	Dublin	Saint John	Yes	Johnson/190
June	Industry	Cork	Saint John	Yes	Johnson/190
June	Jane	Limerick	Saint John	Yes	Johnson/190
June	John Wesley	Cork	Saint John	109	Johnson/191
June	Kangaroo	Cork	Saint John	Yes	Johnson/191
June	Larch	Cork	Saint John	Yes	Johnson/191
June	Lawrence Forrestall	Waterford	Miramichi	52	PANB RS 555[255]
June	Lelia	Galway	Saint John	Yes	Johnson/191
June	Londonderry	Londonderry	Saint John	Yes	Johnson/191
June	Maria	Londonderry	Saint John	Yes	Johnson/191
June	Mary	Baltimore	Saint John	Yes	Johnson/191
June	Mary Campbell	Londonderry	Saint John	Yes	Johnson/191
June	Pons Aelii	Cork	Saint John	Yes	Johnson/191
June	Prince Albert	Dublin	Saint John	Yes	Johnson/191
June	Queen[256]	Cork	Bathurst, NB	15	PANB RS 555

---

[252] No passengers are named in the ship return, but detais men, women and children - page 28, archives.gnb.ca/Irish/Databases/ImmigrationRecords/Documents.aspx?culture=en-CA&F=16226&S=0959&E=1005

[253] A few passengers from the *Pallas* were assisted by the authorities at St. Andrews, NB, in June 1842: Bridget and Humphrey **SULLIVAN** and William **WALLACE** - Daniel F. Johnson, *Irish Emigration to New England Through the Port of Saint John, New Brunswick, Canada 1841 to 1849* (Clearfield Company, Inc., 1996), pp. 228 - 229.

[254] Twelve passengers in the *Royal William* expressed their thanks to Captain Michael **DRISCOLL** in *NBC*, 5 June 1841. Their names were: George H. **BALDWIN**, Patrick **BRYAN**, William **BUTLER**, John **CARDEN**, Daniel **DUNN**, Robert **EDGAR**, James **FITZGERALD**, Henry **FOWLER**, Patrick **KEEFER**, John **KEOHAN**, Richard **PENNEY**, and John **RYAN**.

[255] No passengers are named in the ship return, but details men, women and children - page 13, archives.gnb.ca/Irish/Databases/ImmigrationRecords/Documents.aspx?culture=en-CA&F=16226&S=0959&E=1005

[256] One woman died on passage. The Public Archives of New Brunswick has the ship return at archives.gnb.ca/Irish/Databases/ImmigrationRecords/Documents.aspx?culture=en-CA&F=16226&S=1096&E=1099

Month	Vessel	Port from	Port to	Passengers	Reference
June	Sarah[257]	Sligo	Saint John	Yes	Johnson/191
June	Thomas Hanford	Cork	Saint John	Yes	Johnson/191
June	Thyayirn	Londonderry	Saint John	Yes	Johnson/191
July	George[258]	Cork	Saint John	Yes	NBC, 10 July 1841
July	Jane Duffus	Donegal	Saint John	Yes	Johnson/191
July	Sarah Jane	Donegal	Saint John	Yes	Johnson/191
Aug	Minerva	Belfast	Saint John	Yes	Johnson/191
Aug	Sir James McDonell	Cork	Malpeque, PEI	Yes	Island Magazine, 18
Aug	Trusty	Belfast	Saint John	Yes	Johnson/191
Sep	Caroline	Ballyshannon	Saint John	Yes	Johnson/190
Sep	Dealy	Bantry	Saint John	Yes	Johnson/190
Sep	Kentville	Donegal	Saint John	Yes	Johnson/191
Sep	Londonderry	Londonderry	Saint John	Yes	Johnson/191
-	Consbrook[259]	Belfast	PEI	Yes	O'Grady/61, 155

1842[260]

Month	Vessel	Port from	Port to	Passengers	Reference
Apr	Lord Sandon	Kinsale	Saint John	224	Johnson/193
May	Andover	Cork	Saint John	179	Johnson/192
May	Bolivar[261]	Waterford	Miramichi	136	PANB RS 555
May	British Queen	Cork	Saint John	197	Johnson/192
May	Clyde	Cork	Saint John	Yes	Johnson/192
May	Dealy	Bantry	Saint John	Yes	Johnson/192
May	Eagle[262]	Waterford	Halifax	100	Flewwelling
May	Envoy	Londonderry	Saint John	Yes	Johnson/192
May	John Francis	Cork	Saint John	215	Johnson/193
May	John and Mary	Galway	Saint John	Yes	Johnson/193

---

[257] This appears to be the *Sarah Linden* which brought Ann **McBRIDE**, 33, from Fermoy, County Cork, to join her husband Edward who came to Nova Scotia six months before. On 4 Aug she was at Annapolis, NS, and found her husband had gone on to Boston - NSA, RG 5, Series 'P', Vol. 81, no. 100.

[258] Eight passengers in the *George* expressed their thanks to Captain Richard **POWER** in *NBC*, 10 July 1841. Their names were: John **AIGAN**, Patrick **COMONS** [**CONNORS**], Daniel **COURTENAY**, David **GRADY**, Michael **GRIFFIN**, John **MAHON**, Michael **O'DONNELL**, and Michael **SULLIVAN**.

[259] The *Consbrook*'s passengers came from County Monaghan.

[260] Adams, p. 415, estimates that 10,917 Irish passengers landed in the Maritimes in 1842. We know the names of 17 ships which landed 1,594 souls. The remaining 46 ships in the list could have carried most, but not all, of the remainder. There were eight voyages of ships from Liverpool, England, which may have brought some Irish emigrants to Saint John in 1842, namely, the *Britannia, Elizabeth Grimmer, Mabel, Mary Caroline, Portland* [twice], *Samuel,* and *South Esk* - Johnson, pp. 192 - 194.

[261] No passengers are named in the ship return, but details men, women and children - page 40, archives.gnb.ca/Irish/Databases/ImmigrationRecords/Documents.aspx?culture=en-CA&F=16226&S=0959&E=1005 There were three births on the voyage. One passenger was Joanna **MELTON**, 24, Tipperary, who went to Merigomish, NS, in June 1842, thence to Pictou in November - NSA, RG 5, Series 'P', Vol. 82, no. 99.

[262] Among the passengers in the *Eagle* were a newly-wed couple, James **SPRUIN**, 26, and Mary **MURPHY**, 23, from County Kilkenny. They settled in Halifax and had seven children born there.

Month	Vessel	Port from	Port to	Passengers	Reference
May	Londonderry	Londonderry	Saint John	Yes	Johnson/193
May	Martha Ann	Cork	Saint John	133	Johnson/193
May	Medina	Dungarvan	Miramichi	79	PANB RS 555[263]
May	Midas	Galway	Saint John	133	Johnson/193
May	Morgiana	Belfast	PEI	145	Island Magazine, 26
May	Promise	Newry	Saint John	Yes	Johnson/193
May	Sir James McDonell	Cork/Youghal	PEI	131	Island Magazine, 26
May	Thomas Gelston	Belfast	PEI	280	Island Magazine, 26
May	Westmorland	Cork	Saint John	177	Johnson/194
June	Agnes	Sligo	Saint John	82	Dobson I/3
June	Albion	Baltimore	Saint John	153	Johnson/192
June	Argyle	Cork	Saint John	Yes	Johnson/192
June	Ariel	Limerick	Miramichi	67	PANB RS 555[264]
June	Caroline	Sligo	Saint John	Yes	Johnson/192
June	Carrywell	Belfast	Saint John	Yes	Johnson/192
June	Cordelia	Belfast	Saint John	76	Johnson/192
June	Countess of Arran	Donegal	Saint John	Yes	Dobson I/36
June	Creole	Londonderry	Saint John	Yes	Johnson/192
June	Dykes	Sligo	Saint John	145	Dobson I/43
June	Eliza Ann[265]	Cork	St. Andrews	Yes	PANB, mfm. 7890
June	Erin	New Ross	Miramichi	20	PANB RS 555[266]
June	Jessie	Waterford	Saint John	Yes	Johnson/192
June	John[267]	Waterford	Saint John	91	Johnson/192
June	John Wesley	Cork	Saint John	Yes	Johnson/193
June	Kingston	Cork	Saint John	Yes	Johnson/193
June	Lady Douglas	Drogheda	Saint John	Yes	Johnson/193
June	Lady Milton	Londonderry	Saint John	Yes	Johnson/193
June	Lavinia	Tralee	Saint John	Yes	Johnson/193
June	Lelia	Galway	Saint John	Yes	Johnson/193

---

[263] No passengers are named in the ship return, but details men, women and children - page 37, archives.gnb.ca/Irish/Databases/ImmigrationRecords/Documents.aspx?culture=en-CA&F=16226&S=0959&E=1005

[264] No passengers are named in the ship return, but details men, women and children - page 34, archives.gnb.ca/Irish/Databases/ImmigrationRecords/Documents.aspx?culture=en-CA&F=16226&S=0959&E=1005

[265] The authorities at St. Andrews, NB, assisted 44 passengers from the *Eliza Ann* in 1842. While most family groups are easily distinguished, the exact groupings of the Sheean family are vague in some instances. Those passengers were Bridget, Margaret, Catherine and Michael **CLARY**; Margaret and Patrick **CONNELL**; William, Mary, Owen and Margaret **FINTON**; Garrett **FITZGERALD**; Catherine and John **McCARTY**; John **MOORE**; Joanna, Catherine, William, Elizabeth and Ellen **SHAY**; Daniel, Sr., Ellen, Mary 1st, Joanna Jr., Mary 2nd, and Daniel, Jr. **SHEEAN**; John, Judy and Catherine 1st, **SHEEAN**; Edward **SHEEAN**, Sr.; Jerry Sr., Mary 3rd, Michael, Jerry Jr., Thomas, Catherine 2nd, Patrick, Edward, Catherine 3rd, Barbara, and Joanna **SHEEAN**; Joanna, Catherine, William, Elizabeth and Ellen **SHAY**; Ellen, Joseph, Francis and James **TURNBULL** - Public Archives of New Brunswick, RS 8 [PANB, microfilm F7890].

[266] No passengers are named in the ship return, but details men, women and children - page 32, archives.gnb.ca/Irish/Databases/ImmigrationRecords/Documents.aspx?culture=en-CA&F=16226&S=0959&E=1005 The vessel called in at Newfoundland on the voyage out.

[267] The *John* called at Halifax coming out from Ireland to take on provisions - Johnson, p. 209.

Month	Vessel	Port from	Port to	Passengers	Reference
June	Maria	Londonderry	Saint John	Yes	Johnson/193
June	Martha	Cork	Saint John	151	Johnson/193
June	Mary	Cork	Saint John	Yes	Johnson/193
June	Odessa	Londonderry	Saint John	Yes	Johnson/193
June	Pandora	Waterford	Halifax	40	Flewwelling
June	Silkworth[268]	Cork	Saint John	Yes	Johnson/194
June	Thomas	Sligo	Saint John	Yes	Johnson/194
June	Thomas Hanford	Cork	Saint John	Yes	Johnson/194
July	Clifton	Cork	Saint John	Yes	Johnson/192
July	Comet	Dublin	Saint John	Yes	Johnson/192
July	Defiance	Cork	Saint John	Yes	Johnson/192
July	Friendship	Londonderry	Saint John	Yes	Johnson/192
July	Jessie	Limerick	Saint John	Yes	Johnson/192
July	Pons Aelii[269]	Cork	Saint John	54	Johnson/193
July	Susan Jane	Sligo	Saint John	Yes	Johnson/194
July	Trial	Dublin	Saint John	99	Dobson I/142
Aug	Aisthorpe	Sligo	Saint John	144	Dobson I/4
Aug	St. George	Cork/NL	PEI	10	Island Magazine, 26
Sep	Indemnity	Cork	Saint John	Yes	Johnson/192
Sep	Londonderry	Londonderry	Saint John	Yes	Johnson/193
Sep	Midas	Galway	Saint John	Yes	Johnson/193
Sep	Morgiana	Belfast	PEI	66	Island Magazine, 26
Sep	Pandora	Waterford	Miramichi	4	PANB RS 555[270]

1843[271]

Month	Vessel	Port from	Port to	Passengers	Reference
May	Chieftain	Belfast	PEI	208	Island Magazine, 26
May	Eagle[272]	Waterford	Halifax	88	*MH*, 29 May 1843
May	Louisa	Cork	Saint John	Yes	Johnson/194
May	Mary Jane	Limerick	PEI	Yes	Island Magazine, 26
May	Rosebank	Belfast	PEI	150	Island Magazine, 26

---

[268] We know the names of five passengers because they drowned within a week of their arrival when the small craft they were in was upset in Saint John Harbour. Their names were Mrs. **COLEMAN** of Cork City, Ellen **HURLEY** of "Kennagh" [Kinneigh], County Cork, Mr. and Mrs. **MORGAN**, Tipperary, and James **SHAY**, County Kerry - *Weekly Chronicle*, 8 July 1842.

[269] The *Pons Aelii* called at Halifax coming out from Ireland and left 88 passengers there.

[270] The passengers were a woman with three children, according to the ship return - page 43, at archives.gnb.ca/Irish/Databases/ImmigrationRecords/Documents.aspx?culture=en-CA&F=16226&S=0959&E=1005

[271] A. A. MacKenzie, p. 31, states that 60 Irish immigrants landed at Arichat, Cape Breton, in 1843. No vessel is named. Adams, p. 415, estimates that 3,574 Irish passengers landed in the Maritimes in 1843, but considers that figure to be too large. We know the names of four ships which landed 362 souls. The remaining ten ships listed here for 1843 could have carried some of the remainder.

[272] Twelve passengers in the *Eagle* published their thanks to the captain in *NS*, 5 June 1843. Their names were John **ADDIS**, Edward **BUTLER**, John **CARUE** [Carew], John **CONNORS**, David **DAYDELANY**, Mathew **DOYLE**, James **HEADYN**, Rody **HEFFERNAN**, James **HENECY**, James **KEATING**, Thomas **MURPHY**, and Patrick **TOBIN**.

Month	Vessel	Port from	Port to	Passengers	Reference
May	Sally	Belfast	Saint John	Yes	Johnson/194
June	Don	Waterford	Saint John	Yes	Johnson/194
July	Martha	Cork	Saint John	Yes	Johnson/194
July	Thomas Naylor	Cork	Saint John	Yes	Johnson/194
July	Victory	Youghal	Saint John	Yes	Johnson/194
Sep	Antelope	Dublin	PEI	16	Island Magazine, 26
Sep	Mary Jane	Dublin	PEI	Yes	Island Magazine, 26
Sep	Tagus	[Sligo]	Shippagan	Yes	On line[273]
-	Fanny	Belfast	PEI	Yes	Monaghan/65

1844[274]

Month	Vessel	Port from	Port to	Passengers	Reference
May	Coxon	Cork	Saint John	189	Johnson/195
May	Eagle[275]	Waterford	Halifax	120	*NS*, 27 May 1844
May	John Francis[276]	Cork	Saint John	Yes	Johnson/195
May	Martha	Cork	Saint John	113	Johnson/195
May	Nero	Limerick	Saint John	Yes	Johnson/195
May	Pallas	Cork	Saint John	138	Johnson/195
May	Thomas Hanford	Cork	Saint John	32	Johnson/195
June	Antelope	Dublin	PEI	40	Island Magazine, 26
June	Asia[277]	Londonderry	Saint John	334	Johnson/195
June	British Queen	Dingle	Saint John	Yes	Johnson/195
June	Brothers	Dublin	Shippagan	Yes	On line[278]
June	Clio	Cork	Saint John	Yes	Johnson/195
June	Envoy	Londonderry	Saint John	Yes	Johnson/195
June	Fellowship	Londonderry	Saint John	126	Johnson/195
June	Isadore	Cork	Saint John	Yes	Johnson/195
June	Redwing	Galway	Saint John	Yes	Johnson/195
June	Rose	Belfast	Saint John	Yes	Johnson/195

---

[273] See www.gloucester.restigouche.net/ships

[274] The *Mars, Pearl*, and *Woodstock*, out of Liverpool, England, may have carried some Irish emigrants to Saint John in 1844 - Johnson, p. 195.

[275] The Halifax newspaper, *The Times*, 28 May 1844, states that there were 114 passengers. Possibly six had died on the voyage, or the *Novascotian* had published an estimate in round numbers.

[276] Three passengers from the *John Francis* were admitted to the Alms House in Saint John on 10 Feb 1845: Nancy **BUCKLEY**, widow, 30, and her daughter Jane, 5, of Cork, also a son John, 2 months old in Feb 1845; Mary **HARRINGTON**, 23, from Cork, and Catherine **HARRINGTON**, her infant, who died 17 Oct 1845. Both women delivered a child after landing at Saint John - Johnson, p. 74.

[277] Elizabeth **McBRIDE**, 19, Derry, a passenger in the *Asia*, was admitted to the Alms House, Saint John, 10 Feb 1845 - Johnson, p. 74. The vessel also called at Richibucto, NB - Dobson III, p. 11.

[278] See www.gloucester.restigouche.net/ships

Month	Vessel	Port from	Port to	Passengers	Reference
June	Sir George Prevost[279]	Newry	Cape Breton	120	Dobson I/135
June	Wanderer	Baltimore	Saint John	Yes	Johnson/195
July	Blanche	Donegal	Saint John	Yes	Johnson/195
July	Bristol[280]	Newry	Saint John	20	PANB/RS 555
July	Caroline	Ballyshannon	Saint John	Yes	Johnson/195
July	Independence[281]	Dublin	PEI	360	Island Magazine, 26
July	Kitty	Cork	Saint John	Yes	Johnson/195
July	Thorney Close[282]	Donegal	Saint John	102	Johnson/195
Sep	Antelope	Dublin	PEI	Yes	Island Magazine, 26
Sep	Mary Jane	Dublin	PEI	Yes	Island Magazine, 26
Sep	Sovereign[283]	Newry	Saint John	Yes	Johnson/195
Oct	Londonderry	Londonderry	Saint John	57	Johnson/195
Oct	Midas	Galway	Saint John	Yes	Johnson/195
Oct	Nancy[284]	Ireland/Liverpool	Halifax	Yes	Johnson/74
-	Fanny[285]	Belfast	PEI	Yes	Monaghan/65
-	Margaretta	Ireland	PEI	Yes	Monaghan/65

1845[286]

---

[279] The *Sir George Prevost* was bound for Québec, but was wrecked off Gabarus, Cape Breton, on 6 June 1841. The passengers were saved. In a claim connected with the rescue, the Lloyd's agent named fifteen of the survivors - NSA, MG 100, Vol. 229, item 1. Their names were: John **CAVEL**, a boy, Lucindy **COLLINS**, Catherine **CONNERY**, Patrick **DOREN** and his wife, Thomas and Mary **DOREN**, John **FARNIGEN**, Hugh and Ann **HANNAWAY**, Thomas **KELLY**, Catherine **MICHAELMARRY** [McElmurray], John **O'NIEL**, Michael **RUNNELS** [Reynolds], and Nancy **TIMMONS**.

[280] The *Bristol's* arrival is mentioned in a letter from William F. O'Dell, Provincial Secretary of New Brunswick, 5 Aug 1844.

[281] The *Independence* left 156 passengers in PEI and continued to Québec with remaining 204. O'Grady, *Exiles & Islanders*, p. 155, says the *Independence* had sailed from Belfast, rather than Dublin.

[282] The *Thorney Close* carried passengers from counties Donegal and Fermanagh. Three of its passengers were admitted to the Alms House, Saint John: Margaret, 24, and daughter Margaret, 15 months, **MORROW**, Donegal; and Mrs. Margaret **REILLEY**, 32, Fermanagh - Johnson p. 75.

[283] James **COLEMAN**, 24, Down, a passenger from the *Sovereign*, was admitted to the Alms House, Saint John, 14 July 1845 - Johnson, p. 75.

[284] The *Nancy* sailed from Liverpool, England, and landed at Halifax on 15 Oct 1844. One Irish passenger was admitted to the Alms House, Saint John, on 15 Apr 1845, namely John **DALTON**, 29, from Kilkenny - Johnson, p. 74.

[285] O'Grady, *Exiles & Islanders*, p. 168, considers Patrick **DUFFY** was a probable passenger.

[286] Adams, p. 415, estimates that 5,570 Irish passengers landed in the Maritimes in 1845. We know of 51 vessels making that voyage that year. This could account for all, or almost all, of the voyages in 1845. The *Britannia* and the *Clyde*, out of Liverpool, England, may have carried some Irish emigrants to Saint John in 1845 - Johnson, p. 196.

Month	Vessel	Port from	Port to	Passengers	Reference
May	Albion[287]	Cork	Saint John	Yes	Johnson/196
May	Ann[288]	Donegal	Saint John	Yes	Johnson/196
May	Coxon	Cork	Saint John	Yes	Johnson/196
May	Creole	Londonderry	Saint John	Yes	Johnson/196
May	Eliza Ann[289]	Cork	Saint John	Yes	Johnson/196
May	Governor Douglas[290]	Baltimore	Saint John	Yes	Johnson/196
May	Hope	Dublin	Shippagan	Yes	On line[291]
May	Isadore	Cork	Saint John	Yes	Johnson/197
May	John Wesley[292]	Cork	Saint John	Yes	Johnson/197
May	Leviathan	Baltimore	Saint John	Yes	Johnson/197
May	Londonderry	Londonderry	Saint John	Yes	Johnson/197
May	Ocean	Cork	Saint John	Yes	Johnson/197
May	Pons Aelii[293]	Cork	Saint John	Yes	Johnson/197
May	Redwing[294]	Galway	Saint John	Yes	Johnson/197
May	Sophia[295]	Waterford	Saint John	Yes	Johnson/197
May	St. Lawrence[296]	Cork	Saint John	Yes	Johnson/197

[287] An *Albion* passenger, Thomas **HEALY**, 23, Cork, was admitted to the Alms House in Saint John, on 30 June 1845 - Johnson, p. 76.

[288] Six *Ann* passengers were admitted to the Alms House in Saint John: Unity **CAULFIELD**, 24; Bridget **DIVERS**, 19; Biddy **DONNELL**, 23; James, 23, and Mrs. Hannah **HIGGINS**, 22; Bridget **KENNEDY**, 25, all from Donegal - Johnson, p. 76.

[289] The *Eliza Ann* carried passengers from counties Cork and Waterford. Five of them were admitted to the Alms House at Saint John: John **CARTY**, 28, and Mrs. Bridget **SWEENEY**, 30, both of Waterford; Hanora **HEANEY**, 26; John **LAWTON**, 26; William **MURPHY**, 53, all from Cork - Johnson, p. 77. Forty-five of the passengers left the vessel when it encountered ice conditions and boarded the *Countess of Durham* and the *Neptune* in order to be taken to Québec. The *Neptune* safely brought eighteen of them to that port - Johnson, p. 210.

[290] Mary **CAIN**, 17, from Cork, a passenger in the *Governor Douglas*, was admitted to the Alms House in Saint John from 17 June to 21 November 1846 - Johnson, p. 77.

[291] See www.gloucester.restigouche.net/ships

[292] Three passengers who arrived in the *John Wesley* were admitted to the Alms House in Saint John: Ellen **COLLINS**, 27; William **GEANEY** , 24; and Catherine **McARTY**, 19, all from Cork - Johnson, p. 77.

[293] Roger **CONNER**, 25, from Cork, a passenger in the *Pons Aelii*, was in the Alms House in Saint John from 5 to 17 June 1845 - Johnson, p. 78.

[294] Three passengers in the *Redwing*, all from Galway, were admitted to the Alms House in Saint John: Mrs. **BYRNES**, 30 (died 10 Dec 1846); Ann, 29, and Ellen, 30, **EAGAN** - Johnson, p. 78.

[295] The *Sophia* left 10 passengers at Halifax before proceeding to Saint John with the remainder. The Halifax newspaper, *The Times,* 27 May 1845, did not say how many went on.

[296] Two *St. Lawrence* passengers from Cork were admitted to the Alms House in Saint John: Margaret **HORNETT**, 26; and Peter **SULLIVAN,** 22 - Johnson, pp. 78-79.

Month	Vessel	Port from	Port to	Passengers	Reference
May	Triumph[297]	Baltimore	Saint John	Yes	Johnson/197
May	Virgilia[298]	Londonderry	Saint John	Yes	Johnson/197
June	Agnes	Sligo	Saint John	29	Dobson I/3
June	Brothers	Cork	Saint John	Yes	Johnson/196
June	Caroline	Londonderry	Saint John	Yes	Johnson/196
June	Caroline[299]	Ballyshannon	Saint John	Yes	Johnson/196
June	Champlain	Cork	Saint John	Yes	Johnson/196
June	Cygnet	Sligo	Saint John	Yes	Johnson/196
June	Dominica[300]	Cork	Saint John	Yes	Johnson/196
June	Henry Patterson[301]	Cork	Saint John	Yes	Johnson/196
June	Lady Mary Fox[302]	Cork	Saint John	Yes	Johnson/197
June	Lord Fitzgerald[303]	Galway	Saint John	Yes	Dobson III/65
June	Martha[304]	Cork	Saint John	Yes	Johnson/197
June	Mary[305]	Cork	Saint John	Yes	Johnson/197

---

[297] Two passengers in the *Triumph* were admitted to the Alms House in Saint John: Mary **O'BRIEN**, 20, Cork; and Jerry **SULLIVAN**, 14, Cork - Johnson, p. 79.

[298] Four passengers from the *Virgilia* were admitted to the Alms House in Saint John: Robert **HOWIE**, 19; Dennis **LYNCHIGAN**, 19; Mary **McLAUGHLIN**, 21; and John **PORTER**, 24, all from Donegal - Johnson, p. 79.

[299] Margaret **LENNAN**, 17½, from Fermanagh, a *Caroline* passenger, was admitted to the Alms House in Saint John on 5 May 1846 - Johnson, p. 76.

[300] Five people from the *Dominica* were admitted to the Alms House in Saint John: Norrie **CUNNINGHAM**, 30; Martin **JOYCE**, 26; Ellen **SMITH**, 23; Johanna **SWEENEY**, 21; Mary **WARREN,** 28. All five were from Cork - Johnson, p. 76.

[301] Thirteen passengers can be identified from depositions sworn at Saint John on 19 and 20 June 1845 - Public Archives of New Brunswick, mfm. F16225 (Emigration records). See Johnson, p. 210, for their names and places of origin.

[302] The *Lady Mary Fox* carried passengers from counties Cork and Kerry. Three entered the Alms House in Saint John: Timothy **CONNOLLY**, 32, Cork; Mary **LOVETT**, 22, Kerry; Margaret **SULLIVAN**, 20, Cork (she died 21 March 1846) - Johnson, pp. 77 - 78.

[303] Four passengers in the *Lord Fitzgerald* were admitted to the Alms House in Saint John: Mary **BROWN**, 32 (died 10 July 1845); Judy **DOOLEY**, 20; Margaret **LALLEY**, 24; and Ellen **MANION**, 23, all from Galway - Johnson, p. 78.

[304] The *Martha* carried passengers mainly from the counties of Cork and Kerry. Sixteen of them were admitted to the Alms House in Saint John. A list of these may be seen in Johnson, pp. 88 - 89.

[305] Two passengers in the *Mary*, both from Cork, were admitted to the Alms House in Saint John: Mrs. Margaret **BAKER**, 22; and Mrs. **KEARNS**, 47. The latter died 17 October 1845, ten days after being admitted - Johnson, p. 78.

Month	Vessel	Port from	Port to	Passengers	Reference
June	New Zealand[306]	Londonderry	Saint John	Yes	Johnson/197
June	Sarah[307]	Cork	Saint John	Yes	Johnson/197
June	Thorney Close[308]	Donegal	Saint John	Yes	Johnson/197
June	Velocity	Waterford	Saint John	Yes	Johnson/197
June	Warrior[309]	Drogheda	Saint John	Yes	Johnson/197
July	Catharine	Cork	Halifax	108	*AR*, 19 July 1845
July	Eliza Gillis[310]	Galway	Saint John	Yes	Johnson/196
July	Harriet	Londonderry	Saint John	Yes	Johnson/196
July	Jane[311]	Cork	Saint John	Yes	Johnson/197
July	Time	Cork	Saint John	Yes	Johnson/197
July	Wakefield[312]	Newry	Saint John	Yes	Johnson/197
Aug	Ann[313]	Limerick	Saint John	Yes	Johnson/196
Aug	Danube	Sligo	Saint John	Yes	PANB/RS 555
Aug	Hornet	Limerick	Saint John	Yes	Johnson/196
Aug	Woodland Castle	Cork	Saint John	Yes	Johnson/197
Sep	Dealy	Bantry	Saint John	Yes	Johnson/196
-	Atlas	Cork	Saint John	Yes	Johnson/196
-	Bache McEvers	Donegal	Saint John	Yes	Johnson/196
-	Ellen and Margaret	Cork	Saint John	Yes	Johnson/196
-	Non Pareil	Cork	Saint John	Yes	Johnson/197

[306] Three passengers – Robert **FENTON**, John **McKENNA** and Samuel **GORDON** – signed a testimonial thanking the *New Zealand*'s captain and crew - *New Brunswick Courier*, 28 June 1845. Counties Donegal and Londonderry supplied most of the passengers in the *New Zealand*. Two of them were admitted to the Alms House in Saint John: Mary I. **CUTHBERT**, 19, Londonderry; and Catherine **STRAWBRIDGE**, 17, Donegal - Johnson, p. 78.

[307] Mrs. Elizabeth **POWER**, 19, of Cork, a passenger in the *Sarah*, was at the Alms House in Saint John from 30 August 1845 until 20 January 1846 - Johnson, p. 78.

[308] The *Thorney Close* carried passengers from counties Donegal and Leitrim. Three of them were admitted to the Alms House at Saint John: Mrs. Mary **ARMSTRONG**, 24, Leitrim; Edward **HAGGARTY**, 18; and Mrs. Margaret **McGOWAN**, 21, both from Donegal - Johnson, p. 79.

[309] Rosa **McARRON**, 25, from County Meath, a passenger in the *Warrior*, was admitted to the Alms House in Saint John, 5 December 1845, where she died 8 January 1846 - Johnson, p. 79.

[310] Five people from the *Eliza Gillis* were admitted to the Alms House in Saint John: Catherine **CAREY**, 22; Patrick **HARDIMAN**, 19; Catharine **KRIAN**, 22; Mary A. **MEALEY**, 15, all from Galway, and Hannah **O'BRIEN**, 23, Bandon, County Cork - Johnson, p. 77.

[311] James **O'CONNELL**, 12¼, a passenger in the *Jane*, was admitted to the Alms House in Saint John from 13 February to 11 March 1846 - Johnson, p. 77.

[312] Mary **McMAHON**, 21, County Down, a passenger in the *Wakefield*, was in the Alms House at Saint John from 21 March to 15 June 1846. Her son William appears to have been born there on 15 April 1846 - Johnson, p. 79.

[313] The *Ann* in August carried passengers from counties Limerick and Clare. Two were admitted to the Alms House in Saint John, on 26 Aug 1845: Bridget **LAWLER**, 28, and Eli **LAWLOR**, 18, both from County Clare - Johnson, p. 76.

Month	Vessel	Port from	Port to	Passengers	Reference
-	Pallas[314]	Cork	Saint John	Yes	Johnson/197
-	Sun	Donegal	Saint John	Yes	Johnson/197

1846[315]

Month	Vessel	Port from	Port to	Passengers	Reference
Jan	Conservative[316]	Dublin	Yarmouth, NS	Yes	Johnson/83
Apr	Avon	Belfast	Saint John	Yes	Dobson II/12
Apr	St. Martin	Dublin	Saint John	Yes	Dobson II/115
May	Alarm[317]	Cork	Saint John	119	Johnson/198
May	Albion[318]	Cork	Saint John	160	Johnson/198
May	Brothers[319]	Bantry	Saint John	Yes	Johnson/198
May	Coxon[320]	Cork	Saint John	194	Johnson/198
May	Creole[321]	Londonderry	Saint John	284	Johnson/198
May	Dealy[322]	Bantry	Saint John	Yes	Johnson/198

---

[314] A passenger in the *Pallas*, John CROWLEY, 28, Cork, was admitted to the Alms House in Saint John, on 26 Feb 1846 - Johnson, p. 78.

[315] A party of 69 Irish immigrants from Tralee landed at Halifax in 1846, but the name of the ship which brought them has not been discovered. They may have been landed at Halifax from the *Sir James McDonnell*, en route from Tralee to Saint John, NB, in May 1846. People with County Kerry origins named **BOWLER, HOULIHAN** and **MORIARTY** turned up in Halifax at the right time and may have been among the 69 passengers left at Halifax. The *Coronation, Emerald, Emigrant,* and *Oregon* may have carried some Irish emigrants to Saint John in 1846 - Johnson, pp. 198 - 200.

[316] A passenger in the *Conservative*, John CUNNINGHAM, 23, Louth, was admitted to the Alms House in Saint John, in June 1846 - Johnson, p. 83. The ship presumably continued there from Yarmouth.

[317] Two of the passengers from the *Alarm* were admitted to the Alms House in Saint John: Mary CLELAN, 21, and Julia COTTER, 20, both from Cork - Johnson, p. 80.

[318] The *Albion* carried passengers mainly from County Cork. Two passengers died in Quarantine at Partridge Island: Dennis CARTY, 25, and George THOMAS, 55, both from Cork - Johnson, p. 211. Twenty-seven of the passengers were admitted to the Alms House in Saint John - Johnson, pp. 80 - 81.

[319] Seven passengers from the *Brothers* were admitted to the Alms House, Saint John: Mrs. Norrie, 32, John, 3½, and Mary, 15 months, COLLINS; Julia CONNEL, 18; Margaret CONNER, 22; Margaret CRONIN, 22; and Ellen McARTY, 23, all from Cork - Johnson, p. 82.

[320] Nine passengers from the *Coxon* were admitted to the Alms House in Saint John: John CONDEN, 26; Catherine DONOVAN, 10; Honora DRISCOL, 24; Joanna HERON, 22; Mrs. Ellen, 32, and John, 9 months, HERRICK; Jerry KEILLEY, 10; Mary MURPHY, 26, all from Cork; also James MURPHY, 30, Waterford - Johnson, p. 83.

[321] The *Creole* carried passengers mainly from the counties of Donegal and Fermanagh. Six were admitted to the Alms House in Saint John: Rose, 38, James, 3, and William, 9 months, HARKINS, from Donegal; Jane, 38, widow, Thomas, 7, and John, 9 months, LYNN, from Fermanagh - Johnson, p. 84.

[322] The *Dealy* carried passengers mainly from western County Cork. Thirteen of the passengers were admitted to the Alms House in Saint John. A list of these may be seen in Johnson, pp. 84-85. In the case of Ann MORRIS, 21, the home community is specified as Bandon.

Month	Vessel	Port from	Port to	Passengers	Reference
May	Envoy[323]	Londonderry	Saint John	298	Johnson/199
May	George Ramsay[324]	Kinsale	Saint John	Yes	Johnson/199
May	Harriet[325]	Londonderry	Saint John	154	Dobson III/46
May	Hornet	Limerick	Saint John	37	Johnson/199
May	Lady Napier[326]	Westport	Saint John	90	Johnson/199
May	Mary[327]	Cork	Saint John	107	Johnson/199
May	Pallas[328]	Cork	Saint John	189	Johnson/200
May	Princess[329]	Cork	Saint John	303	Johnson/200
May	Rose Macroom	Waterford	Saint John	Yes	Johnson/200
May	St. Lawrence	Baltimore	Saint John	Yes	Johnson/200
May	Sir James McDonell[330]	Cork/Tralee	Saint John	135	Johnson/200
May	Sophia	Waterford	Halifax	82	*Times*, 2 June 1846
May	Thomas Hanford	Cork	Saint John	160	Johnson/200
May	Triumph	Castletown	Saint John	Yes	Johnson/200
May	Velocity	Waterford	Saint John	Yes	Johnson/200
May	Victoria[331]	Galway	Saint John	Yes	PANB/RS 555

[323] The *Envoy* carried passengers mainly from the counties of Londonderry, Donegal and Tyrone. Forty of the passengers were admitted to the Alms House in Saint John. A list of these may be seen in Johnson, pp. 85 - 86. Three others died in quarantine at Partridge Island, May-June 1846 - Johnson, p. 80.

[324] John **DONOVAN**, 32, Kinsale, a passenger in the *George Ramsay*, was admitted to the Alms House in Saint John, on 17 Nov 1846, and died there, 28 Dec 1846 - Johnson, p. 86.

[325] Seven passengers from the *Harriett* were admitted to the Alms House, Saint John: David, 20, and John, 22, **CURRY**; Mary **DEVLIN**, 20; Ellen **HANNA**, 18; Ellen **McAFFREY**, 21 (died 1 July 1846), all from County Tyrone; Mrs. Bridget, 36, and Catherine, 14, **SWIFT**, from Fermanagh - Johnson, pp. 86 - 87.

[326] Three passengers from Mayo were admitted to the Alms House in Saint John on 24 June 1846: Anthony, 30, Mary, 26, and Mary, 5, **BYRNE** - Johnson, p. 87.

[327] The *Mary* carried passengers from the counties of Cork and Kerry. Two of the passengers were admitted to the Alms House in Saint John: William **TOBIN**, 30, Cork, and Mary **TOBIN**, 20, Kerry - Johnson, p. 89.

[328] Nine of the passengers were admitted to the Alms House, Saint John: Edmund **BARRETT**, 27; Edward **CLELAN**, 30; David **CROWLEY**, 20; Sarah **KNOWLES**, 35 (died 24 June 1846), all from Cork; Mary **LANDRIGAN**, 36, Fermanagh; Catherine **ROACH**, 19, Cork; Catherine **SHEHAN**, 20, Cork; Margaret **SULLIVAN**, 20, Cork; and John **WELCH**, 20, Cork. Another passenger was the mother of Biddy **McARNEY**, admitted on 15 Sep 1846 - Johnson, p. 89.

[329] Three passengers from the *Princess* were admitted to the Alms House in Saint John: Julia **GRIFFIN**, 19, Cork; Michael **McANARNEY**, 26, Killarney; and Daniel **MAHONY**, 52, Cork - Johnson, p. 90.

[330] Three of the passengers were admitted to the Alms House, Saint John: Thomas **KIRBY**, 5; James **SULLIVAN**, 26; and Catherine **SULLIVAN**, 40, all from Kerry - Johnson, p. 92.

[331] Moses Perley, the New Brunswick Emigration Officer, advised on 27 May 1846 that the brig *Victoria* from Galway arrived on 17 May. "The master reported that he had touched at Prospect near Halifax when sixty-two passengers land[ed] . . . of their own free will."

Month	Vessel	Port from	Port to	Passengers	Reference
May	Warrior[332]	Drogheda	Saint John	Yes	Johnson/200
June	Alexander[333]	Londonderry	Saint John	155	Johnson/198
June	Ann Wise[334]	Sligo	Saint John	134	Johnson/198
June	Ariel	Cork	St. Andrews	Yes	PANB/RS 555
June	Aulaby[335]	Cork	Saint John	Yes	PANB/RS 555
June	Bache McEvers	Cork	St. Andrews	137	PANB/RS 555
June	British Queen[336]	Newry	Saint John	Yes	Johnson/198
June	Charles[337]	Youghal	Saint John	Yes	Johnson/198
June	Charlotte	Ballyshannon	Saint John	Yes	Johnson/198
June	Coronation	Ireland	Saint John	Yes	PANB/RS 555
June	Ellen and Margaret	Cork	Saint John	95	Johnson/199
June	Faugh-a-Ballagh[338]	Dublin	Saint John	Yes	PANB/RS 555
June	Garland	Castletown	Saint John	135	Johnson/199
June	Herrings	Dublin	Shippagan	Yes	On line[339]
June	Jane	Cork	Saint John	68	PANB/RS 555
June	Jessie	Sligo	Saint John	100	Dobson I/81
June	John	Waterford	Halifax	29	*Times*, 9 June 1846
June	John Begg[340]	Galway	Saint John	Yes	Johnson/199

[332] Edward **FITZSIMMONS**, 18, Louth, a passenger in the *Warrior*, was an inmate of the Alms House in Saint John, from 22 Aug to 28 Oct 1846 - Johnson, p. 93.

[333] **WEIGHTMAN**, master of the brig *Alexander* (arrived 24 June 1846), was fined at Saint John for *"the irregular and insufficient issue of provisions and water"* to the passengers - Johnson, p. 211. Most of the passengers came from counties Londonderry and Donegal. Four were admitted to the Alms House at Saint John: Sally **FERRY**, 37, Derry; Nancy **McCARTY**, 22, Derry; Ellen **McCOLGAN**, 20, Donegal; and William **McLAUGHLIN**, 20, Derry - Johnson, pp. 81 - 82, 211.

[334] **ALLWOOD**, master of the *Ann Wise* (arrived 24 June 1846), was fined at Saint John for having *"a deficiency of provisions"* - Johnson, p. 212. Three passengers from Sligo were admitted to the Alms House in Saint John: Mrs. Bridget, 40, William, 18 (died 25 Mar 1847), and John, 4, **McDONOUGH**.

[335] Three passengers from the *Aulaby* were admitted to the Alms House in Saint John: Michael **COUGHLAN**, 40; Laurence, 27, and Honora, 22, **DONOVAN**, all from Cork - Johnson, p. 82.

[336] A passenger from the *British Queen*, Rose **McCULLOUGH**, 15, Tyrone, was admitted to the Alms House in Saint John, 20 Dec 1846, and died there, 4 Jan 1847 - Johnson, p. 82.

[337] The *Charles* carried passengers from counties Waterford, Cork and Kerry. Five of them were admitted to the Alms House, Saint John: Edwin **DOYLE**, 30, Waterford; Ellen **DUNN**, 16, Cork; Bridget **LANE**, 22, Cork; Catherine **LANE**, 19, Kerry; and Michael **MURRAY**, 30, Waterford - Johnson, p. 83.

[338] The *Faugh-a-Ballagh* carried passengers mainly from the counties of Westmeath and Cavan. Two were admitted to the Alms House in Saint John: Mary **CONNER**, 16, Westmeath, and Michael **MONOHAN**, 20, Cavan - Johnson, p. 86.

[339] See www.gloucester.restigouche.net/ships

[340] Biddy, 24, and John, no age, **HEAD**, Galway, passengers in the *John Begg* were admitted to the Alms House in Saint John, 12 Oct 1846. John died 13 Dec 1846 - Johnson, p. 87.

Month	Vessel	Port from	Port to	Passengers	Reference
June	John Francis[341]	Cork	Saint John	214	Johnson/199
June	Leviathan	Cork	Saint John	Yes	PANB/RS 555
June	Linden[342]	Galway	Saint John	Yes	Johnson/199
June	Lord Fitzgerald	Galway	Saint John	Yes	Johnson/199
June	Lord Glenelg[343]	Cork	Saint John	233	Johnson/199
June	Margaret Thompson[344]	Donegal	Miramichi	Yes	Dobson I/95
June	Martha[345]	Cork	Saint John	153	Johnson/199
June	Moy	Limerick	Saint John	Yes	Johnson/199
June	Midas[346]	Galway	Saint John	Yes	PANB/RS 555
June	Ocean[347]	Cork	Saint John	224	PANB/RS 555
June	Pero	Cork	St. Andrews	141	PANB/RS 555
June	Pons Aelii[348]	Castletown	Saint John	Yes	Johnson/200
June	Princess Royal[349]	Cork	Saint John	113	Johnson/200
June	Racer[350]	Dingle	Saint John	180	Johnson/200

---

[341] Four passengers in the *John Francis* were admitted to the Alms House, Saint John: Timothy **DOGAN**, 30; John **HAYES**, 28; Ellen **LEARY**, 23 (died 11 July 1846); and William **MURPHY**, 26, all from Cork - Johnson, p. 87.

[342] Two passengers in the *Linden* were admitted to the Alms House, Saint John: Biddy **CAIN**, 40, Clare; and Mrs. Catherine **FOLARA**, 40, Galway - Johnson, p. 88.

[343] The *Lord Glenelg* carried passengers from the counties of Cork and Limerick. Four of them were admitted to the Alms House, Saint John: Mrs. Ellen **DUNANE**, 28, Cork; Joanna **GUINEY**, 20, Limerick; James, 22, and Mrs. Mary, 24, **KEATING**, Cork - Johnson, p. 88.

[344] The *Margaret Thompson* was abandoned at sea. The master, **LACEY**, had been fined for "*not having supplied the emigrants with the quantity or quality of provisions as required by the Passengers Act*" - Johnson, p. 213.

[345] Fifteen passengers from the *Martha* were admitted to the Alms House, Saint John. All were young adults from Cork or Kerry. A list of these may be seen in Johnson, p. 88. One of them, Lawrence **SULLIVAN**, 22, from Cork, died there 16 June 1846, three days after his admission.

[346] Mrs. Margaret **JOYCE**, 28, Galway, a passenger in the *Midas*, was admitted to the Alms House, Saint John, on 22 August, and died there, 13 Sep 1846 - Johnson, p. 88.

[347] Four passengers in the *Ocean* were admitted to the Alms House, Saint John: William, 24, and Bridget, 24, **BRYANT**; Edward **GLEESON**, 27; and Richard **MURRAY**, 23, all from Cork - Johnson, p. 89.

[348] Thomas **BAKER**, 23, Cork, a passenger in the *Pons Aelii*, was admitted to the Alms House, Saint John, 13 July 1846 - Johnson, p. 90.

[349] Two of the passengers from the *Princess Royal* were admitted to the Alms House, Saint John: John, 21, and Mrs. Margaret, 22, **FITZGERALD**, both of Limerick - Johnson, p. 90.

[350] **POWER**, master of the *Racer*, was fined at Saint John "*for having an excess of passengers under the Passengers Act*" - Johnson, p. 214. Thirty-six of the passengers were admitted to the Alms House in Saint John, 19 of them within a week of arrival. One, Eleanor **FIELDING**, 68, from Kerry, died on 16 July 1846. A list of the 36 admissions may be seen in Johnson, pp. 90 - 91.

Month	Vessel	Port from	Port to	Passengers	Reference
June	Recovery[351]	Sligo	Saint John	Yes	Dobson I/124
June	Regina[352]	Baltimore	Saint John	Yes	Johnson/200
June	Renewal[353]	Castletown	Saint John	Yes	Johnson/200
June	Richard N. Parker[354]	Cork	Saint John	93	Dobson III/89
June	Sophia	Baltimore	Saint John	Yes	Johnson/200
June	Springhill	Sligo	Saint John	200	Dobson I/137
June	Themis[355]	Bantry	Saint John	98	Johnson/200
June	Victoria[356]	Youghal	Saint John	79	Johnson/200
June	Virgilia[357]	Londonderry	Saint John	172	Johnson/200
June	Volant	Londonderry	St. Andrews	Yes	PANB/RS 555
June	Wellington[358]	Galway	Saint John	Yes	Johnson/200
June	Woodland Castle[359]	Cork	Saint John	117	PANB/RS 555
July	Blanche	Donegal	Saint John	Yes	Johnson/198

[351] A list of seven passengers from Galway on board the *Recovery* and the *Chieftain* (1846) was published by Charles Addington, *Some Passengers from Ireland to New Brunswick, 1846* (London, ON, 1985). Two of those in the *Recovery* were Mrs. Catherine **REILLEY**, 23, Mayo; and John **COAN**, 29, Galway, who were admitted to the Alms House, Saint John - Johnson, p. 91.

[352] Four passengers from the *Regina* were admitted to the Alms House, Saint John: Dennis **HAYES**, 18; John **LAVIS**, 18; James **LEAVIS**, 16; and Dennis **SPILLANE**, 18, all from Cork - Johnson, p. 91.

[353] **COOPER**, master of the *Renewal*, was fined at Saint John "*for not supplying the proper quantity and quality of provisions and for excess number of passengers under the Passengers Act*" - Johnson, p. 214. Two of his passengers were admitted to the Alms House, Saint John: John **HAWKES**, 17, Cork, and John **SULLIVAN**, 16, Cork - Johnson, p. 91.

[354] Nine passengers from the *Richard N. Parker* were admitted to the Alms House, Saint John: John **CONWAY**, 26; Michael **DELAY**, 33; Daniel **HORNE**, 21; Charles **McARTY**, 30; Mary **MAHONY**, 30; Mrs. Mary, 30, and Joanna, 2, **O'NEILL**, all from Cork; also Mary **HORN**, 22; and Deborah **REGAN**, 23, both from Kerry - Johnson, p. 92.

[355] Two of the passengers from the *Themis* were admitted to the Alms House, Saint John: Margaret **McARTY**, 20, Kerry; and Peter **O'BRIEN**, 28, Cork - Johnson, p. 92.

[356] Four of the passengers from the *Victoria* were admitted to the Alms House, Saint John: James, 6, and Robert, 4, **CRAWFORD**, Cork; Patrick **DELANEY**, 20, Galway; and Edward **HANNEN**, 23, Galway - Johnson, p. 92.

[357] Six of the passengers in the *Vigilia* were admitted to the Alms House, Saint John: George **CAMPBELL**, 28, Donegal; Mrs. Dorah **CUMMING**, 22, Cork; Timothy, 32, Michael, 32, and John, 4, **FOLEY** of Cork; and Ann Jane **McLELLAN**, 21, Londonderry. Another passenger must have been the mother of John **BYRNE**, whose "mother came in the *Virgilia*". The child was an inmate from 20 Feb to 11 March 1847 - Johnson, p. 93.

[358] Mrs. Mary **MULLINS**, 25, a passenger in the *Wellington* from Galway, died in the Alms House, Saint John, on 16 May 1847, seventeen days after her admission - Johnson, p. 93.

[359] Five passengers from the *Woodland Castle* were admitted to the Alms House, Saint John: Dennis **KILLENAN**, 24; Mrs. Ellen, 44, and Richard, 20, **MOORE**; Joanna, 25, and Patrick, 1½, **SCANLAN**, all from Cork - Johnson, p. 93.

Month	Vessel	Port from	Port to	Passengers	Reference
July	Bristol	Londonderry	Saint John	Yes	Johnson/198
July	Burman[360]	Sligo	Saint John	Yes	Johnson/198
July	Elizabeth	Cork	Saint John	34	Johnson/198
July	Harry King[361]	[Castletown]	Saint John	Yes	Johnson/199
July	Mary Campbell[362]	Londonderry	Saint John	Yes	Johnson/199
July	Richard Watson	Sligo	Saint John	164	Dobson I/126
Aug	Brothers	Newry	Saint John	Yes	Johnson/198
Aug	Caroline[363]	Ballyshannon	Saint John	<30	PANB/RS 555
Aug	Chieftain[364]	Galway	Saint John	Yes	PANB/RS 555
Aug	Danube[365]	Ballyshannon	Saint John	Yes	Johnson/198
Aug	Dealy	Bantry	Saint John	Yes	PANB/RS 555
Aug	Donegal	Donegal	Sainr John	Yes	PANB/RS 555
Aug	Envoy	Londonderry	Saint John	Yes	PANB/RS 555
Aug	Pearl	Londonderry	Saint John	Yes	PANB/RS 555
Sep	Leviathan[366]	Cork	Saint John	Yes	Johnson/87

---

[360] **CANN**, master of the *Burman* (arrived July 1846), was fined at Saint John for having "*a deficiency of provisions*" - Johnson, p. 212. Probably in this ship was Mary **DRISCOL**, 25, Cork, admitted to the Alms House, Saint John, having arrived 9 July 1846 in the "*Brehm*". Were *Burman* and *Brehm* mistakes for *Burmah*?

[361] Five passengers in the *Harry King* were admitted to the Alms House, Saint John: Mrs. Joanna, 40, Mary, 16, Alice, 9, and Thomas, 7, **HUSSEY** from Kerry, and Humphrey **SULLIVAN**, 20, Cork - Johnson, p. 87.

[362] Three of these passengers were admitted to the Alms House, Saint John: Eliza **McDERMOTT**, 15, Donegal; Mrs. Maria, 28, and Sophia, 10, **STEWART** from Londonderry - Johnson, p. 89.

[363] The Emigration Agent had complaints from passengers about provisions, but he could take no action as *the Shipping Act did not apply to vessels carrying fewer than 30 passengers* [my italics] - Report of 7 Aug 1846.

[364] Six passengers in the *Chieftain* expressed their thanks to Captain **DUFFY** and Chief Mate **McKENZIE**. They state that the ship sailed from Galway and "lost its mainmast six days out and safely reached Saint John after a passage of 47 days." The passengers were mainly from counties Galway and Clare. Signatories were: James **DAVIN**, Bryan **DUGGAN**, John **SELLORS**, Thomas **SMYTH**, Thomas **THORNTON**, and Patrick **WALSH** - *Morning News*, 10 Aug 1846. Three other passengers -- Catherine **DEVENEY**, 30, from Galway; Mary **FLANAGAN**, 26; and Sarah **O'BRIEN**, 27, both from County Clare – were admitted to the Alms House, Saint John - Johnson, p. 83.

[365] **McNAGHTEN**, master of the *Danube* (arrived 4 August 1846), was prosecuted at Saint John for "*not having a proper supply of provisions and water, for having made use of temporary hold-beams and for having sailed without proper medicines in breach of the Passengers Act*" - Johnson, p. 212. Six of the passengers were admitted to the Alms House, Saint John: Mary **BYRNE**, 21 (her child John was born there on 4 Dec 1846); Margaret **BYRNE**, 21, Donegal; Mary **DEVER**, 20, Donegal; Eleanor **DUNLEVY**, 18, Donegal; Charles **McHUGH**, 26, Donegal or Ballyshannon; and Thomas **MEHAN**, 23, Donegal - Johnson, p. 84.

[366] Jeremiah **HEALEY**, 20, Cork, a passenger in the *Leviathan*, was admitted to the Alms House, Saint John, 20 Feb 1847 - Johnson, p. 87.

Month	Vessel	Port from	Port to	Passengers	Reference
Oct	Catherine[367]	Killala	Yarmouth, NS	Yes	Johnson/82
Oct	Harriet	Limerick	Saint John	Yes	Dobson III/46
Oct	Renewal[368]	Baltimore	Saint John	Yes	Johnson/200
Nov	Londonderry[369]	Londonderry	Saint John	79	Johnson/88
-	Britannia	Baltimore	Saint John	Yes	Johnson/198
-	Cynthia Ann	Drogheda	Saint John	Yes	Johnson/198
-	Emulous	Newry	Saint John	Yes	Johnson/199

1847[370]

Month	Vessel	Port from	Port to	Passengers	Reference
Mar	Lady Napier[371]	Dublin	Saint John	Yes	Dobson III/62
Apr	Falcon	Limerick	Saint John	Yes	Dobson III/38
Apr	Forager	Londonderry	Saint John	-	Dobson III/40
May	Aeolus[372]	Sligo	Saint John	493	Dobson I/2

---

[367] Eight passengers from the *Catherine* were admitted to the Alms House, Saint John: Widow, 40, and John, 12, **FINAN**; Mrs. Nancy, 34, Mary, 9, Bridget, 7, John, 4, and Michael, 2, **KILLANE**; and Biddy **McINNES**, 10, all from Mayo - Johnson, pp. 82 - 83.

[368] Three of the passengers from the *Renewal* were admitted to the Alms House, Saint John: Mary **DONOVAN**, 23; Ellen **GLENHORN**, 20; Ellen **LEAHORN**, 22, all from Cork - Johnson, p. 92.

[369] John **McCUTCHEON**, 25, Tyrone, a passenger in the *Londonderry*, was admitted to the Alms House, Saint John, 15 Apr 1847 - Johnson, p. 88.

[370] This was the worst year of famine emigration from Ireland to the Maritime Provinces. Most of these emigrants went on to the United States as soon as they were able. Coleman, p. 185, states that 17,074 Irish passengers were embarked for New Brunswick from Ireland, that 823 died on voyage, 697 in quarantine, and 595 in hospitals, for a net immigration of 14,959. The mortality rate was 12.38%, close to one in eight people. Johnson, in his book, *Irish Emigration to New England . . .*, gives the names of many of those who perished in Quarantine or in other institutions in Saint John. Coleman underestimated at least the numbers embarked. Ninety-nine of the ships in the present list conveyed 18,537 souls to New Brunswick ports, while a further 43 vessels brought across unknown numbers of Irish emigrants to the province.

[371] Although Dobson III, p. 62, places the *Lady Napier*'s arrival as being 2 March 1847, no one from the vessel turns up in records at Saint John until 24 September, when Bridget **FEHIN**, 19, Mayo, was admitted to the Alms House. Four other passengers from the vessel turn up in the admissions register on 20 March *1848*: Michael, 25, Biddy, 27, Ann, 10, and Michael, 5, **MEENAN** from Tyrone - Johnson, p. 143. Perhaps this voyage should be attributed to a date later in the year 1847.

[372] Twenty-six passengers died during the crossing - *New Brunswick Courier*, 5 June 1847. Twenty-five passengers signed a testimonial of thanks to Captain Michael **DRISCOLL** of the *Aeolus* for his good treatment of them and their fellow passengers, 31 May 1847. Punch, *Erin's Sons: Irish Arrivals in Atlantic Canada*, Vol. II, p. 74, lists their names. Seven other passengers died in Quarantine at Partridge Island in Saint John Harbour, between 31 May and 2 July 1847, namely: Unity **BURNS**, 11; Patrick **CRADE**, 7; Mary **HARTT**, 25; David **HENRY**, 55; Biddy **KILBRIDE**, 15; Mary **McLAUGHLIN**, 40; and Sally **TOHER**, 18 - Cushing, p. 25. Seventy-four passengers were admitted to the Alms House, Saint John, where seven more of them died. - Johnson, pp. 114 - 116. The passengers came from the estates of Sir Robert Gore Booth in County Sligo, and were described as "scattering fast" and finding employment - Coleman, p. 248.

Month	Vessel	Port from	Port to	Passengers	Reference
May	Aldebaran[373]	Sligo	Saint John	418	Dobson I/4
May	Alexander Edmund	Cork	Saint John	Yes	Dobson III/6
May	Amazon[374]	Ireland/Liverpool	Saint John	262	Johnson/201
May	Ariel	Cork	Saint John	Yes	Dobson III/10
May	Barbara	Galway	Halifax	296	Flewwelling
May	Caledonia[375]	Ireland/Liverpool	Saint John	Yes	Johnson/201
May	David[376]	Galway	Saint John	74	Cushing/61
May	Dealy[377]	Bantry	Saint John	169	Cushing/61
May	Governor Douglas[378]	Baltimore	Saint John	261	*PANB/RS* 555
May	Hannah[379]	Sligo	Saint John	211	Cushing/62

[373] Thirty-six passengers in the *Aldebaran* died at sea and two other in Quarantine immediately after arrival - *The Weekly Observer*, 18 May 1847. Eighty-four died in Quarantine at Partridge Island. Three survived and were admitted to the Alms House, Saint John - Johnson, p. 116. See Appendix IV for particulars of this "coffin ship".

[374] Fifty-four passengers from the *Amazon* died in Quarantine at Partridge Island - Cushing, pp. 23 - 39, *passim*. Since the vessel arrived on 2 May (Cushing, p. 60), and only began to discharge passengers on 18 June, it appears to have arrived in terrible condition. Twenty-four of its passengers were admitted to the Alms House, Saint John, where another five of them died - Johnson, pp. 116 - 117. Another of the passengers, John **BURNS**, escaped Quarantine on the night of 29 May 1847 - Johnson, p. 216.

[375] The *Caledonia* had 10 passengers who were admitted to the Alms House, Saint John: Thomas **HANEBERRY**, 29, Galway (died 25 June 1847), and two family groups: Michael, 30, and Jane **DONELLY**, 25, and children Daniel, 2½, and Peter, 20 months, from County Kildare; and William **McLOON**, 53, Tyrone, and his children Bernard, 13, Thomas, 12, William 6, and Mary, 3 - Johnson, pp. 126 - 127. Five others died in Quarantine at Partridge Island: Dennis **HOULAHAN**, 3; William **LIGAM**, 4; James **LUNNEY**, 28; Anne **McMANUS**, 50; and Ellen **WISEMAN**, 25 - Cushing, pp. 26, 28, 30.

[376] The *David* reached Saint John on 31 May 1847 via Halifax - Dobson III/27. Three passengers were admitted to the Alms House, Saint John in 1848 [sic]: Martin **FOLEY**, 30; and Bridget **MADDEN**, 19, both from Galway; and Patrick **MADDEN**, 3½, Cork - Johnson, p.129.

[377] The *Dealy* made port on 28 May and soon afterwards four of its passengers died in Quarantine at Partridge Island - Cushing, pp. 25, 28, 61. Eight passengers were admitted to the Alms House, Saint John, where four died: Mary **SULLIVAN**, 22, Cork (died 4 July 1847); Margaret **HORGAN**, 30, Cork (died 12 July 1847); Mary **DONNELL**, 10, Limerick (died 18 Aug 1847); and Mary **DONOVAN**, 20, Cork (died 20 Aug 1847). The survivors were Mrs. Anne **CONNELL**, 40, Sligo; Mary, 22, and Jerry, 19, **SULLIVAN**, Cork; Margaret **SWEENEY**, 17, Cork; and Catherine **TOOMEY**, 28, Cork - Johnson, pp. 129 -130. Four others died in Quarantine at Partridge Island: Catherine **COLLINS**, 20; Bridget **CONNY**, 10; Ellen **HALEY**, 17; and Rachel **KINGSTON**, 33 - Cushing, pp. 25, 28.

[378] The *Governor Douglas* embarked with 261 passengers and arrived at Saint John on 1 June - Cushing, p. 62. It arrived with 236 passengers, 26 of them sick with fever - Cushing, p. 17. Fifteen died in Quarantine at Partridge Island - Cushing, pp. 25, 28. The Alms House, Saint John, admitted 22 passengers; two died: Mary **DOUGAN**, 20; and Patrick **McCARTHY**, 40, both from Cork - Johnson, pp. 134 - 135.

[379]Thirteen passengers from the *Hannah* died in Quarantine at Partridge Island - Cushing, pp. 26 - 54, *passim*. The ship reached Quarantine on 22 May but was not permitted to land passengers in the city until after 3 July, after which 37 passengers were admitted to the Alms House, Saint John, most of them within the next two months - Johnson, pp. 135 - 136.

Month	Vessel	Port from	Port to	Passengers	Reference
May	Inconstant[380]	Cork	Saint John	114	Cushing/62
May	James[381]	Cork	Saint John	156	Johnson/202
May	Lady Constable[382]	Ireland/Liverpool	PEI	440	Monaghan/4/58
May	Lady Gordon	Belfast	Saint John	-	Dobson III/61
May	Marchioness of Clydesdale[383]	Londonderry	Saint John	374	Dobson I/96; III/67
May	Marquess of Normanby	Cork	Saint John	11	Dobson III/70
May	Mary[384]	Cork	Saint John	77	PANB/RS 555
May	Mary	Cork	Saint John	87	Cushing/63
May	Mary[385]	Cork	Halifax	46	Dobson III/73,

---

[380] Three passengers in the *Inconstant* died in Quarantine at Partridge Island following arrival on 22 May 1847: Catherine **HENNISAY**, 25; Ellen, 25, and Ellen, 20, **McCARTY** - Cushing, p. 25. By 3 June the ship was allowed into the harbour to discharge its passengers - *New Brunswick Courier*, 5 June 1847. Thirty-seven of them were admitted to the Alms House, Saint John, where seven died - Johnson, pp. 136 - 137.

[381] Nancy **LEARY**, 22, from Cork, a passenger in the *James*, was admitted to the Alms House, Saint John, 24 Aug 1847 - Johnson, p. 137.

[382] The *Lady Constable* was described as a "fever ship". There were 25 deaths on the passage. A further 8 passengers died after the ship reached port. Up to 35 passengers can be named with certainty or with reasonable confidence. From County Fermanagh came Aeneas **McCABE** and his son James; Owen **McCARVILLE**; Patrick **McCLUSKY** [and his wife Ellen **DOUGHERTY** of Rosslea, with 4 sons, of whom only Philip survived]; Dennis **ROONEY**; Philip **ROONEY** and his wife Mary Dougherty. From County Monaghan came Daniel **HUGHES**, John A. **RANAHAN** and Terence **SLAVIN**. Robert and Margaret **McALLISTER** came from County Antrim, while Owen **O'NEILL** was from County Armagh. Most likely from County Fermanagh were Patrick **DUNN**, John **FINEGAN**, John **GOODMAN**, Edward **KELLY** and Bernard **McTEAGUE**. From somewhere in northern Ireland came James **FARMER**, Patrick **GORMLEY**, Mr. & Mrs. Matthew **KELLY**, John **McCARVILLE**, James **McMAHON**, Felix **MULLIGAN** and Patrick **YOUNG**. Since all the foregoing were drawn from northern counties, the presence of four Munster Irish in the vessel can only be speculation: Michael and Mary **CHRISTOPHER** from County Waterford, Edward **FEEHAN** and Daniel **MULLEN** from County Tipperary, *cf.*, O'Grady, *Exiles & Islanders*, pp. 153, 290, n. 14. Another passenger, Michael **NEAL**, 30, from County Leix, was housed in the Alms House in Saint John, NB, from 7 July to 20 August 1847, and again from 20 March to 19 April 1848 - Johnson, p.143. Two other passengers were Michael **MULLIN** and his wife Anna from Dunmore, County Galway. After landing at Charlottetown, they went to Pictou, NS, in August, where Michael deserted his wife and she was assisted to go to Halifax, 30 Aug 1847 - NSA, RG 5, Series 'P', Vol. 84, no. 2.

[383] The passengers are named in Brian Mitchell, *Irish Passenger Lists 1847-1871*, pp. 2 - 5. The vessel landed 309 passengers, with 65 unaccounted for. Nine died during the voyage - NBC, 3 July 1847.

[384] Disentangling the several ships named *Mary* in 1847 is difficult. There would seem to have been four distinct vessels, as their arrival times fall within too short a time for there to have been one vessel making two transatlantic crossings under sail.

[385] The *Mary* had a very troubled voyage, reaching Boston on 28 May 1847, being turned away from there and again from Halifax. The passengers mutinied and had to be subdued, but the vessel made Saint John Harbour by 12 June. Seven passengers died at the Quarantine station on Partridge Island and a further thirty-one were admitted to the Alms House in Saint John, where four more died. The people were all natives of counties Cork and Kerry. The figure Dobson found for the number of passengers – 46 – seems low when one can account for 38 people in the Quarantine and Alms House records, ten of them children below the age of 14. The names and ages of the thirty-eight passengers are given in Punch, Vol. III, pp. 84 - 86.

Month	Vessel	Port from	Port to	Passengers	Reference
May	Mary Harrington[386]	Donegal	Saint John	135	Cushing/63
May	Midas[387]	Galway	Saint John	163	Cushing/63
May	Mountaineer[388]	Cork	Halifax	279	Flewwelling
May	Nova Scotia	Cork	Saint John	-	Dobson III/80
May	Ocean[389]	Castletown	Saint John	89	PANB/RS 555
May	Pallas[390]	Cork	Saint John	204	Cushing/63
May	Princess Royal[391]	Cork	Saint John	129	Cushing/64
May	Richard White	Cork	Miramichi	45-50	On line[392]
May	Sea Bird[393]	Newry	Saint John	346	Cushing/6

[386] "Those who arrived on the *Mary Harrington*, the first vessel to arrive with immigrants at Saint John [in 1847], were all bound for the United States and were described as 'a rather superior class of emigrant'." - Spray, "The Difficulties", p. 111. Despite that positive observation, one passenger – Patrick **KERRIGAN**, 20 – died in Quarantine - Cushing, p. 74, and eighteen were admitted to the Alms House, Saint John: Patrick **CLANCY**, 26, Leitrim; Ann **CONNERS**, 15, Sligo (still in Saint John on 18 May 1848); Catherine 'Kitty', 8 or 10, Owen, 8, and Biddy, 4 or 5 (died 7 Aug 1847) **DEALY**, Donegal; Francis and Mrs. Bridget **ELLIS**, both 28, Donegal; James, 36, Mrs. Catherine, 23 (died 24 May 1847), and Anne Jane, 4 months **FOLIS**, Fermanagh; Dennis **GALLAGHER**, 24, Leitrim; Mary **GALLAGHER**, 14, Donegal; John, 35, and Anne, 18, **GALLAGHER**, Fermanagh; Dennis **HILLEY**, 30, Donegal; John **HARRINGTON**, 40, Kerry; John, 25, and James 23, **SLAVIN**, Donegal - Johnson, p. 153.

[387] Ten passengers in the *Midas* died during the voyage - Johnson, p. 221. Two passengers from the *Midas* died in Quarantine at Partridge Island: John **SHAUGHNESSY**, 30; and Martin **WALSH**, 18 - Cushing, p. 22. Eleven were admitted to the Alms House, Saint John, where one died - Johnson, p. 154.

[388] The *Mountaineer* actually sailed from Liverpool, England, and reached Halifax on 15 May 1847. Its passengers were taken onward to Saint John, NB, and several were admitted to the Alms House there: Jerry **CONNELL** from Cork, on 20 July, died 28 July 1847; Daniel **DONOVAN**, 37, from Cork, on 30 Aug 1847; Thomas **FLEMING**, 22, from Mayo, on 30 July, died 9 Aug 1847; Michael **GANCEY**, 34, from Cork, on 10 July 1847; and Owen **SWEENEY**, 20, from Cork, on 2 Aug 1847 - Johnson, p. 156.

[389] One passenger from the *Ocean* died in Quarantine at Partridge Island: Mary **RAFTER**, 32 - Cushing, p. 26. Twenty-three were admitted to the Alms House, Saint John, where two of them died: Norry **HURLEY**, 1, and Mary **SULLIVAN**, 14, both from Cork - Johnson, pp. 156 - 157.

[390] The *Pallas* arrived on 22 May and was quarantined at Partridge Island, where 26 passengers died, before being permitted to land its passengers at Saint John on 21 June - Cushing, p. 29. Another 29 passengers were admitted to the Alms House, Saint John, where seven died - Johnson, pp. 157 - 158. Capt. Robert **HALL** of the *Pallas*, age 51, a native of Aberdeen, Scotland, died at the Quarantine Station on July 1st of typhus fever - *New Brunswick Courier*, 3 July 1847.

[391] The *Princess Royal* sailed from Limerick and came via Cork. On arrival at Saint John on 22 May 1847 the vessel was held in Quarantine until 3 July - Cushing, p. 64. Three of the passengers were admitted to the Alms House, Saint John: Thomas **MURRAY**, 27, Clare; Mrs. Ellen, 24, and Michael, 20 months **WAUL** [Wall], Limerick - Johnson, p. 161.

[392] This voyage is mentioned at www.theshiplist.com/1847/Miramichi

[393] The *Sea Bird*, 492 tons, P. Morrison, master, sailed from Warrenpoint/Newry about April 1st and arrived at Saint John on 22 May 1847, with 346 passengers - Cushing, pp. 10, 64. Three of the passengers from the *Sea Bird* were admitted to the Alms House, Saint John: Mrs. Catherine **McKAY**, 26, Down; John, 50, and Mrs. Betty, 50, **MURPHY**, Armagh - Johnson, p. 165.

Month	Vessel	Port from	Port to	Passengers	Reference
May	Shakespeare[394]	Ireland/Liverpool	Saint John	29	Cushing/64
May	Sir Charles Napier[395]	Londonderry	Saint John	429	Dobson III/96
May	Susan[396]	Cork	Saint John	Yes	Dobson III/99
May	Thorney Close[397]	Londonderry	Saint John	137	Cushing/64
May	Three Sisters	Cork	Saint John	-	Dobson III/102
June	Aeneas[398]	Cork	Saint John	62	Dobson I/2; II/2
June	Anne[399]	Kinsale	Saint John	Yes	Dobson II/9
June	Bolivar	Ireland	Miramichi	250	On line[400]
June	Eliza[401]	Youghal	Saint John	70	Cushing/61

[394] Twenty of the 29 passengers in the *Shakespeare* were admitted to the Alms House, Saint John, where six died. Apart from four individuals, there were three family groups: William, 35 (died 27 Aug 1847), and Catherine, 40, **CLANCEY**, Tipperary, with seven daughters (Mary, 15, Ellen, 14, Norry, 12, Peggy, 10, Judy, 9, Catherine, 3, and Eliza. 1); Patrick **HEGARTY**, 37, Cork, with three children (Jerry, 5 [died 27 Aug], Daniel, 2 [died 23 July], and Mary, 8 months); three children named **HESSON** from Cork (Michael, 13, Mary, 11, and John, 9). Of the individuals admitted, Ellen **GREGG**, 18, Londonderry, survived, while three others died, namely, John **COUGHLIN**, 40, Cork; John **GAVENEY**, 20, Monaghan; and Mary **MILLS**, 18, Louth - Johnson, p. 166.

[395] Passenger list in Mitchell, pp. 8 -11. Since 434 passengers embarked, seven appear to have died on passage - Cushing, p. 64. Four passengers from the *Sir Charles Napier* died in Quarantine at Partridge Island: Jane **BOYCE**, 37; Thomas,12, William, 6, **BOYER**; and John **MITCHEL**, 18 - Cushing, pp. 26, 29, 37. Fifteen of the passengers were admitted to the Alms House, Saint John - Johnson, pp. 166-167. Six of them do *not* appear in the passenger list (cf., Mitchell, pp. 8 - 11): Mary **ALLAN**, 25, Cork; Mary, 30, and Ann, 3, **RYAN**, Leitrim; Cornelius **MULHERRIN**, 57, Donegal; Eliza **CARSON**, 23, Donegal, and perhaps Barry **DEVLIN**, 10, Tyrone (unless Barry was the Daniel, 5, shown in that family on the passenger list). The two men in the Alms House listed as John **CURRAN**, one 18 from Tyrone, the other 30 from Cavan, *might* be the John **CARREN** from Castlederg and John **CURNIN** from Enniskillen (Mitchell, pp. 9, 10).

[396] Two passengers from the *Susan* were admitted to the Alms House, Saint John: Richard , 30, and Catherine, 14, **SULLIVAN**, Cork - Johnson, p. 168.

[397] Eight passengers in the *Thorney Close* inserted a card of thanks to the captain and crew for their good treatment. They mention that six children and a Mrs. **MAGWOOD** had died during the voyage. A further seventeen passengers are named in various records from Saint John at the time. *Cf.*, Punch, *Erin's Sons: Irish Arrivals in Atlantic Canada*, Vol. III, p. 83 - 84.

[398] The *Aeneas* sailed on 23 May and arrived on 26 June. Six of its 62 passengers were admitted to the Alms House, Saint John, where four died. The survivors were Mary **LEE**, 22, Cork; and Richard **LEARY**, 19, Cork. One of the deceased, William **LEE**, 50, Cork, was probably the father of Mary Lee. The others who died during September were Mary **NEAGLE**, 2; Maurice **NEHEL**, 50; and Elizabeth **NEIL**, 45, all from Cork. The last two may have been a couple, despite the different spelling - Johnson, p. 121.

[399] Libby **MURRAY**, 50, Cavan, a passenger in the *Anne, was* admitted, 4 Aug 1847, to the Alms House, Saint John, where she died, 31 Aug 1847 - Johnson, p. 121.

[400] This voyage is mentioned at www.theshiplist.com/1847/Miramichi It carried on to Québec.

[401] This and the following entry may in fact refer to the same voyage of the *Eliza*.

Month	Vessel	Port from	Port to	Passengers	Reference
June	Eliza Ann[402]	Galway	Saint John	65	Cushing/61
June	Eliza McCarthy[403]	Cork	Saint John	Yes	Dobson II/37
June	Eliza Parker[404]	Waterford	Saint John	28	Dobson II/37
June	Elizabeth Grimmer[405]	Waterford	Saint John	Yes	Dobson II/39
June	Eliza Liddell[406]	Sligo	Shippagan	164	Spray/122
June	Ellen[407]	Cork	Saint John	86	PANB/RS 555
June	Enterprise	Kinsale	Saint John	60	*NBC*, 12 June 1847
June	Friends[408]	Waterford	Saint John	Yes	Dobson II/46

---

[402] Five passengers from the *Eliza Ann* were admitted to the Alms House, Saint John: Patrick **FLYNN**, 19, Galway; Michael **HAHAR** [Mahar?], 22, Galway (died 22 Aug 1847); Edward **HICKSON**, Kerry; Mary **MULHERRIN**, 25, Galway (died 7 Sep 1847); and Fergus **O'BRIEN**, 20, Galway - Johnson, p. 130.

[403] Margaret **FORESTER**, 19, County Clare, a passenger in the *Eliza McCarthy*, was admitted to the Alms House, Saint John, on 19 July 1847 - Johnson, p. 130.

[404] The *Eliza*, or *Eliza Parker*, carried 96 passengers, but left 68 at Halifax, before taking the remaining 28 to Saint John - Susan L. Morse, appendix to her unpublished thesis, "Immigration to and Emigration from Nova Scotia 1839-1851" (Dalhousie University, 1946). The vessel reached Saint John on 21 June 1847. Seven from the "*Eliza*" were admitted to the Alms House at Saint John: Julia **CAIN**, 17, from Waterford; Thomas **CLANCY**, 22, from Waterford; Catherine **DONOVAN**, 20, from Waterford; Mary **HALY**, 28, from Waterford; Mary **HALY**, 2, from Waterford, died 9 Sep 1847; Michael **RYAN** or **REGAN**, 18, from Waterford; and Patrick **TIERNY**, 34, from Cork. Six from the "*Eliza Parker*" were also admitted: Hannah, 12, and Eliza, 5, **COLEMAN**, Cork; Joanna **LEARY**, 70, Cork; Betty **MOORE**, 16, Cork; Catherine **RIGGIN**, 20, Waterford; and John **RYAN**, 57, Waterford (died 26 Aug 1847) - Johnson, p. 130. If, as I believe, the references are to one and the same ship, 13 of the 28 passengers brought to Saint John are accounted for.

[405] Samuel **McNUTT**, 18, Donegal, a passenger from the *Elizabeth Grimmer*, admitted on 5 Aug, died 15 Aug 1847, at the Alms House, Saint John - Johnson, p. 131.

[406] According to Dobson I, p. 147, the *Eliza Liddell* sailed from Sligo either with 171 passengers to Saint John, NB, or with 77 passengers to Shippagan, NB. There is no mention of the vessel at Saint John that year. The Gloucester County authorities reported the ship's arrival in early July at Shippagan with 128 passengers, and reported that 36 had died during the passage, so that 164 seems to be the actual number of Irish aboard. *Cf.*, Spray, "The Difficulties", p. 122. The passengers came from the estates of Lord Palmerston in County Sligo. One was Owen **GILGAN**, traveling with his wife and four children. It was he who wrote to **DORAN**, a local magistrate, describing what he termed "our deplorable condition here; we are poor patients in great destitution, bordering on starvation." - Coleman, p. 250.

[407] This would seem to be the same voyage mentioned in Dobson I/49, where the vessel is called the *Ellis*. Forty of the passengers were admitted to the Alms House, Saint John, where six of them died. These passengers were drawn mainly from counties Cork, Galway and Clare - Johnson, p. 131 - 132. The confusion within the one record of the ship's name – *Ella, Ellen, Ellis* – reflects the chaotic circumstances prevailing when the record was written.

[408] Three passengers from the *Friends* died in Quarantine at Partridge Island; William **CONNER**, 25; Winnifred **KENNEDY**, 14; and Jane **REARDON**, 32 - Cushing, pp. 26, 28. Harriett **PHELAN**, 28, Tipperary, was admitted to the Alms House, Saint John - Johnson, p. 133. The ship stopped in at St. John's, NL, on the outbound voyage - Johnson, p. 219.

Month	Vessel	Port from	Port to	Passengers	Reference
June	Garland[409]	Cork	Saint John	138	Dobson III/41
June	Gem[410]	Galway	Saint John	123	Dobson III/41
June	Helen Anne[411]	Galway	Saint John	Yes	Dobson III/47
June	Herbert	Waterford	Saint John	Yes	Dobson III/48
June	John Clarke[412]	Londonderry	Saint John	528	PANB/RS 555
June	Linden[413]	Galway	Saint John	189	Cushing/63
June	Loosthauk[414]	Ire/Liverpool	Miramichi	462	Dobson I/91
June	Malvina[415]	Baltimore	Saint John	185	Dobson III/67
June	Margaret Elizabeth[416]	Youghal	Saint John	Yes	Dobson II/83

[409] Four passengers from the *Garland* were admitted to the Alms House, Saint John: Daniel, 45, and Daniel Jr., 5, **MAHONY**, Cork; Thomas **MITCHELL**, 16, Galway; and Peggy **MURPHY**, 14, Cork - Johnson, p, 133. Another, George **ILISAN**, 21, died in Quarantine at Partridge Island - Cushing, p. 28.

[410] Two passengers from the *Gem* died in Quarantine at Partridge Island: Thomas **BARKER**, 30; John **BURKE**, 30 - Cushing, pp. 28, 30. Nine were admitted to the Alms House, Saint John: Ellen, 35, Ellen, 30, and Biddy, 20, **BRODERICK**; and Mary **DILLON**, 22, Galway; Mary **FITZGERALD**, 22, Kerry; Jane, 26, and Julia, 9 months, **KELLY**, Leix; Margaret, 7, and Michael, 1, **NAULTY**, Galway - Johnson, pp. 133 - 134.

[411] Johnson, p. 202, states that the *Helen Anne* was out of Galway, but the Alms House record suggests that it was from Kinsale, and lists one passenger admitted to that institution on 10 July 1847 as being from Cork, namely Denis **SULLIVAN**, 21 - Johnson, p. 136.

[412] Passenger list in Mitchell, pp.18-21. Three of the *John Clarke*'s passengers died in Quarantine at Partridge Island: Sarah **CALVIN**, 19; Patrick **DOHERTY**, 25; and Betsey **JOHNSTON**, 31 - Cushing, p. 28. Only Doherty from Ballyboe, County Donegal, matches the published list. The two women are not found there. Nine of the passengers were admitted to the Alms House, Saint John - Johnson, pp.138 - 139. Three names do not match the Mitchell list: Dan **HAGGERTY**, 31, Donegal; Hugh **McDADE**, 28, Derry; and John **MOHAN**, 27, Donegal.

[413] The master of the *Linden*, Austin **YORK**, was fined £20 under the Passengers' Act for *"failing to provide sufficient water and provisions for his passengers"* - *New Brunswick Courier*, 3 July 1847. Sixty of the passengers were admitted to the Alms House, Saint John (56 people, several twice; 9 of the 56 died) or the Emigrant Hospital (4 people, of whom one died) - Johnson, pp. 146 - 148.

[414] The *Loosthauk* sailed from Liverpool but with Irish passengers, of whom 117 died on voyage, which touched in at Miramichi before continuing on to Québec. One passenger was Michael **DEE**, age 20. Some details on this unfortunate voyage may be found at www.theshiplist.com/1847/Miramichi

[415] Six of the *Malvina*'s passengers died in Quarantine at Partridge Island: Hugh **BOYCE**, 60; James **CARNEY**, 26; Mary **DONOHUE**, --; Stephen **HICKEY**, 28; Ellen **RYAN**, 21; and Matthew **SHEA**, 44, all from Cork - Cushing, pp. 26, 28, 37, 40, 55. Eleven others were admitted to the Alms House, Saint John: Catherine, 20 [died 23 July 1847], and Mrs. Johanna, 30, **CARNEY**; Denis **DALY**, 25; Ellen **DONNELLY**, 27 [died 20 July 1847]; Mary **DRISCOLL**, 30; Patrick **HAGGERTY**, 37; Daniel, 26, and Mary, 26 [died 8 Aug 1847] **HEGARTY**; John **HEGGARTY**, 10 [died 7 Sep 1847]; and James **KELLY**, 20, all from Cork - Johnson, p. 150.

[416] Eight passengers from the *Margaret Elizabeth* were admitted to the Alms House, Saint John, where four of them died: John **FINN**, 40, Sligo; John **DONOVAN**, 2½, Cork; Michael, 25, and Ellen, 22, **KEEFFE**, Waterford. The survivors were John, 30, Mrs. Catherine, 30, Mary, 8, and Michael, 1½, **DONOVAN**, Waterford - Johnson, p. 151.

Month	Vessel	Port from	Port to	Passengers	Reference
June	Mary Dunbar[417]	Cork	Saint John	Yes	Dobson II/89
June	Mary Grimmer[418]	Cork	Saint John	Yes	Dobson II/89
June	Mary Murray[419]	Cork	Saint John	Yes	Johnson/203
June	Nancy[420]	Killala	Saint John	106	Dobson III/77
June	Perseverance[421]	Cork	Saint John	123	Cushing/64
June	Progress[422]	Londonderry	Saint John	138	*NBC*, 5 June 1847
June	Redwing	Galway	Halifax	140	An Nasc/10
June	Rose	Cork	Saint John	56	Dobson III/91
June	Sarah	Ireland	Saint John	81	PANB/RS 555
June	Thomas Begg	Ireland/Liverpool	Saint John	Yes	Dobson I/140
July	Abrona[423]	Cork	Saint John	73	PANB/RS 555
July	Ambassadress[424]	Ireland/Liverpool	Saint John	498	PANB/RS 555
July	Bache McEvers[425]	Cork	Saint John	166	*NBC*, 10 July 1847

---

[417] Three of the passengers were admitted to the Alms House, Saint John: Michael **COLLINS**, 25, Cork; Johanna **DONOVAN**, 20, Cork (died 5 July 1847); and Daniel **HAYES**, 21, Cork - Johnson, p. 152.

[418] Two of the passengers were admitted to the Alms House, Saint John: Alexander, 16 (died 28 Aug 1847), and John, 14 (died 12 Sep 1847) **McNUTT**, Donegal - Johnson, pp. 153 - 154.

[419] Four of the passengers were admitted to the Alms House, Saint John: Mary **BRANNEN**, 19, Kerry; Gubby [*sic*] **BRESNAHAN**, 14, Kerry; Mary **HARRINGTON**, 14, Kerry; and Mary **WALSH**, 21, Cork - Johnson, pp. 153 - 154.

[420] Four passengers from the *Nancy* were admitted to the Alms House, Saint John on 1 Sep 1847: Peter, 45, Mrs. Anne, 45 (died 19 Sep 1847), Mary, 7, and Biddy, 10 months, **JORDAN** from Mayo. - Johnson, p. 156.

[421] Seventeen passengers from the *Perseverance* died in Quarantine at Partridge Island - Cushing, pp. 25-29. A further 28 were admitted to the Alms House, Saint John - Johnson, p. 159.

[422] Passenger list in Brian Mitchell, pp. 14-15. Five passengers died on passage - Cushing, p. 17. Six passengers from the *Progress* were admitted to the Alms House, Saint John. Another said to be from the *Progress* was Hugh **COYLE**, 14, Donegal, who does not appear in the list published by Mitchell - Johnson, p. 161.

[423] Nineteen of the passengers from the *Abrona* were admitted to the Alms House, Saint John, where five of them died (three were members of the **DESMOND** family of Cork: Denis, 50, on 24 Aug, Mrs., 55, on 21 Aug, and Johanna, 7 months, on 25 Aug 1847) - Johnson, pp. 106.

[424] The *Ambassadress* sailed from Liverpool, carrying Irish passengers. Nineteen passengers died on voyage, and 14 more died in Quarantine at Partridge Island - Cushing, pp. 28, 30, 36, 38. Another 123 were admitted to the Alms House, Saint John, where 27 died - Johnson, pp. 117-121, names them with their ages and places of origin. Dobson I, p. 7, calls the ship the *Ambassador*.

[425] The *Bache McEvers* arrived on 4 July with 147 passengers - Cushing, p. 60. Twelve died in Quarantine at Partridge Island - Cushing, pp. 28, 30, 38, 40. Eighteen others were admitted to the Alms House, Saint John, where three died - Johnson, p. 122.

Month	Vessel	Port from	Port to	Passengers	Reference
July	Blanche[426]	Donaghadee	Saint John	73	PANB/RS 555
July	British Queen[427]	Londonderry	Saint John	123	Cushing/26
July	Caledonia[428]	Cork	Saint John	67	PANB/RS 555
July	Caroline[429]	Ballyshannon	Saint John	88	PANB/RS 555
July	Charles Richards[430]	Sligo	Saint John	174	Dobson I/30
July	Chieftain[431]	Galway	Saint John	337	PANB/RS 555
July	Elizabeth Mary[432]	Cork	Saint John	Yes	Dobson II/3
July	Envoy[433]	Londonderry	Saint John	266	Dobson I/51

[426] The *Blanche* arrived on 6 July 1847 and two passengers died in Quarantine at Partridge Island: Mary **MAHON**, 30; Francis **McARTHUR**, 28 - Cushing, pp. 28, 30. Three passengers were admitted to the Alms House, Saint John: Catherine **HEGARTY**, 17, Donegal; Sarah **McCOUGHEL**, 21, Donegal; and Michael **WADE**, 24, Kerry - Johnson, p. 123.

[427] The *British Queen* embarked on 3 June 1847 with 125 passengers and had 123 when she arrived on 17 July - Cushing, pp. 26, 61. Three passengers were admitted to the Alms House, Saint John: Patrick **ALLEN**, Cork; Jane, 21, and Margaret, 4, **MURDOCK**, Derry - Johnson, p. 126.

[428] The *Caledonia* reached Partridge Island on 2 July 1847, where four passengers died in Quarantine - Cushing, pp. 28, 30, 60. Four passengers were admitted to the Alms House, Saint John: Ellen, 11, and Catherine, 9, **KEATING**, Waterford; Michael **MAHONY**, 24, Kerry; and Bridget **SHIFNA**, 27, Donegal - Johnson, p. 127.

[429] Three passengers from the *Caroline* were admitted to the Alms House, Saint John: Daniel **GILMARTIN**, 22, Leitrim; Mary **KENNEDY**, 20, Tipperary; and Bridget **SHEFNA**, 10, Donegal - Johnson, p. 127. The vessel sailed on 28 May and reached Saint John on 6 July 1847 - Cushing, pp. 26, 61.

[430] The *Charles Richards* arrived at Québec on 16 July 1847, so may have bypassed Saint John.

[431] Recorded information concerning the *Chieftain* is contradictory as to dates and the number of passengers. The vessel seems to have sailed from Galway on 23 May - Johnson, p. 201. It arrived on 5 July (Johnson, p. 127) or 6 July (Johnson, p. 201, and Dobson III, p. 23). I believe we can discount the arrival date of 2 August (Dobson I, p. 32). It seems likely that 344 passengers embarked (Cushing, p. 22) and that 325 arrived (Dobson III, p. 23). There were only 65 passengers according to Cushing, p. 61, but that can be disregarded, since 46 of the passengers were admitted to the Alms House, Saint John, where 9 of them died - Johnson, pp. 127-129. Twelve of the passengers placed a notice of thanks to Captain William **McDONOUGH** in the Saint John *Daily Morning News*, 14 July 1847. It was signed by six cabin passengers (William **CAVANAGH**, Hugh **CREAN**, Patrick **HENESSY**, Michael **HIGGINS**, William **KEANE**, and Patrick **REYNOLDS**) and six in steerage (James **FLANAGAN**, James **GREADY**, Bryan **KING**, Anne and Denis **MULHEENY**, and William **STAFFLE**).

[432] One passenger from the *Elizabeth Mary* was admitted to the Alms House, Saint John, on 11 Aug 1847: John **DONOVAN**, 29, Waterford - Johnson, p. 131.

[433] Passenger list in Mitchell, pp. 32-34. Two passengers died on the voyage and the others were landed on Partridge Island on 31 July, by which time there were 17 cases of smallpox - Johnson, p. 218. Eleven of the passengers died in Quarantine at Partridge Island - Cushing, pp. 37 - 54, *passim*. Eleven others were admitted to the Alms House, Saint John - Johnson, p. 133. Thirty-three passengers signed a notice of appreciation to Captain **LAIDLER** on 23 July 1847 - *New Brunswick Courier*. See pp. 115 - 122, *infra*, for two versions of the passenger list of the *Envoy,* and the notice of appreciation.

Month	Vessel	Port from	Port to	Passengers	Reference
July	Gowrie[434]	Cork	Saint John	71	Cushing/62
July	John Begg[435]	Galway	Halifax	97	An Nasc/10
[July]	John Wesley[436]	Baltimore	Saint John	Yes	Dobson II/71
July	Kingston[437]	Cork	Saint John	76	Cushing/62
July	Lady Bagot[438]	New Ross	Saint John	337	PANB/RS 555
July	Lady Caroline[439]	Warrenpoint	Saint John	105	Cushing/62
July	Lelia[440]	Galway	Halifax	160	An Nasc/10
July	Magnus[441]	Galway	Saint John	131	Cushing/26
July	Mary[442]	Cork	Saint John	Yes	Dobson III/72
July	Osmiller	Dublin	Saint John	Yes	Dobson III/82
July	Portland[443]	Londonderry	Saint John	338	Mitchell/24-26

[434] Two passengers from the *Gowrie* were admitted to the Alms House, Saint John: James **DRISCOLL**, 35; James **SHAUGHNESSY**, 26, both from Cork - Johnson, p. 136. Jerry **BRIAN**, 10; and Mary **PUNCH**, 30, from Cork, died in Quarantine at Partridge Island - Cushing, pp. 40, 54.

[435] The passengers in the *John Begg* were taken onward to Saint John, NB. Three of them were admitted to the Alms House there: Peter **GALOONE**, 24; Stephen **KILMARTIN**, 30; and Thomas **SPELLMAN**, 29, all from Galway - Johnson, p. 138.

[436] One of the passengers in the *John Wesley*, Mrs. Cate **HEGARTY**, 40, Cork, was admitted to the Alms House, Saint John, on 3 July 1847 - Johnson, p. 139.

[437] Mary **SULLIVAN**, 5, a passenger from the *Kingston*, died in Quarantine at Partridge Island - Cushing, p. 28. Twenty-one others were admitted to the Alms House, Saint John, where six died - Johnson, pp. 141 - 142.

[438] When the *Lady Bagot* arrived on 17 July the report was "All well on arrival" - Cushing p. 62. However, 25 were admitted to the Alms House, Saint John, where eight died between 1 August and 11 September 1847 - Johnson, p. 142.

[439] This was one of the happier voyages in 1847. The *Lady Caroline* conveyed 105 passengers who arrived on 23 July with "no death or sickness on passage". None died in Quarantine and only Elizabeth **LAUGHLIN**, 23, Down, was an inmate of the Alms House, Saint John - Johnson, p. 143.

[440] The passengers in the *Lelia* were taken onward to Saint John, NB. Tom **FOLAN**, 15, from Galway, was admitted to the Alms House at Saint John on 24 July 1847 - Johnson, p. 146.

[441] The *Magnus* sailed on 3 June and arrived on 24 July, after being driven aground on Partridge Island, where twelve passengers subsequently died in Quarantine - Cushing, pp. 37 - 55, *passim*, and p. 63. Ten passengers died from fever during the crossing - Johnson, p. 220. Twenty-one others were admitted to the Alms House, Saint John, where two died - Johnson, pp. 149 - 150.

[442] Two of the *Mary*'s passengers died in Quarantine at Partridge Island - Cushing, pp. 28, 37.

[443] Passenger list in Mitchell, pp. 24-26, lists 338 passengers. Dobson I, p. 118, claims that the *Portland* conveyed only 287 passengers. Of the passengers, 38 were admitted to the Alms House, Saint John, and 9 of them died - Johnson, pp. 160-161. I suspect that three people who arrived on the "Buksa?" (Johnson, p. 126) were actually people from the *Portland*, as no such ship existed as the *Buksa*, their surnames, origin and dates of admission match similarly named people in the list from the *Portland*. They were Hanora, 25, Mary, 1½, and John, 6 months (died 30 Aug 1847), **WARREN** from Cork.

Month	Vessel	Port from	Port to	Passengers	Reference
July	Royal Mint[444]	Ireland/Liverpool	Saint John	148	PANB/RS 555
July	Ruby[445]	Sligo	Saint John.	105	Dobson III/92
July	Sally[446]	Cork	Saint John	96	NBC, 10 July 1847
July	Seraph[447]	Cork/Boston	Saint John	120	NBC, 10 July 1847
July	Susan Anne[448]	Castletown	Saint John	59	Cushing/64
July	Theobald Mathew[449]	Galway	Saint John	Yes	Dobson III/101
July	Trafalgar[450]	Cork	Saint John	127	Cushing/26
July	Ward Chipman[451]	Cork	Saint John	505	Cushing/26

[444] The *Royal Mint*, with mainly Irish passengers, reached Partridge Island on 18 July 1847, where seven people died - Cushing, pp. 29, 30, 37, 64. The ship began to discharge its passengers on 30 July, and 17 were admitted to the Alms House, Saint John, where two of them died - Johnson, pp. 161-162. They were drawn from nine Irish counties as well as one each from Scotland and England. In addition 19 passengers died during the crossing - Johnson, p. 222.

[445] The *Ruby* arrived on 2 July 1847 with 105 passengers, of whom two died in Quarantine at Partridge Island: Patrick **KENNEDY**, 40; and Mary **LONG**, 59 - Cushing, p. 29. Forty-one others were admitted to the Alms House, Saint John, where 11 died - Johnson, pp. 162 - 163.

[446] The *Sally* arrived on 5 July 1847 with 96 passengers, of whom two died in Quarantine at Partridge Island: Mary **COCHRANE**, 30; and John **QUINN**, 37 - Cushing, p. 29. Twenty-one were admitted to the Alms House, Saint John, where three died - Johnson, pp. 163 - 164.

[447] The *Seraph* of Cork went first to Boston but when the ship master refused to post bond that his passengers would not become a public charge, the ship proceeded to Saint John - *New Brunswick Courier*, 10 July 1847. When the ship arrived on 6 July the number of passengers was 114 - Cushing, p. 64. Six passengers died in Quarantine at Partridge Island: Thomas **BLACKSON**, 26; Daniel **CLARK**, 32; Corley **DONAGHEY**, 25; John **McHUIRE**, 26; Will **PINE**, 30; and John **TREAGH**, 50 - Cushing, pp. 29, 30, 38. Another six were admitted to the Alms House, Saint John, where one, Esther **O'CONNOR**, 24, Cork , died on 17 August 1847, a day after being admitted. It seems likely that Margaret **O'CONNOR**, 14, Cork, admitted the same day, was her sister. Others from the *Seraph* were James **CONNERS**, 48, Cork; Mathew **CONNOR**, 14, Cork; Patrick **LYNCH**, 20, Kerry; and Walker **O'CONNERS**, 15, Cork - Johnson, pp. 165 - 166.

[448] The *Susan Anne* was bound for Boston - Cushing, p. 64, but put into Saint John on 17 July 1847 and left some of its passengers, since six were admitted to the Alms House, Saint John: Denis, 27, and Patrick, 6 months, **CLEARCY**, Cavan; Michael **DOWNEY**, 50, Cork; Mary **HARRINGTON**, 18, Cork; Jerry **SULLIVAN**, 25, Kerry; and Cornelius **SULLIVAN**, 22, Cork - Johnson, 169.

[449] Two passengers from the *Very Rev. Theobald Mathew* died in Quarantine at Partridge Island: Will **KAIN**, 23; and Patrick **QUINN**, 26 - Cushing, p. 29. Another passenger, Hanora **THORNTON**, 26, Galway, was admitted to the Alms House, Saint John - Johnson, p. 169.

[450] The *Trafalgar* sailed on 5 June 1847 with 127 passengers who seem to have arrived safely, but 12 died in Quarantine at Partridge Island - Cushing, pp. 26, 29-30, 37-38, 40, 64. Another 12 passengers were admitted to the Alms House, Saint John, where Hanora **HURLEY** from Cork died 9 Aug 1847, age 26, and John **DONAHUE** from Cork died 10 Aug 1847, age 30 - Johnson, p. 169.

[451] The *Ward Chipman* embarked with 505 passengers on 12 June 1847, and arrived with 482 on 22 July - Cushing, pp. 26, 64. Another 36 died in Quarantine at Partridge Island - Cushing, pp. 30 - 45, *passim*. Six died out of a further 88 passengers who were admitted to the Alms House, Saint John - Johnson, pp. 169 -172. That gives a total mortality of 65 out of 505.

Month	Vessel	Port from	Port to	Passengers	Reference
Aug	Adeline[452]	Cork	Saint John	61	Cushing/26
Aug	Alice[453]	Galway	Saint John	125	PANB/RS 555
Aug	Bethel[454]	Galway	Saint John	247	PANB/RS 555
Aug	Bloomfield[455]	Galway	Saint John	74	Dobson III/14
Aug	British Merchant[456]	Cork	Saint John	371	Dobson I/21
Aug	Cushlamachree[457]	Galway	Saint John	337	Dobson I/37
Aug	Glory[458]	Cork	Saint John	Yes	Johnson/134

[452] The *Adeline* (called the *Adelaide* in some secondary sources), sailed on 15 June and arrived on 3 August 1847. Five passengers were admitted to the Alms House, Saint John: Mary **COAN**, 10, Kerry (died 18 Sep 1847); Mary **CONNELL**, 18, Cork (died 6 Mar 1848); Daniel, 23, and John, 23, **DONOVAN**, Cork; and Jerry **KENNEDY**, 30, Cork - Johnson, p. 107.

[453] The *Alice* embarked on 8 July with 131 passengers, and arrived in Saint John shortly before 7 August 1847 with 125 souls aboard - Cushing, pp. 30, 60. Three of the passengers died in Quarantine at Partridge Island: Bridget **CONNOR**, 4; John **LOWREY**, 7; and Michael **MAHON**, 37 - Cushing, pp. 38, 40, 43. The Immigration Office had received a request for information concerning five of the passengers in the *Alice*: Martin, James, Honor and Ellen **MALONE**, and Thomas **HYNES** - Johnson, p. 215.

[454] The *Bethel* arrived on 27 Aug 1847, and 23 of its passengers died in Quarantine at Partridge Island - Cushing, pp. 43-45, 54. Another 29 were admitted to the Alms House, Saint John, where Mary **BOCHAN**, 5, Galway, died on 25 Sep 1847 - Johnson, pp. 122 - 123. All the passengers originated in Galway or northern County Clare.

[455] The *Bloomfield* was driven on shore by a gale on 6 Augus 1847t, and the passengers were found to be in a "destitute and starving state." The master, Patrick **BEEGAN**, was fined £50 and costs *"for not supplying the passengers by that vessel with sufficient water and provisions, as required by the Passengers' Act."* - NBC, 21 Aug 1847. There had been two deaths on passage - Cushing, p. 30. Thirty-four of the passengers were admitted to the Alms House, Saint John, where eight of them died - Johnson, pp. 123-124. A sum of £11/10/6 was remitted to Michael **CORNEY** of Kinsale, brother of John Corney who died at Partridge Island in Quarantine - Johnson, p. 217.

[456] The *British Merchant* sailed with 371 passengers and arrived at Saint John on 5 August 1847 with 338 - Cushing, p. 30. The 33 deaths on passage were followed by 56 deaths in Quarantine at Partridge Island - Cushing, pp. 36 - 54, *passim*. A further 8 deaths occurred among the 49 passengers who were admitted to the Alms House, Saint John - Johnson, pp. 124 - 126. That was a total mortality of 97out of 371 passengers, more than one in four.

[457] The *Cushlamachree* reputedly sailed with 172 passengers on 6 July 1847 - Cushing, p. 30, yet arrived with 337 - Cushing, p. 61, which suggests either a mathematical error in one of the accounts or that the vessel took on additional passengers after departing Galway. The latter is supported by the presence of several people from Cork among the disembarked passengers at Saint John. Nine people from the vessel were admitted to the Alms House, Saint John: David **GOGGIN**, 22, Cork (died 27 Dec 1848); Randle **McDONNELL**, 55, Roscommon; John **MELOY**, 13, Galway; Edward **MURPHY**, 48, Cork; John **SALLORY**, 27, Galway (died 19 Sep 1847); Mrs. Judy, 40, Michael, 30, and Biddy, 5, **TRACY**, Galway; and John **TRAHEE**, 55, Cork - Johnson, p. 129.

[458] Dennis **GARAVAN**, 20, Cork, a passenger from the *Glory, was* admitted to the Alms House, Saint John on 6 Aug 1847 - Johnson, p. 134.

Month	Vessel	Port from	Port to	Passengers	Reference
Aug	Jane[459]	Limerick	Saint John	98	Cushing/26
Aug	John Francis	Cork	Saint John	Yes	Dobson I/83
Aug	John S. DeWolfe[460]	Killala	Saint John	362	Cushing/62
Aug	Leviathan[461]	Baltimore	Saint John	131	Cushing/30
Aug	Londonderry[462]	Londonderry	Saint John	182	Cushing/63
Aug	Midas[463]	Galway	Saint John	138	Cushing/63
Aug	Numa[464]	Sligo	Saint John	256	Dobson I/110
Aug	Ocean	Castletown	Saint John	Yes	Dobson III/81
Aug	Pallas	Cork	Saint John	338	Dobson I/113
Aug	St. Lawrence	Cork	Saint John	133	Cushing/46
Aug	Sea[465]	Ireland/Liverpool	Saint John	243	Cushing/64
Aug	Sir James McDonell[466]	Dublin	Saint John	156	Cushing/64
Aug	Warrior[467]	Belfast	Saint John	97	Cushing/30

[459] Two passengers of the *Jane* died in Quarantine at Partridge Island: Michael, 4, and Bridget, 3, **COSTELLO** - Cushing, p. 40. Seventeen were admitted to the Alms House, Saint John - Johnson, p. 138. Nine passengers signed a testimonial thanking Captain **McLEAN** and his crew for their attentions during the crossing, namely: John **DAVIES**, Robert **DOBIE**, Patrick **JUDGE**, Thomas **McAVOY**, John **O'BRIEN**, Henry D. **O'REILLY**, MD, John **REES**, Michael **TENANT**, and David **WILSON** - *New Brunswick Courier*, 21 Aug 1847.

[460] Eighteen passengers from the *John S. DeWolf* died in Quarantine at Partridge Island - Cushing, pp.54, *passim*. Sixty-seven others were admitted to the Alms House, Saint John, where seven died - Johnson, pp. 139 - 141.

[461] The *Leviathan* embarked 131 passengers on 6 July, and arrived with 127 on 12 August 1847 - Cushing, pp. 30, 62. Five died in quarantine at Partridge Island: Bridget **BURKE**, 6 months; Daniel **HOLLAND**, 40; Arthur **LACEY**, 29; Patrick **SMELLIE**, 31; and Eleanor **WHEELAN**, 33 - Cushing, pp. 37, 38. Another three were admitted to the Alms House, Saint John: Daniel **DALY**, 30, Cork; Owen, 32, and Mrs. Mary, 26, **SAVAGE**, Cork - Johnson, p. 146.

[462] Passenger list in Mitchell, pp. 34-35. Fourteen of the passengers from the *Londonderry* were admitted to the Alms House, Saint John, where James **McGINN**, 30, Tyrone, died on 12 July 1848. These passengers were from Donegal, Londonderry and Tyrone - Johnson, pp. 148 - 149.

[463] Fifty-five passengers from the *Midas* were admitted to the Alms House, Saint John, where five died - Johnson, pp. 154 - 156.

[464] Although the *Numa* sailed for Saint John in May 1847, it seems to have landed its passengers at Grosse Isle, Québec, in August.

[465] The *Sea* arrived on 27 August 1847 and lost two passengers in Quarantine at Partridge Island - Cushing, pp. 40, 55, 64. Thirty-three passengers, one of them English, were admitted to the Alms House, Saint John, and four of them died there - Johnson, pp. 164 - 165.

[466] Fifty passengers from the *Sir James McDonell* were admitted to the Alms House, Saint John, where ten of them died - Johnson, pp. 167 - 168.

[467] The *Warrior* sailed on 8 July with 97 passengers and arrived on 20 August 1847 with 95 - Cushing, pp. 30, 65. Four of the surviving passengers were admitted to the Alms House, Saint John: Margaret **CAIN**, 13, Derry; James **DONELLY**, 35, Derry; Mary **MAGIVERN**, 54, Antrim; and Arthur **O'NEIL**, 50, Tyrone (who died 12 Sep 1847) - Johnson, p. 172.

Month	Vessel	Port from	Port to	Passengers	Reference
Aug	Yeoman[468]	Sligo	Saint John	540	PANB/RS 555
[Sep]	Creole[469]	Londonderry	Saint John	Yes	Dobson Ii/36
Sep	John	Waterford	Saint John	27	Cushing/42
Sep	Lady Dunblain	Killybegs	Saint John	50	Cushing/32
Sep	Lady Sale[470]	Sligo	Saint John	350	Cushing/41
Sep	Lord Fitzgerald[471]	Galway	Saint John	78	Cushing/32
Sep	Pekin[472]	Sligo	Saint John	72	Dobson I/114
Sep	Pero[473]	Cork	Saint John	153	Cushing/41-42
Oct	Aldebaran	Dublin	Saint John	Yes	*NBC*, 6 Nov 1847
Oct	British Queen[474]	Londonderry	Saint John	44	PANB/RS 555
Oct	Caroline	Limerick	Saint John	83	Cushing/61

[468] Thirty-seven passengers from the *Yeoman* died in Quarantine on Partridge Island, Saint John Harbour, between late August and 31 October 1847. Their names and ages may be found in Punch, *Erin's Sons: Irish Arrivals in Atlantic Canada,* Vol. II, p. 75. The *New Brunswick Courier*, 28 Aug 1847, reported that the "passengers by the *Yeoman* have been well fed and cared for on the voyage . . .". Forty-four others were admitted to the Alms House, Saint John, where six of them died - Johnson, pp. 172 - 174. The *Yeoman* had 950 tons burden, making it one of the larger sailing vessels in the emigrant trade to the region up to that time. Its people were described as being "in good order" and had come from the estates of Sir Robert Gore Booth - Coleman, p. 249.

[469] Three passengers in the *Creole* were admitted to the Alms House, Saint John, on 19 Sep 1847: Catherine, 30, Anne, 7, and John, 1, **KIRK** from County Tyrone - Johnson, p. 129.

[470] Twenty-one out of 350 passengers embarked in the *Lady Sale* died on passage - Cushing, p. 41. Nineteen others died of fever in Quarantine on Partridge Island, Saint John Harbour, between their arrival on 9 September and the end of October 1847. Their names and ages may be found in Punch, *Erin's Sons: Irish Arrivals in Atlantic Canada,* Vol. II, pp. 75 - 76. Eighty-six passengers were admitted to the Alms House, Saint John, where two of them died - Johnson, pp. 143 - 146. Nine widows with 57 children were among the passengers - Johnson, p. 220.

[471] Four passengers from the *Lord Fitzgerald* died on passage - Cushing, p. 42. Twelve died in Quarantine at Partridge Island - Cushing, pp. 43, 45, 54. Another fourteen passengers were admitted to the Alms House, Saint John, where Bridget **LYNCH**, 21, Galway, died, 22 Apr 1848 - Johnson, p. 149.

[472] The *Pekin* reached Saint John on 24 Sep 1847. Three of its passengers died in Quarantine at Partridge Island: Mary, 5, and Winnifred, 3, **MORROW,** and Bridget **QUINAN**, 1 - *NBC,* 20 Nov 1847. Two passengers were admitted to the Alms House, Saint John on 20 March 1848: Francis **MURRAY**, 26, Roscommon; and John **RADEKIN**, 50, Sligo - Johnson, p. 158.

[473] The *Pero* embarked 153 passengers on 15 July 1847, and 21 died on passage (12 children and infants from smallpox) - Cushing, pp. 41-42. Another 17 died in Quarantine at Partridge Island - Cushing, pp. 43, 45, 55. A further nine passengers from the *Pero* were admitted to the Alms House, Saint John - Johnson, p. 158.

[474] Three passengers from the *British Queen* were admitted to the Alms House, Saint John: Patrick **ALLEN**, 33, Cork; Jane, 21, and Margaret, 4, **MURDOCK**, Londonderry - Johnson, p. 126. It is a bit unusual to find a passenger from Cork, such as Allen, sailing from Londonderry.

Month	Vessel	Port from	Port to	Passengers	Reference
Oct	David[475]	Galway	Saint John	91	Cushing/37
Oct	Fanny[476]	Londonderry	Saint John	223	Cushing/49
Oct	Independence[477]	Belfast	Miramichi	432	Dobson I/51
Oct	James	Limerick	Saint John	129	PANB/RS 555
Oct	John Hawkes[478]	Limerick	Miramichi	114	Dobson III/58
Oct	Lord Ashburton	Sligo	Saint John	584	Dobson I/91
Oct	Victoria	Ireland	Miramichi	Yes	On line[479]
Nov	Aeolus[480]	Sligo	Saint John	428	Dobson I/2
Nov	Alert	Waterford	Saint John	Yes	Dobson III/5
Nov	Brown	Dublin	Saint John	Yes	Dobson III/18
Nov	Meodkes	Wexford	Saint John	-	*NBC*, 13 Nov 1847
Nov	Triumph[481]	Sligo	Saint John	46	PANB/RS 555
-	Alexander	Sligo	Saint John	Yes	Dobson I/6
-	Avon	Belfast	Miramichi	500	Dobson I/15
-	Commerce	[Sligo]	Saint John	Yes	Dobson I/34
-	Conqueror	Ireland	Saint John	Yes	Dobson II/34
-	Fredericton	Ireland	Saint John	Yes	Dobson I/57
-	Highland Mary[482]	Ireland	Saint John	Yes	Dobson I/70

---

[475] Three passengers in the *David* were admitted to the Alms House, Saint John: Martin **FOLEY**, 30, Galway; Bridget **MADDEN**, 19, Galway; and Patrick **MADDEN**, 3½, Cork - Johnson, p. 129. Three died in Quarantine at Partridge Island: Patrick **CONNER**, 18 months; Mary, 3 months, and Patrick, 39 **NAUGHTEN** - *New Brunswick Courier*, 20 Nov 1847.

[476] Ann **MULLIN**, 22, Kerry, a passenger in the *Fanny*, was admitted to the Alms House, Saint John, on 29 Dec 1848 - Johnson, p. 133.

[477] This ship called at Miramichi en route to Québec. See www.theshiplist.com/1847/Miramichi

[478] This voyage is mentioned at www.theshiplist.com/1847/Miramichi From Miramichi, it carried on to Québec. If the ship embarked 147 passengers and delivered 114 at Québec, it is probable that some of the 33 died on the voyage or disembarked at Miramichi.

[479] This voyage is mentioned at www.theshiplist.com/1847/Miramichi

[480] No fewer than 174 passengers, tenants from Lord Palmerston's estates in County Sligo, and landed from this voyage of the *Aeolus*, were admitted to the Alms House, Saint John, where 14 died. Some hint of their subsequent dispersal may be observed in the comment that Ellen **McGOWAN**, 16, Sligo, discharged 24 Oct 1848, went to Philadelphia. Biddy **MOOHAN**, 23, Sligo, was "sent to Boston" after her discharge on 7 June 1848. A second person of that name, age 10, was discharged on 17 Oct 1848 and was also "sent to Boston" - Johnson, pp. 107 - 113.

[481] These people were tenants from the estate of John ffolliott, M.P. for Sligo.

[482] Although Johnson, p. 136, reports that the *Highland Mary* arrived at Montréal in 1847, two of its passengers were admitted to the Alms House, Saint John late that year, namely John, 58, and John Jr., 15, **SULLIVAN**.

Month	Vessel	Port from	Port to	Passengers	Reference
-	Lotus[483]	Ireland/Liverpool	Saint John	Yes	Dobson I/92
-	Magna Charta	Sligo	Saint John	Yes	Dobson I/93
-	Mayflower	Limerick	Pictou, NS	39	*NS*, 31 May 1847

1848[484]

Month	Vessel	Port from	Port to	Passengers	Reference
Apr	Lockwood[485]	Cork	Saint John	Yes	Dobson I/90
Apr	Londonderry[486]	Londonderry	Saint John	194	Mitchell/38-41
May	Ayrshire[487]	Newry	Halifax	Yes	Dobson I/15
May	Bache McEvers[488]	Cork	Saint John	116	PANB/RS 555
May	Charles[489]	Youghal	Saint John	95	PANB/RS 555
May	Clare[490]	Donegal	Saint John	91	PANB/RS 555
May	Exchange	Sligo	Saint John	58	PANB/RS 555
May	Frederick[491]	Cork	Saint John	Yes	Dobson II/45

---

[483] James **KEEFFE**, 36, a passenger from County Clare, was admitted to the Alms House, Saint John, on 3 October 1848 - Johnson, p. 149.

[484] People were being dropped off along the coast during this period and the ships that brought them eluded contemporary record keepers. On 24 March 1848, a group of Irish people petitioned the government for a barrel of flour for each of the four families, comprising 24 individuals. They said that they were "poor Irish emigrants . . . landed in Guysborough last summer . . . that the season of the year for putting a crop into the ground had passed before their arrival . . . that at the present time they are entirely destitute of provisions, and without the means of procuring any . . ." - NSA, RG 5, Series "P", Vol. 84 #64 (mfm. 23184). The heads of the families were William **FOLEY**, Peter **MELEDY**, John **WATKINS** (all signed), and Owen **HARNEY**, who made his mark.

[485] Four of the passengers from the *Lockwood* were admitted to the Alms House, Saint John: Mrs. Catherine, 27, and Daniel, 1½, **DRISCOLL**; Mary **DUNAVAN**, 28; and Margaret **O'NEILL**, 19, all from County Cork - Johnson, p. 179.

[486] Passenger list in Mitchell, pp. 38-41. Sixteen passengers from the *Londonderry* were admitted to the Alms House, Saint John, where three of them died: Fanny **DOHERTY**, Jr., 6, from Derry; James **McGINN**, 30, from Tyrone; and Biddy **SWEENEY**, 19, from Donegal - Johnson, pp. 179 - 180.

[487] The *Ayrshire* proceeded from Halifax towards Québec, but went aground on the Ile d'Orléans in the Saint Lawrence River below Québec.

[488] Mary **BARRY**, 24, Waterford, a passenger in the *Bache McEvers*, died in the Alms House at Saint John, on 4 July 1849 - Johnson, p. 175. Perley, the Emigration Agent, reported, 10 May 1848, "The passengers by this vessel, almost without exception, expressed their desire to proceed to the United States as quickly as possible."

[489] Seventeen passengers from the *Charles* were admitted to the Alms House, Saint John, where three of them died: Patrick **FOLEY**, 25; John **MURRAY**, 25; and Bridget **SCANLAN**, 30, all of Waterford - Johnson, p. 176.

[490] Margaret **DONELLY**, 20, Tyrone, a passenger from the *Clare*, died in the Alms House at Saint John, 10 May 1849 - Johnson, p. 176.

[491] John **CASEY**, 23, Cork, a passenger from the *Frederick*, died in the Alms House at Saint John, 5 May 1849 - Johnson, p. 177.

Month	Vessel	Port from	Port to	Passengers	Reference
May	John Francis[492]	Cork	Saint John	183	PANB/RS 555
May	Leviathan[493]	Baltimore	Saint John	94	PANB/RS 555
May	Lord Sandon[494]	Kinsale	Saint John	167	PANB/RS 555
May	Princess[495]	Dublin	Saint John	-	Dobson I/120
May	Redwing[496]	Galway	Saint John	Yes	Dobson I/124
May	Sir James McDonell[497]	Cork	Saint John	220	PANB/RS 555
May	Star	New Ross	St. Andrews	383	On line[498]
May	Triumph[499]	Limerick	Saint John	103	PANB/RS 555
June	Adeline Cann[500]	Waterford	Saint John	98	PANB/RS 555
June	Aeolus	Sligo	Saint John	Yes	Dobson I/2, 3

---

[492] Nine passengers from the *John Francis* were admitted to the Alms House, Saint John: William **COONEY**, 23, Tipperary; Mary **COUGHLIN**, 20, Cork; Thomas **DOHEY**, 18, Cork; Mrs. Ann **FOGARTY**, 42, Waterford; Ed **FOGARTY**, 5, Waterford; Mary **LYONS**, 14, Cork; Alice **LYONS**, 8, Cork; Timothy **McARTY**, 16, Cork; and Dennis **McARTY**, 14, Cork - Johnson, p. 178.

[493] Seven passengers from the *Leviathan* were admitted to the Alms House, Saint John. One family group was "sent to Boston", namely Mrs. **MELLSOP** 28, from Cork, with her children Joseph, 10, Elizabeth, 8, Thomas, 5, and William, 2½. The other passengers admitted were Ellen, 20, and Patrick, 2, **SULLIVAN**, also from Cork - Johnson, p. 178.

[494] Nine passengers from the *Lord Sandon* were admitted to the Alms House, Saint John: Mrs., 30; Ellen, 8, John, 6, and Mary, 3, **BOCHAN**; Timothy, 40, Joanna, 7, and John 5, **GRIFFIN**; Mary **LEAREY**, 40 (died 10 May 1849); and Judy **LEARY**, 15 months, all from Cork - Johnson, p. 181.

[495] The *Princess* was wrecked at Cape Sable, Nova Scotia, 21 August 1848.

[496] Seven passengers from the *Redwing* were admitted to the Alms House, Saint John: John **BURK**, 30, Galway; Mary **FITZPATRICK**, 28, Galway; Michael **GLYNN**, 19, Galway (died 1 June 1848); Ann **MOOHAN**, 20, Galway; Michael **NOON**, 25, Galway; John **RILEY**, 12, Mayo; and Mary **REILLEY**, 10, Mayo - Johnson, p. 182.

[497] Seven passengers from the *Sir James McDonell* were admitted to the Alms House, Saint John: John **BRANNEN**, 25, Cork; Michael **CALLAGHAN**, 26, Kerry; Tom **CLIFFORD**, 40, Kerry; Kitty **DEALEY**, 20, Cork; Kitty or Kate **DRISCOL**, a.k.a. **BLAKE**, 20, Cork; Ellen **FLEMING**, 19, Cork; and Catherine **MORRISON**, a.k.a. **BLAKE**, 24, Cork. The last named woman had a child born in Oct 1848, but young John Morrison died 17 Feb 1849, when 3 months old - Johnson, pp. 181 - 182.

[498] These were tenants from the estates of Lord Fitzwilliam, in eight civil parishes in the south of County Wicklow - the "Fitzwilliam Emigration Books" forming MS 4974 and 4975, National Library of Ireland. A list of 295 of the passengers with precise places of origin and age may be viewed at www.archives.gnb.ca/Irish/Databases/Fitzwilliam/search.aspx?culture=en-CA Database © Jim Reese.

[499] Two passengers from the *Triumph* were admitted to the Alms House, Saint John: Bridget **BYRNES**, 20, from Limerick; and Anthony **GRIFFIN**, 20, from Clare - Johnson, p. 183.

[500] Perley, the Emigration Agent, wrote, 29 June 1848, that "about two-thirds of the whole number on board, embarked at once in the steamer for Boston (without landing) and the rest will follow by next opportunity."

Month	Vessel	Port from	Port to	Passengers	Reference
June	Commerce[501]	Galway	Saint John	Yes	Dobson II/27
June	Envoy[502]	Londonderry	Saint John	214	Mitchell/41-42
June	Grace Darling[503]	Newry	Saint John	Yes	Johnson/205
June	Linden[504]	Galway	Saint John	Yes	Johnson/205
June	Lord Maidstone[505]	Londonderry	Saint John	355	Johnson/205
June	Springhill[506]	Donegal	Saint John	103	PANB/RS 555
July	Agnes Jermyn[507]	Sligo	Saint John	Yes	Johnson/205
July	Blanche[508]	Donegal	Saint John	Yes	Johnson/205
July	Concord	Limerick	Saint John	Yes	Johnson/205
July	Dealy[509]	Castletown	Saint John	128	PANB/RS 555
July	Ellis	Cork	Saint John	Yes	Dobson I/49
July	Hornet[510]	Limerick	Saint John	Yes	Dobson I/73

---

[501] Six passengers from the *Commerce* were admitted to the Alms House, Saint John: Peggy **CAINEY**, 26; Phelix, 35, and Patrick, 7, **CARROL**; Michael **NAILON**, 22; Biddy **POTTER**, 20; and Thomas **RYAN**, 21, all from Galway - Johnson, p. 176.

[502] The *Envoy* continued to Québec. It is unclear how many passengers landed at Saint John.

[503] The *Grace Darling* reached New York with passengers on 13 Oct 1848 - Dobson III, p.44.

[504] Twenty-one passengers from the *Linden* were admitted to the Alms House, Saint John, where five of them died: Michael **BROWN**, 50, Clare, on 12 July 1848; Mary **BROWN**, Clare, 2, on 10 Feb 1849; James **LAWLESS**, 35, Galway, on 17 Oct 1848; Conor **SEXTON**, 55, Clare, on 13 Oct 1848; and Honor **SEXTON**, 3, Clare, on 15 Aug 1848 - Johnson, pp. 178 - 179.

[505] Passenger list in Mitchell, pp. 42-45. Dobson I, p. 87 refers to the vessel as the *Lady Maidstone*. Eight passengers were admitted to the Alms House, Saint John: Dr. William **GRAHAM**, 38, Derry; Rose **McINTYRE**, 22, Tyrone; James, 39, Mrs. Jane, 36, Wm. John, 14, James, 11, Martha, 8, and David, 6, **PEACOCK**, Derry - Johnson, pp. 180 - 181.

[506] Three passengers from the *Springhill* were admitted to the Alms House, Saint John: Thomas, 20, and George, 18, **CLARK**; and Margaret **MILLER**, 20, all from County Donegal - Johnson, p. 182.

[507] Six passengers from the *Agnes Jermyn* were admitted to the Alms House, Saint John: Tommy **LYNCH**, 13, Kerry (died 25 Aug 1848); William, 30, and wife, Michael, 14, Lott, 12, and Mary, 8 (died 24 Oct 1848) **McANARTNEY**, all of Clare - Johnson, p. 175.

[508] Four passengers from the *Blanche* were admitted to the Alms House, Saint John: Bridget **McMURRAY**, 16, Leitrim; Margaret **MEEHAN**, 22, Donegal; Jane **MULDERG**, 24, Donegal; and Patrick **QUINN**, 19, Donegal - Johnson, p. 175.

[509] Two passengers from the *Dealy* were admitted to the Alms House, Saint John: Mary **DRISCOL**, 16; and Jerry **SULLIVAN**, 19, both from Cork - Johnson, p. 177.

[510] Six passengers from the *Hornet* were admitted to the Alms House, Saint John: Bridget, 30, Robert, 3, and Patrick, 6 months **BENTLEY**, Clare; John, 30 or 32, and John Jr., 8, **MEENEY**, Clare; and James **REILLEY**, 35, Limerick (died 17 Sep 1849) - Johnson, pp. 177 - 178.

Month	Vessel	Port from	Port to	Passengers	Reference
July	Princess Royal[511]	Cork	Saint John	Yes	Dobson II/107
July	William Penn	Galway	Saint John	Yes	Dobson I/152
Aug	Aeneas	Castletown	Saint John	Yes	Johnson/205
Aug	British Queen[512]	Londonderry	Saint John	122	PANB/RS 555
Aug	Lady Lifford	Limerick	Saint John	Yes	Johnson/205
Aug	Londonderry[513]	Londonderry	Saint John	143	Mitchell/47-48
Aug	Steven Heath[514]	Cork	Saint John	Yes	Dobson I/137
Sep	William Kerry[515]	Galway	Saint John	Yes	Dobson II/139
Oct	Douglas[516]	Dublin	PEI	14	Dobson I/41
Oct	Margaret[517]	New Ross	Saint John	Yes	Dobson II/83
-	Mary Sultana	Ireland	Saint John	Yes	Dobson I/101
-	Sophia[518]	Waterford	Halifax	58	Flewwelling

[511] One family group from the *Princess Royal* was admitted to the Alms House, Saint John, on 18 Jan 1849: Mrs. Joanna **MURPHY**, 30, Cork, and her children William, 8, Eliza, 6, Michael, 4, and Jane, 1½ - Johnson, p. 182.

[512] Four passengers from the *British Queen were* admitted to the Alms House, Saint John: John, 30, Mrs. Eliza, 24, Mary Ann, 5, and Margaret, 1½, **DOGHERTY**, all from Donegal - Johnson, pp. 175 - 176.

[513] Passenger list in Mitchell, pp. 47 - 48. Sixteen of them were admitted to the Alms House, Saint John, where three died - Johnson, pp. 179 - 180.

[514] One family group from the *Steven Heath* was admitted to the Alms House, Saint John: Michael, 62 ("deserted"), and Mrs. Ann, 46, **GALLAGHER**, from Waterford, and children Ann, 13, Ellen, 10, and Susan, 6 - Johnson, p. 182.

[515] John **NEAGLE**, 26, Clare, a passenger from the *William Kerry*, was admitted to the Alms House, Saint John, on 24 Oct 1848 - Johnson, p. 185.

[516] Edward A. Clohossey, "Excerpts from a Family History," *The Abegweit Review*, 6:1 (Spring 1988), p. 129, states that Patrick **CLOHOS[S]EY**, 27 years old, and his sister Catherine, from Freshford, County Kilkenny, came out from Waterford in late summer 1848. A letter to the young people from their parents, signed, "Mr. and Mrs. Edmond Clohosy", is dated 28 Dec 1848 and is replying to a letter sent to the parents upon the children's arrival, probably in October. The *Douglas* seems the most likely ship in which the pair traveled.

[517] John **HENNESY**, 37, Wexford, a passenger in the *Margaret*, was admitted to the Alms House, Saint John, several times in 1848 and 1849 - Johnson, p. 181.

[518] On 25 April 1848, sixty-one Irish immigrant men petitioned the government of Nova Scotia for work . Many came from counties Waterford, Cork and Kerry, suggesting that they had probably traveled out in the *Sophia* from Waterford. Since a few came from Galway, they may have arrived in May 1847 in the *Barbara,* which sailed out of that port. The names of the petitioners and what became of some of them may be found in Punch, *Erin's Sons: Irish Arrivals in Atlantic Canada to 1863*, Vol. IV, pp. 164 - 165. At least twenty-eight of the petitioners had reached Boston later in 1848.

Month	Vessel	Port from	Port to	Passengers	Reference
			1849[519]		
May	Albion[520]	Cork	Saint John	172	PANB/RS 555
May	Londonderry[521]	Londonderry	Saint John	156	Mitchell/48-49
May	Pallas[522]	Cork	Saint John	201	PANB/RS 555
May	Sophia[523]	Waterford	Saint John	Yes	Dobson II/121
May	Waterford[524]	Limerick	Saint John	156	PANB/RS 555
June	Governor Douglas[525]	Westport	Saint John	Yes	Dobson II/51
June	John[526]	Westport	Saint John	98	PANB/RS 555
June	Nancy[527]	Westport	Saint John	Yes	Dobson II/95

---

[519] The *Ann Hall* (40 passengers), *Coronation*, and *Goliah* [*Goliath*?] (40 passengers), out of Liverpool, England, may have taken some Irish emigrants to Saint John in 1849 - Johnson, pp. 206 - 207.

[520] Three passengers from the *Albion* were admitted to the Alms House, Saint John: Jerry **HOUR[LIH]AN**, Mrs. Peggy, 35, and Patrick, 19, **HOURLIHAN**, Cork - Johnson, p. 184.

[521] Passenger list in Mitchell, pp. 48 - 49. Four of the passengers from the *Londonderry* were admitted to the Alms House, Saint John: Ann **McAFFRY**, 26, Fermanagh; Margaret **SALISBURY**, 3 months, died 9 Oct 1849, daughter of Ann **McAFFRY**; Robert **SAUNDERS**, 26, Fermanagh; and Walter **WELSH**, 71, Fermanagh - Johnson, p. 185. Perley reported that most of the passengers were going to the United States.

[522] Fifteen passengers from the *Pallas* were admitted to the Alms House, Saint John: Timothy, 45, and Hanora, 44, **HALLISEY** from Cork, with six children: Dennis, 14, Mary, 12, Timothy, 10, Margaret, 8, Ann, 6, and Hanora, 4; Mrs. Hanora **MURPHY**, 40, Cork, with her children: Nancy, 11, Mary, 9, Thomas, 7, Paddy, 5, and Daniel, 4; and Daniel **CADOGAN**, 23, Cork - Johnson, p. 186. Perley reported that most of these passengers were going to the United States.

[523] The *Sophia* called into Halifax between 25 and 31 May 1849, and left 58 passengers there - Punch, *An Nasc*, p. 10. A family group from this vessel was admitted to the Alms House, Saint John: Mrs. Bridget **LAWLESS**, 41, Waterford, and her children: Mary, 11, Patrick, 10, Alice, 9, Lilly, 6, and James, 4 - Johnson, p. 187.

[524] Thirteen passengers in the *Waterford* died on the voyage, and are named in Punch, *Erin's Sons: Irish Arrivals in Atlantic Canada*, Vol. II, p. 60. Another six passengers were admitted to the Alms House, Saint John: Michael, 40, Catherine, 34, and their daughter Honora, 5, **CONNORS**, from Limerick; Catherine **KINNEY**, 19, Limerick; Kitty **WELSH**, 18, from Clare; and Ellen **WHALEN**, 23, from Limerick. - Johnson, p. 188.

[525] Seven passengers from the *Governor Douglas* were admitted to the Alms House, Saint John: Ellen, 32, Ellen Jr., 11, James, 6, **FALLAHER**, Mayo; Thomas **GRADY**, 19, Mayo; Philip **McCALL**, 22, Mayo; Peter **O'MEALY**, 16, Galway; and John **TOOLE**, Mayo - Johnson, p. 185.

[526] Perley reported that most of these passengers were bound for the United States.

[527] Twelve passengers from the *Nancy* were admitted to the Alms House, Saint John, where one died. Two children in the group were Patrick, 10, and Catherine, 7, **MITCHELL** from County Mayo. A note states that their father was dead and their mother in the United States - Johnson, pp. 185 - 186.

Month	Vessel	Port from	Port to	Passengers	Reference
July	Alexander Stewart	Cork	Saint John	106	PANB/RS 555
July	Blanche[528]	Donegal	Saint John	67	PANB/RS 555
July	British Queen[529]	Londonderry	Saint John	87	PANB/RS 555
July	Eliza	Sligo	Saint John	102	PANB/RS 555
July	Eliza Edwards[530]	Tralee	Saint John	78	PANB/RS 555
July	Jane	Castletown	Saint John	68	PANB/RS 555
July	Sarah[531]	Londonderry	Saint John	81	PANB/RS 555
July	Whitehaven[532]	Sligo	Saint John	Yes	Johnson/207
Aug	Aeneas	Castletown	Saint John	62	PANB/RS 555
Aug	Charlotte[533]	Donegal	Saint John	Yes	Johnson/207
Aug	Ocean	Castletown	Saint John	Yes	PANB/RS 555
Aug	Granville[534]	Ballina	Saint John	Yes	Johnson/207
Aug	Ruby[535]	Westport	Saint John	Yes	Dobson II/113
Aug	Standard[536]	Limerick	Saint John	139	PANB/RS 555
Sep	Velocity[537]	Waterford	Saint John	Yes	Dobson II/133

[528] Mrs. **HAGERTY**, a passenger from the *Blanche*, was admitted to the Alms House, Saint John, on 30 July 1849. There is a notation, "deliv'd child in street" - Johnson, p. 184.

[529] Passenger list in Mitchell, p. 56. Perley reported that they were mostly bound for the United States.

[530] Three passengers in the *Eliza Edwards* were admitted to the Alms House, Saint John: Patrick **BRICK**, 32, Kerry; Roger **CROW**, 48, Tipperary; and Michael **O'DONNELL**, 35, Kerry - Johnson, p. 184.

[531] Passenger list in Mitchell, pp. 55 - 56. Five of the passengers from the *Sarah* were admitted to the Alms House, Saint John: Mrs. Jane, 23, and Mary Jane, 2, **ANDERSON**, Tyrone; Margaret, 20, and her son William **THOMSON**, Tyrone; and Mary **WATSON**, 30, Derry - Johnson, p. 187. Only Margaret Thomson from Beragh, County Tyrone, appears in the list published in Mitchell.

[532] Mrs. **KILMARTIN**, 22, Guernsey, a passenger from the *Whitehaven*, was admitted to the Alms House, Saint John, on 11 Jan 1850 - Johnson, p. 188.

[533] A family group from the *Charlotte* was admitted to the Alms House, Saint John: Ned **SLEVIN**, 40, his wife Mary, 30, of Donegal, and their children Michael, 7, and Biddy, 15 months - Johnson, p. 184.

[534] Five passengers from the *Granville* were admitted to the Alms House, Saint John: Cecilia **BARNES**, 24; Michael **CALLAHAN**, 9; Mary **CANE**, 32; Martin, 21, and Mrs. Celia, 17, **LOFTUS**, all from County Mayo - Johnson, p. 185.

[535] Nine passengers from the *Ruby* were admitted to the Alms House, Saint John: Catherine **KEARNEY**, 19, Mayo; Bridget, 34, Mary, 13, Sarah, 10, Bridget, 8, Ann, 5, and Catherine 4, **MURRAY**, Mayo; Thomas **O'HARA**, 36, Sligo; and Bridget **RODY**, 17, Mayo - Johnson, p. 187.

[536] Mrs. Ellen **COLEMAN**, 27, Limerick, a passenger from the *Standard*, was admitted to the Alms House, Saint John, on 30 Jan 1850 - Johnson, p. 187.

[537] Ann **MORISSY**, 24, Waterford, a passenger from the *Velocity*, was admitted to the Alms House, Saint John, on 2 Nov 1849 - Johnson, p. 188.

Month	Vessel	Port from	Port to	Passengers	Reference
Oct	Unicorn[538]	Ireland/Liverpool	Saint John	Yes	Johnson/187
-	Envoy[539]	Londonderry	Saint John	Yes	Dobson II/41
-	Hibernia	Wexford	Saint John	Yes	Johnson/207
-	Rover	Baltimore	Saint John	Yes	Johnson/207

1850

Month	Vessel	Port from	Port to	Passengers	Reference
May	Albion	Cork	Saint John	183	PANB/RS 555
May	Garland[540]	Cork	Saint John	Yes	Dobson I/59
May	Mary	Cork	Saint John	96	PANB/RS 555
[May]	Seraphine[541]	Newry	Saint John	Yes	Dobson I/134
May	Sophia[542]	Waterford	Halifax	80	Flewwelling
May	Londonderry[543]	Londonderry	Saint John	181	Mitchell/61-62
June	Abby	Limerick	Saint John	Yes	PANB/RS 555
June	Kingston	Cork	Saint John	79	PANB/RS 555
July	Eagle[544]	Londonderry	Saint John	145	PANB/RS 555
Aug	James Redden[545]	Londonderry	Saint John	101	Mitchell/67-68
Aug	Ocean	Cork	Saint John	Yes	PANB/RS 555
Oct	Clytha	Cork	Saint John	118	PANB/RS 555
-	Susan	Cork	Saint John	Yes	Dobson II/124

1851

Month	Vessel	Port from	Port to	Passengers	Reference
Feb	Fanny[546]	Galway	Halifax	74	NSA, MG 100/167/14

---

[538] The *Unicorn* out of Liverpool, England, arrived in Saint John in October 1849. One passenger, Thomas **LEONARD**, 29, from Cork, was admitted to the Alms House, Saint John - Johnson, pp. 187-188.

[539] The *Envoy* continued to Philadelphia. It is unclear how many passengers landed at Saint John.

[540] The *Garland* rescued the people shipwrecked in the *Seraphine*.

[541] The *Seraphine* was abandoned at sea, 24 April 1850, and its people taken to Saint John by the *Garland*.

[542] From Halifax, the *Sophia* went on to Saint John with some passengers - PANB/RS 555, report dated 3 June 1850.

[543] Passenger list in Brian Mitchell, pp. 61 - 62.

[544] Passenger list in Brian Mitchell, pp. 65 - 66.

[545] Passenger list in Brian Mitchell, pp. 67 - 68.

[546] The people had contracted to be transported to New York. Rough weather caused the master to put into Lunenburg and then Halifax, Nova Scotia. They petitioned the government there for rations and for the captain to be obliged to take them to their contracted destination. Their names appear in Punch, *Erin's Sons: Some Irish Arrivals in Atlantic Canada,* Vol. I, p. 142. More detail may be found in *Ibid.*, Vol. IV, pp. 158 - 159.

Month	Vessel	Port from	Port to	Passengers	Reference
May	Barbara[547]	Londonderry	Saint John	164	PANB/RS 555
June	Field Marshall Radetsky	Cork	Saint John	Yes	PANB/RS 555
June	Gould	Castletown	Saint John	Yes	PANB/RS 555
June	Lord Ashburton	Sligo	Saint John	60	Dobson I/91
July	Blanche	Donegal	Saint John	52	PANB/RS 555
July	Princess Royal	Cork	Saint John	98	PANB/RS 555
-	Londonderry[548]	Londonderry	Saint John	162	PANB/RS 555
-	Londonderry[549]	Londonderry	Saint John	94	Mitchell/79-80

1852

Month	Vessel	Port from	Port to	Passengers	Reference
Apr	Mary Ann[550]	Londonderry	Saint John	196	Mitchell/83-84
July	Economy	Cork	Saint John	78	PANB/RS 555
July	Nicholson	Westport	Saint John	78	PANB/RS 555
July	Soflide[551]	Londonderry	Saint John	179	Mitchell/92-93
-	Mary Ann[552]	Belfast	Saint John	137	Mitchell/94-95

[547] Passenger list in Mitchell, pp. 77 - 78.

[548] Passenger list in Mitchell, pp. 71 - 73.

[549] Passenger list in Mitchell, pp. 79 - 80.

[550] Passenger list in Mitchell, pp. 83 - 84.

[551] Passenger list in Mitchell, pp. 92 - 93.

[552] Passenger list in Mitchell, pp. 94 - 95.

VI - ANNUAL NUMBER OF VOYAGES FROM IRELAND TO THE MARITIMES

Research through a range of primary and secondary sources has resulted in a list of over one thousand distinct voyages made by vessels from ports in Ireland to harbours in the three Maritime Provinces. It would not only be presumptuous to consider this list complete, but would fly in the face of the available evidence.

The existence of other, unrecorded, voyages is beyond doubt. What cannot be determined is the ports from which those unidentified vessels made their departure, not where they disembarked their passengers. Adams presents numbers of passengers and ships that cannot be accommodated within the scope of those for which documentary evidence of a ship-by-ship nature has been found.[1] This is particularly true for the years between 1792 and 1815, 1822 and 1825, 1835-1836, and 1839.[2]

Miscellaneous hints of other Irish emigrant voyages can be noted here. O'Grady writes of a family which arrived in Prince Edward Island in 1801 for which no vessel can be ascertained.[3] MacKenzie mentions the arrival of 25 Irish at Sydney, NS, in 1815, others in 1827, and yet again in 1843.[4] Martell recorded 500 young Irishmen at Halifax in 1816 (perhaps by way of Newfoundland), and others at Sydney in 1828, but tells us nothing about the vessels on which they came.[5] The *Henry Arnot* brought 233 Irish to Halifax in late summer 1828, from Brazil, but neither the vessel on which they left Ireland nor their port of origin in Ireland was reported in the newspaper shipping news.[6] The absence of Customs House records for Saint John for the years 1835 and 1836 means that we have no record of the Irish ships which must have left emigrants at that busy port in those years. To judge by the high volume of traffic in the years before and after that gap, we can reasonably assume that there were at least a dozen and probably many more than that.[7]

Unless we learn the names of the passengers aboard vessels sailing out of Liverpool, England, we cannot assume that those ships carried Irish emigrant passengers. Such voyages have been listed here only in cases where that is known for certain. Twelve instances have been accepted for inclusion in this list, although there must have been many more cases of Irish emigrants arriving via ports in England such as Liverpool.[8] Present information does not permit them to be counted in this compilation. "Some Irish, it is quite likely, sailed from Liverpool, England,

---

[1] Adams, pp. 87, 97, 422-425.

[2] See Appendix III for instances of Irish emigrants who arrived by unknown means before 1825.

[3] O'Grady, "The Monaghan Settlers," *The Abegweit Review*, Vol. 4:1 (Spring 1983), pp. 52-53.

[4] MacKenzie, *The Irish in Cape Breton*, p. 31.

[5] Martell, *Immigration to and Emigration from Nova Scotia*, pp. 40, 62.

[6] *Novascotian*, 18 Sep 1828.

[7] The drop from 61 arrivals in 1834 to only 10 discovered from other sources for 1835 suggests that such an assumption is a conservative estimate.

[8] Johnson, *Irish Emigration to New England Through the Port of Saint John,* pp. 190 - 207, *passim*, offers twenty-two such vessels for consideration.

but . . . [Martell put] down all passengers from Newfoundland as Irish. The great majority, it is certain, were Irish, but undoubtedly there were also some English."[9]

A proper comprehension of emigration from Ireland into the three Maritime provinces requires some understanding of how Newfoundland figures in the equation. Forty-five named ships from Ireland reached the Maritimes via St. John's or another port in Newfoundland. We can assume with some degree of confidence that the passengers coming to the mainland in those vessels were from Ireland and that the Irish ships called into St. John's to discharge passengers, light cargo or mail.[10]

Both Ireland and Newfoundland suffered serious economic depression at the end of the prolonged wars between Great Britain and France which had flared between 1792 and 1815. Governor Dalhousie of Nova Scotia reported early in 1817 that many needy Irish had arrived, being "the overflow of an immense Emigration to Newfoundland last summer."[11] A year later, Michael Tobin and Samuel Cunard, Halifax, informed Lord Dalhousie that in "December last we were visited by above 300 Men, Women & Children from Newfoundland, most of whom landed amongst us in a destitute State, many of them being shipwrecked on their way here & had lost the remains of what they may have saved from the fires of 7th & 21 November."[12] As if destitution and fires were not enough trouble, on 8 December 1821 Sir Charles Hamilton at St. John's, Newfoundland, advised Sir James Kempt at Halifax that he tried to discourage people impoverished by "the general failure of the fishery throughout the Island" from removing from there to Nova Scotia. He issued few passes to such folk and reminded Kempt that any ship master taking unauthorized paupers away was liable to a penalty of £200 recoverable by the Vice Admiralty Court at Halifax.[13]

Innumerable smaller vessels, schooners and the like, plied between Newfoundland and the Maritimes with supplies and occasional passengers. Historian, Helen Cowan, observed that Cape Breton, with its isolated landing spots, was "a bootlegger's paradise for merchants in the emigrant

---

[9] Martell, p. 35.

[10] For the extent to which Newfoundland interacted with the Maritimes in terms of population mix, see Terrence M. Punch, "Newfoundland's Links with Nova Scotia," in *Family History Seminar 1987*, Elsa Hochwald, ed. (St. John's, NL: Newfoundland and Labrador Genealogical Society, Inc., 1988), pp. 19 - 35, especially pp. 32-33, for an illustration of the genealogical importance of considering this migratory pattern.

[11] Lord Dalhousie to Lord Bathurst, 2 Jan 1817 (C.O. 217/90).

[12] Michael Tobin and Samuel Cunard to Lord Dalhousie, 9 Feb 1818 (NSA, RG 1, Vol. 305, doc. 121). Nor were those the first fires at St. John's, Newfoundland. There had been another on 14 February 1816 in which 130 houses burned down, rendering over 1,500 people homeless. The November fires in 1817 destroyed a further 300 houses and left 2,000 without shelter as the winter set in. The winter of 1817-18, we are told, was "one of the coldest on record . . . causing indescribable hardships." Coming as those fires did, between the failure of the inshore fishery in 1817 and that of the spring seal-fishery in 1818, the period reads like a chronicle of misery for the poorer classes, most of whom were Irish. *Cf.*, R. G. Moyles, *Complaints is many and various, but the odd Divil likes it*" (Toronto: Peter Martin Associates Limited, 1975), p. 5.

[13] Quoted in Martell, p. 51.

trade."[14] Plessis, the Catholic Bishop of Québec, noted in 1815 that the Catholic coal miners near Sydney were "Irish people . . . [from] Newfoundland [who] had come from there to the mine."[15] In 1832, a Scottish writer observed that Boularderie Island in Cape Breton was inhabited by Scots Highlanders and "numbers of Irish fishermen who were formerly employed at Newfoundland . . ."[16]

It is probably impossible to estimate, let alone tally, the true number of Irish people who reached the Maritimes as "two-boaters". Until the advent of railways at mid-century, a large portion of all the Irish who came into Maritime ports were "two-boaters" who landed here, then continued to the United States in another vessel. Some agents and captains encouraged the practice. For instance, the master of the *Ganges* published a notice in which he guaranteed his passengers conveyance from Saint John to the United States.[17] "From Saint John, passengers often went on to St. Andrews, as a first step in that direction, or northward through the Bay of Fundy toward Sackville [New Brunswick] or Windsor, Nova Scotia. Digby, across the Bay of Fundy from Saint John, offered another point for getting into Nova Scotia."[18]

> Up to 1817 ships advertised for the British Colonies had laid emphasis upon climate, soil, conditions for granting land, and other advantages, but in 1817 and 1818 ships for Halifax, Saint John and St. Andrews were advertised as 'for the United States'. . . . It is impossible to say what proportion of the Irish passengers to Nova Scotia and New Brunswick went on to the United States, but ninety per cent is a reasonable estimate. The capacity of the provinces to absorb settlers was very limited in 1817.[19]

The prevalence of this phenomenon inspired the late Daniel F. Johnson to title his book, *Irish Emigration to New England Through the Port of Saint John, New Brunswick, Canada, 1841 to 1849*.[20] To gain another indication of the dispersal of the Irish arrivals in Saint John onward to the

---

[14] Helen I. Cowan, *British Emigration to British North America* (Toronto: University of Toronto Press, 1928), p. 148. Being aware of this occurrence one comprehends the truth behind a piece of lore common to many families in the Maritimes that the ancestor "jumped ship". Rather than being crewmen some of those people may have been illegal emigrants, inventing a romantic story which their children and grandchildren received as being factually correct.

[15] A. A. Johnston, *History of the Catholic Church in Eastern Nova Scotia* (Antigonish, NS: St. Francis Xavier University Press, 1960), Vol. I, p. 295.

[16] John McGregor, *British America* (Edinburgh, 1832), Vol. I, pp. 388, 401, 406.

[17] *Belfast News Letter*, 31 July 1818. When the British authorities attempted to retain artisans in British realms, shippers liked to point out to emigrants the proximity of St. Andrews, New Brunswick, to the American border, an instance of "a wink being as good as a nod to a blind horse."

[18] Houston and Smyth, p. 90.

[19] Adams, p. 92.

[20] Thousands of people who left the Maritimes and arrived in the United States are named in two CD-ROMs: *Passenger and Immigration Lists: New York, 1820 - 1850*, and *Passenger and Immigration Lists: Boston, 1821 - 1850* [www.genealogy.com]. Boston arrivals, for instance, included the family of William and Elizabeth **BURKE** from Prince Edward Island on 3 September 1849; Michael and Bridget **DALTON** from Saint John, NB on 14 December 1833; and Johanna **AHERN** and her six children from Nova Scotia on 26 April 1847. Other names may be sought in *Passengers who arrived in the United States, September 1821 - December 1823* (reprinted, Baltimore: Clearfield Company, Inc., 2005).

United States, one need go further than the 1851 census of New Brunswick. People were asked to state the year they arrived in New Brunswick. A survey of a few census districts will reveal that most of the settled Irish-born population had arrived from five to fifty years earlier, that is, before the Famine years.[21] It is fairly certain that the Irish in New Brunswick, as elsewhere in Atlantic Canada, were not fleeing "The Great Famine", but had come earlier. Most of the "Famine Irish" who came to the Maritimes during the late 1840s went to New England and beyond. While this pattern of migration through the Maritimes to further destinations intensified during the Famine period, it was scarcely a new phenomenon.

Martell's study found that between 1829 and 1838, at least 3,235 people from Nova Scotia, Newfoundland, etc., departed by sea for Québec, the number being as high as 546 in the year 1832.[22] He also established that a minimum of 2,927 people went from Halifax to American ports between 1817 and 1838: 1,841 to Boston (in 83 vessels), 670 to New York (20 vessels), 256 to Philadelphia (3 vessels), 117 to Baltimore (2 vessels), and 43 to Alexandria (in the ship *Potomac*).[23] In her study of emigration from Nova Scotia, 1839 - 1851, Flewwelling accounted for "1,900 passengers, . . . of these more than a thousand went to the United states, chiefly to Boston . . . Some may have returned, but to more than counter-balance this, there were many others *whose departure was never officially recorded.*"[24] [my italics]

Several natives of Ireland appear among the arrivals in the Rhode Island ports of Providence, Bristol and Warren between 1831 and 1849, having reached Nova Scotia before taking ship at Pictou or Sydney to carry on to the United States. For instance, Mack **BRADLEY**, Patrick **CONER** and Isabele **JONTE** from Ireland were on their way to Utica, NY, and sailed from Pictou, NS, in September 1837. Michael **BURNES**, and Margaret **PENDEGRAS** were going to Providence in July 1835, while their shipmate William **MULONNAY** was headed for Philadelphia.[25]

Table 5 includes only vessels for which contemporary evidence indicates that they visited a Maritime port. I have excluded those going to *Canada*. Until the Confederation of Canada in 1867, *Canada* referred to what are now Québec (Lower Canada) and Ontario (Upper Canada). Nova Scotia and New Brunswick joined with the Canadas in 1867, while Prince Edward Island adhered in 1873. Not reckoned as one of the Maritimes, the fourth Atlantic jurisdiction, Newfoundland and Labrador, did not become a Canadian province until 1949. While people at the time probably used the term "Canada" correctly, later authors sometimes failed to make the distinction, and should be interpreted with care until one has made sure of what they intended by their use of the term.

---

[21] Albert County in south-eastern New Brunswick was home to 422 natives of Ireland, according to the 1851 census. Of these 366, or 87%, had reached the province *before* the famine years 1846-1849 - Punch, Vol. III, pp. 140 - 152.

[22] Martell, p. 112. The number ranged from a low of 123 in 1829 to as high as 546 in 1832. In 1817 two vessels took 41 passengers from Halifax to that port - Martell, p. 102.

[23] Martell, pp. 103, 111. All sailed from Pictou, NS.

[24] Mrs. R. G. Flewwelling, "Immigration to and Emigration from Nova Scotia 1839 - 1851," *Collections of the Nova Scotia Historical Society*, Vol. 28 (1949), p. 98.

[25] Maureen A. Taylor, *Rhode Island Passenger Lists* (Baltimore: Genealogical Publishing Co., Inc., 1995), pp. 41, 44, 56, 107, 147, 157. Taylor reported the names as mis-spelled in the original. Bradley, Connor, Joynt, Burns, Prendergast and Muloney would be more in line with modern spellings.

Table 5 - Annual number of Voyages from Ireland to the Maritimes, 1749 - 1852

Year	No.	Year	No.	Year	No.
1749	9	1811	1	1833	65
1750	4	1812	3	1834	61
1761	2	1815	1	1835	10
1762	3	1816	8	1836	20
1765	1	1817	21	1837	25
1766	2	1818	32	1838	25
1769	2	1819	15	1839	10
1771	2	1820	19	1840	9
1772	3	1821	5	1841	62
1773	1	1822	2	1842	62
1774	1	1823	5	1843	14
1775	1	1824	2	1844	33
1778	4	1825	2	1845	52
1779	2	1826	14	1846	92
1780	2	1827	12	1847	150
1789	1	1828	9	1848	42
1790	1	1829	7	1849	27
1793	1	1830	19	1850	13
1799	1	1831	24	1851	9
		1832	20	1852	5

These 1,050 voyages may be grouped by time period as follows:

(1) Prior to 1816: 56 voyages during a time of relatively low direct emigration from Ireland into the Maritime Provinces. The 1749 and 1750 figures do not represent emigration in the sense we usually think of the word. In 1749 the British government spent public money to build a town and military base at Halifax. Some Irish people were among those engaged to undertake the settlement project. In 1750 a military unit was transferred from Dublin to the new settlement. Ulster Scots made up most of the emigration after that, while the existence of crew lists for 1778-1780 accounts for the few extra ships noted in those years.

(2) From 1817 - 1820: 87 voyages in the post-war influx following on disasters in Newfoundland and an economic downturn in the British Isles. Much of the movement involved Irish going from Newfoundland to the Maritimes. An average of 22 voyages per annum.

(3) From 1821 - 1832: 121 voyages during a time when Ireland began to suffer from its overpopulation and a rising atmosphere of political and economic tension. An average of 10 voyages annually.

(4) From 1833 - 1838: 206 voyages; the larger numbers reported in these years may be somewhat illusory since for four of those years (1833, 1834, 1837, 1838) the Customs House records for Saint John, NB, have survived. An average of 38-37 voyages each year.

(5) From 1839 - 1844: 190 voyages in the years just before the Great Famine in Ireland. An average of 31-32 voyages per annum.

(6) From 1845 - 1849: 363 voyages during the Famine, peaking in 1847. Thanks to the operation of the quarantine station at Partridge Island, Saint John, and of the Alms House, we have more complete records than in the earlier period, hence more ships are accounted for. An average of 73 ships per year.

(7) From 1850 - 1852: 27 voyages in the immediate post-Famine years. Irish emigrants were now going directly to the United States, and immigration to and through the Maritimes fell. An average of 9 voyages annually.

VII - THE NUMBER OF IRISH EMIGRANTS TO THE MARITIMES

The lack of comprehensive records and the vagueness of others make it impossible to project a statistically accurate total of the numbers of immigrants who came to the Maritime Provinces, British North America, or indeed to the entire North American continent. We can collect the scattered evidence, make educated guesses at how many passengers were aboard the many ships on which we know there were Irish emigrants but for which we have no lists of passengers and all too often no newspaper account carrying a ballpark figures such as "about 200". The result of research, even that done by careful properly-qualified historians, is a group of figures that, by any reasonable standard, must be considered tentative in nature. Use of the surviving contemporary evidence presents the emigration historian with the need to accept that figures for different ports and different dates are not based on one consistent source. The figures that follow are, therefore, offered with that caveat.

Irish people were present in the Maritimes in the late seventeenth century. When the Sieur de la Roque prepared his census in 1752 he found settled at Riviére du Moulin-à-scie, near the site of present day Charlottetown, one Michel Caissy, ploughman, native of Acadia, age 38, two years there with his wife and two daughters.[1] A French document of earlier date also mentions the early presence of a few Irishmen. Villebon's Journal, 27 October 1699, refers to "the fishermen sent out last year . . . to establish a fishing industry, deserted Chebucto [Halifax Harbour] where they were stationed, and have gone to Boston, taking a bark belonging to the Company, and almost all the supplies intended for a year's fishing. There remain only five Frenchmen and three Irishmen, the latter are at Port Razoir [Shelburne] where they are to fish."[2]

There were Irish people in the French town of Louisbourg, Cape Breton, throughout its existence, drawn there by economic motives and the opportunity to enjoy the freedom to practice their Catholic faith. Because they were fisher folk or held menial positions, many of those Irish can be found only by careful examination of records. Then we must interpret what the frenchified version of their names might have been originally. A case in point was that of a servant working in *Le Billard* tavern. When François Cressonet dit Beauséjour died in 1742, his widow Marguerite Dugas continued the business with the help of "Salle Forlan" [Sally Furlong].[3]

Irish people were present from the earliest British settlement in the Maritimes, beginning with 200 or so among the founding party at Halifax in 1749. Apart from that group, the only other co-herent migration from Ireland into the region was that arranged by Alexander McNutt in 1761 and following years. A census taken in 1767 is the only pre-confederation population return that covered

---

[1] *Tour of Inspection Made by the Sieur de la Roque*, translated and published in Sessional Paper No. 18 (Ottawa, 1906), p. 101. The Irishman Roger Casey settled in Acadia in the seventeenth century. His descendants were thoroughly assimilated, being sometimes referred to as the Caissy dit Roger.

[2] John Clarence Webster, *Acadia At the End of the 17th Century* (Saint John: The New Brunswick Museum, 1934), pp. 124 - 125.

[3] www.fortresslouisbourg.ca/History-Buildings Furlong has been a County Wexford name since the end of the thirteenth century. An interesting incident followed the loss of Louisbourg by the French in 1758. The British demolished the fortress and in subsequent years an Irish family named **KEHOE** lived in one of the old French buildings in the 1780s. When they answered a knock on their door, a French naval officer entered and assured them he meant no harm. "I just want to recover something that is here," he said, and went to the fireplace, removed a stone, and pulled out a metal box, thanked them and left - www.celiastories. blogspot.com Truth or romance, it the sort of lore that has been passed down among the old-settled Irish families.

the area of all three Maritime Provinces. As of 1 January 1767, there were 2,165 natives of Ireland living in the area: 112 in Prince Edward Island, 37 in New Brunswick, 169 in Cape Breton Island, and 1,847 in mainland Nova Scotia. By then six shipments of Ulster Irish had reached the region, and 531 Irish-born people with their children lived in three townships (Truro, Londonderry, Onslow) around the head of Minas Basin. A further 162 lived nearby in Windsor, Amherst and Newport townships. Southern Irish, mainly Catholic, predominated among the 853 in Halifax and 112 at Canso in the fishery.[4]

There were eighty-eight known charter members of the Charitable Irish Society in Halifax in 1786 and these tended to be the more established element in the Irish population. Again we have an indicator that Irish were reaching these shores in the eighteenth century, even if they were not "immigrants" in the sense people came to think of them a generation later. The were arriving in a small but steady stream for several decades before mass emigration set in after 1815.[5]

A similar pattern of gradual arrival occurred in New Brunswick. The arrival of the *Union* at St. Andrews in 1817 is the first *recorded* arrival of a ship from Ireland carrying emigrants to New Brunswick. Yet the census taken in 1851 in that province reveals that there were then at least 109 natives of Ireland who had lived there for more than 40 years by that time. We may accept that in the intervening 40 years quite a number of early Irish arrivals would have moved away or died. By 1851 there were about 20,750 natives of Ireland residing in New Brunswick, most of them having arrived within the previous 15 or 20 years.[6]

Finally, there is Prince Edward Island which had even seen an abortive attempt to rename the colony, then known as St. John Island, as New Ireland,[7] indicating that there was an Irish element in the island's population throughout the period before 1800. The 1798 census contained at least 218 people we may consider Irish.[8] At least six ships brought people from Ireland thither before that date. O'Grady reckoned that "10 percent of the population" of 4,382 persons in 1798 was Irish.[9]

My calculation, based on the ships for which mention has been found, is that perhaps 4,000 natives of Ireland came to the Maritimes directly from Ireland before 1810; as many again probably

---

[4] D. Allison, "Notes on the Census of 1767," *Collections of the Nova Scotia Historical Society*, Vol. VII (1891), pp. 45 - 72.

[5] Terrence M. Punch, " 'Gentle as the snow on a rooftop': The Irish in Nova Scotia to 1830," *The Untold Story: The Irish in Canada*, Robert O'Driscoll & Lorna Reynolds, eds. (Toronto: Celtic Arts of Canada, 1988), Vol. I, pp. 215 - 227.

[6] Punch, *Erin's Sons: Irish Arrivals in Atlantic Canada*, Vol. I, pp. 40 - 42. The 1851 census of New Brunswick lacks Kent and Gloucester counties, most of Queens County, three parishes in York County, and – most relevant to the Irish -- three of the seven parishes in Saint John. Had we those returns, the number of Irish might be larger.

[7] In 1780 the General Assembly passed "An Act for altering the Name of this Island from *Saint John* to that of *New Ireland*", but this was not approved by the British government. Confronted by too many similarly named places, the government eventually renamed it Prince Edward Island in honour of the Duke of Kent. By convention, the other two locations are written as St. John's, Newfoundland, and Saint John, New Brunswick.

[8] Punch, *Erin's Sons: Irish Arrivals in Atlantic Canada*, Vol. IV, p. 78 - 79.

[9] O'Grady, *Exiles & Islanders,* p. 13. For present purposes I have placed the figure at 400.

came into the region by way of Newfoundland. Father Jones at Halifax commented in 1797 that most of his congregation had come from Placentia, in Newfoundland, a circumstance which finds support in the parish records which begin in 1800.[10]

There was little immigration during the later years of the Napoleonic Wars, i.e., until 1815, in which year Adams reckoned that only about 1,500 Irish came out to mainland North America, but that 5,000 emigrated to Newfoundland.[11] As the Newfoundland economy was on the verge of a major collapse, much of that migration found its way to the Maritimes between 1817 and 1820, when 15 voyages with passengers are on record. An unknown number crossed to Nova Scotia and Prince Edward Island in schooners and small craft, and it seems probable that virtually all the Irish who went to Newfoundland at that time went on to the Maritimes, together with numbers of the Irish fishermen and their families who had been in Newfoundland before 1815.

As for the number of emigrants from Ireland to British America, Adams says there were "few" in 1815, 500 in 1816, 5,000 in 1817, and 13,500 in 1818.[12] Apart from those from Newfoundland, the ships comprised in the lists presented in this volume account for 105 to the Maritimes in 1816, meaning that the balance went to Québec or arrived in vessels not on record. In 1817, 11 vessels brought 855 Irish to the region. Five other ships with passengers add 390 Irish (at an average of 78 per vessel, based on the numbers carried in the 11 ships whose numbers of passengers are known), giving a total to the Maritimes of 1,245 for 1817. Again in 1818 we know that 15 ships brought 2,644 Irish to the Maritimes. The remaining recorded arriving ships would have brought a further 1,936 people if their passengers matched the average of 176 found in the 15 whose numbers are known, making a total of 4,580 Irish to Maritime ports in 1818. Together we have just under 6,000 Irish entering Maritime ports between 1815 and 1818. This is a reasonable number, given Adams tally of 19,000 for all of British North America in those four years.[13]

From 1819 until 1824 we lack acceptable estimates of the passenger traffic between Ireland and Maritime ports. Adams gives a figure for arrivals at Saint John, New Brunswick, for each of those years, totaling 18,772 passengers: 2,644 (1819), 3,025 (1820), 2,067 (1821), 5,226 (1822), 4,761 (1823), and 1,049 (1824).[14] Known voyages during those years offer only 16 vessels bound for New Brunswick ports, and even if each was assumed to be carrying 200 emigrants, there would remain 15,000 or so to be accounted for. Adams' tally exceeds the total number of reported vessels reaching the Maritimes – 48 -- in those six seasons, and even if all of those were assumed to be carrying 200 passengers, we would have accounted for barely half of the traffic Adams estimated.

---

[10] Between 1800 and 1814, 37 natives of Newfoundland were married in the Catholic parish at Halifax; and 12 of these stated that they came from Placentia and 7 others may have been. All had Irish surnames, and all were in Nova Scotia *before* the post-war influx. This amounted to between one fifth and one third of the total

[11] Adams, p. 71. Prince Edward Island and Cape Breton Island were being counted apparently as "mainland" by Adams in this instance.

[12] Adams, p. 426.

[13] Adams, p. 420 claims that 5,113 Irish came from Belfast to the Maritimes in 1818-1819. If that is accurate, either many of the vessels in which they came have escaped notice or some of those attributed to other Ulster ports, e.g., Londonderry, must be counted into the Belfast total.

[14] Adams, p. 422. See Appendix III for some probable arrivals in the years 1821 - 1825.

From 1825 to 1845 Adams presents a list of Irish arrivals in British North America which adds up to 451,826, exclusive of the year 1836 which was unreported.[15] That averages out to 22,591 per annum. If 1836 was a typical year, then there were nearly 475,000 Irish emigrants in the 21 year period. For the years 1827 - 1836 Adams claims that 341,000 Irish emigrated to North America, and breaks down that figure as 160,000 to Québec, 114,000 to the United States, and 65,000 to New Brunswick, which leaves only 2,000 for Nova Scotia and Prince Edward Island.[16] However, the known numbers on the reported ships coming to those two provinces in those ten years was at least 8,376. Some adjustment in Adams' estimate would seem in order.

The numbers adduced for the port of Saint John by Houston and Smyth are also a shade low. Their total stands at 9,579 Irish passengers to the port in 1833 and 1834.[17] The lists in this volume add up to 9,717 direct to Saint John, with a further four vessels for which the number of passengers is not known. An additional 300 or 400 would not be far off the mark, giving a total of something above 10,000 Irish emigrants through Saint John in the two years.

For the years 1837 to 1845 Adams supplies further annual numbers of Irish entering Maritime ports, giving a tally of 53,081 in all for the years immediately preceding the Famine emigration.[18] By year his numbers are 8,612 (1837), 1,061 (1838), 4,506 (1839), 8,631 (1840), 8,778 (1841), 10,917 (1842), 3,574 (1843), 1,432 (1844), and 5,570 (1845). In none of these years is the *known* total of Irish passengers as high as that. However, in 1844 the present list found 1,770 emigrants in 14 vessels, an average of 126 in each, but a further 19 vessels certainly brought out more, which widens the difference between Adams' 1,432 Irish passengers and the 1,770 accounted for by 14 ships. By contrast, we are lacking data on quite a number of voyages in years such as 1842.

It is indicative of onward migration, presumably to the United States, that there were about 160,000 natives of Ireland in all British North America in 1842,[19] and Adams' research indicates that 472,476 Irish immigrated into the colonies from 1825 to 1845, allowing 20,650 for 1836, a year for which no official figure was to hand.[20] If we disregard Adams' estimate for 1836, the number is 451,826, about the same as Houston and Smyth's estimate of 450,000. Something like 25% of that number entered the Maritime Provinces and it is evident that a substantial portion of those, perhaps as many as three quarters traveled onward to the United States within a few months or years of their landing in New Brunswick or Nova Scotia.

---

[15] Adams, pp. 413 - 414.

[16] Adams, p. 196. His numbers for the Maritimes in several of those years are 6,103 (1830), 15,461 (1831), 17,803 (1832), 9,558 (1833), 10,479 (1834), and 2,679 (1835), in all 62,083 Irish people.

[17] Houston and Smyth, p. 35.

[18] Adams, p. 415.

[19] Houston and Smyth, p. 25

[20] Adams, pp. 413 - 414. Adams relied principally upon the annual Parliamentary Papers published by the British government for many of his figures.

Terry Coleman noted that approximately 43,000 Irish emigrated to British North America in 1846,[21] while Houston and Smyth give a more precise total of 40, 667.[22] Of the 92 ships noticed as reaching the Maritimes in 1846, no fewer than 82 landed at Saint John, New Brunswick, bringing a reported 9,690 Irish emigrants, of whom 4,500 immediately went on to the United States. Peter Toner found that only ten per cent of the Irish arrivals in that city in 1846 were there by the time of the 1851 census.[23]

The year 1847 produced the largest and most extraordinary ballooning of Irish emigration ever experienced. Landing mainly at Québec and Saint John, 104,518 Irish refugees from the Great Famine arrived.[24] Three times as many Irish entered British North America that year than in the preceding three years 1844-45-46 together.[25] An estimated 35,000 Irish disembarked at Saint John in 1847. Some of these were paupers and poor tenants who were dispatched to the colonies on ships chartered by landlords such as Sir Robert Gore Booth and Lord Palmerston.[26] Moses Perley, the government emigration agent at Saint John, writing to the provincial secretary, John Saunders, described the process as "a shovelling out of hopeless paupers."[27] Eighteen additional vessels from Sligo and Killala, areas where Palmerston was a major landowner, arrived at Saint John in 1847; the 15 vessels whose passenger complement we know had 4,373 souls on board. Many of these were Palmerston tenants as he claimed to have sent out 2,000 people at his own expense that year.[28]

Other reasons for the arrival of more emigrants in British North America and fewer in American ports in 1847 include the divergence between the British and American passenger acts. The Americans mandated 14 feet of deck space per adult passenger, whereas the British act at

---

[21] Coleman, p. 167.

[22] Houston and Smyth, p. 26.

[23] Houston and Smyth, p. 25. Peter Toner's research, reported in Houston and Smyth, p. 217, discovered that "no more than 15 per cent" of the Irish in Saint John in 1851 had arrived there in the Famine period, 1845 - 1850. This accords with my study of the Irish in Halifax, where the percentage of Irish who arrived, 1846 - 1849, could have been as low as 1 per cent of those who remained in that city by 1855. A similar pattern prevails in Cape Breton Island and Prince Edward Island. It is apparent that the Famine of the late 1840s was not responsible for much of the permanent Irish population of the Maritime Provinces.

[24] Houston and Smyth, p. 26.

[25] Coleman, p. 164. Coleman was being conservative, as there were 85,100 in those three years. He could have compared 1847 to the preceding four years, as even by counting 1843 with the following three, the total is 99,768, still rather fewer than the 1847 number.

[26] Gore Booth's charters included the *Aeolus* in May, the *Yeoman* in August, and the *Lady Sale* in September. They carried 1,421 passengers among them. Palmerston's charters included the *Eliza Liddell* in June and the *Aeolus* in the autumn, between them carrying 592 Irish.

[27] Letter dated 28 July 1847 and quoted by Coleman, p. 249. A balanced account may be found in Gerald Moran, *Sending out Ireland's Poor: assisted emigration to North America in the nineteenth century* (Dublin: Four Courts Press, 2004).

[28] Coleman, p. 250.

the time accepted that each adult need have only 10 feet of space, meaning that quite a few more passengers could be shipped to a destination within the British Empire. As a further disincentive to sail to American harbours, the ports of New York and Boston began to enforce pauper laws more strictly. This further discouraged the bringing of anyone classed as a pauper into Massachusetts or New York, and most of the Irish during the Great Famine fell into that category.[29]

For the three years after the tragic migration of 1847, the numbers coming to British North America fell off markedly, to 24,809 (1848), 33,392 (1849), and 26,444 (1850). We have 20 vessels embarking 2,957 to Maritime ports in 1848, an average of 148 souls per voyage. If we apply that average to the 22 ships for which we have no figures, we find a total of 6,213 Irish arrivals that year. In 1849, 14 vessels conveyed 1,573 Irish to the Maritimes, an average of 112 per shipload. By prorating that average for all 27 ships that arrived, we have 3,024 Irish arrivals in 1849. Finally, for 1850, when 8 vessels are known to have had 983 Irish, an average of 123 each, we can apply that average to all 13 known arrivals that year and arrive at a total Irish immigration to the Maritimes in 1850 of 2,214 souls. Clearly the trend was for fewer Irish emigrants to come to the Maritime Provinces following the height of the Great Famine. Changing conditions allowed more Irish people to go directly to the United States, and limited the arrivals in the Maritimes mainly to those driven here by marine conditions and to those for whom the region was their intended destination. Later on, the Irish, in common with other groups in the region, continued to migrate to economic opportunity in Upper Canada (Ontario) and the United States.

By adding all the arrivals of Irish in Maritime ports down to 1852 – there were 1,372 souls recorded in 1851 and 1852 – we arrive at a total of about 230,000. Allowing for deaths on voyage and in quarantine, nearly 220,000 Irish emigrants were landed in the region. At a retention rate of about one in five, the remaining 175,000 must have removed to the United States or the Canadas, since very few returned to Ireland to live. Something like 45,000 remained to enrich the cultural diversity of the three provinces of New Brunswick, Nova Scotia, and Prince Edward Island. At a very modest estimate, there are several million people alive today in North America who can count one of those Irish arrivals in Maritime Canada among their ancestors.

---

[29] Coleman, pp. 165 - 166.

VIII - MARITIME PORTS OF ARRIVAL

Map 5 indicates the location of the ports to which vessels from Ireland came between 1749 and 1852. Those linked to the Gulf of St. Lawrence (the west side of Cape Breton, Prince Edward Island, Pictou, Bathurst, Shippagan, Miramichi, Richibucto, Pugwash and Wallace) were timber suppliers to the British Isles. Saint John and St. Andrews were convenient landing places for those intending to proceed to the United States. To a lesser extent this was also true of Halifax. Some locations on the map were not emigration ports, but the scene of marine mishaps, e.g., Beaver Harbour, Cape Negro, Barrington, Sable Island. The very small numbers shown for some ports on Table 6 demonstrate that such harbours were not destinations but accidental havens.

Map 5 - The Maritime Provinces Ports of Arrival of Irish Emigrant Vessels

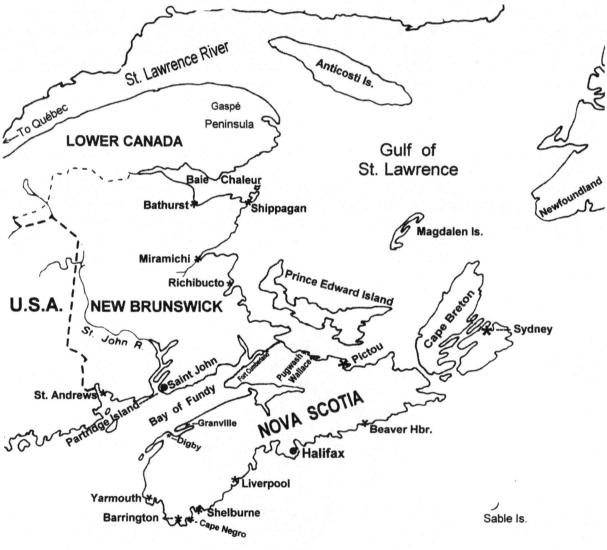

THE MARITIME PROVINCES

Table 6 - Maritime Ports of Arrival of Irish Passengers, 1749 - 1852

Maritime Port	To 1816	1817-1820	1821-1832	1833-1838	1839-1844	1845-1849	1850-1852	Total
Saint John, NB		23	24	139	139	331	25	681
Halifax, NS	47	41	49	30	5	11	2	185
Prince Edward Island	8	12	29	13	29	2		93
St. Andrews, NB		6	2	11	1	5		25
Miramichi, NB		1	5		11	8		25
Pictou, NS			6	3		1		10
Sydney/Cape Breton, NS			1	5	2			8
Shippagan, NB					2	3		5
Wallace/Pugwash, NS			2	2				4
Bathurst/Baie Chaleur, NB				2	1			3
Yarmouth, NS (note 1)		1				2		3
Barrington, NS (note 2)			1					1
Cape Negro, NS (note 2)		1						1
Fort Cumberland, NS	1							1
Granville, NS			1					1
Liverpool, NS			1					1
Richibucto, NB				1				1
Shelburne, NS (note 2)		1						1
"New Brunswick"		1						1
TOTAL BY TIME PERIOD	56	87	121	206	190	363	27	1050
Voyages per year	n/a	22	10	34	32	73	9	

Comments

1. The three ships mentioned as being at Yarmouth were probably destined for Saint John.
2. These three "ports" were actually at or near locations of ships going aground or being otherwise forced to put into land.
3. No annual average can be made for the pre-1816 period as there are no surviving records for most of that period.
4. During the period 1816 - 1852, when there were voyages every year, the average annual number was about 27.

Patterns may be observed in the voyages between Irish ports and destinations in the Maritimes. There was considerable traffic between Londonderry and Saint John, New Brunswick, from 1818 onwards.[1] During the eighteenth century ships coming out from Londonderry had brought Ulstermen to settle around the head of Minas Basin in Nova Scotia's townships of Truro, Londonderry and Onslow. From 1832 well into the 1860s Saint John, conveniently situated if one intended to go to the United States, enjoyed a virtual monopoly of the shipping from Londonderry. Since Londonderry was the major embarkation port for those emigrating from the River Foyle and its inland tributaries, Saint John received a great number of Irish people originating in counties Londonderry, Tyrone and Fermanagh, as well as eastern Donegal and north-western Antrim. "Very few Derry ships plied the routes to the Miramichi or to Nova Scotia, and . . . few went to Prince Edward Island."[2]

Another pattern was the prevalence of Saint John as the destination for Irish emigrating from ports on Sligo Bay: Killala, Ballina, and Sligo. Seventy-three out of seventy-nine voyages originating there were destined for Saint John, while another proceeded there after a call at Yarmouth, Nova Scotia. The ports on Donegal Bay – Donegal, Ballyshannon, and Killybegs – followed an even more pronounced pattern of sailing to Saint John, with all but one of forty groups of emigrants going thither. The ports on the bays of Sligo and Donegal served a catchment area that included the counties of Sligo and Leitrim, as well as coastal County Donegal and northern County Mayo. Certain vessels were particularly active in the 1830s and 40s on the run from that part of Ireland to Saint John, namely the *Britannia*, with 9 voyages, the *Caroline* with 6, the *Agnes* and the *Zephyr*, 4 each. To some extent the path of emigration here was determined by the fact that landlords, such as D'Arcy, Gore-Booth, and Palmerston, had chartered ships to take away their distressed tenantry.

Western County Cork and County Kerry were served by the ports within the jurisdiction of the customs house at Baltimore – Castletown-Bere, Bantry, and Baltimore – and by the ports at Tralee and Dingle. All 47 voyages from the south-western corner of Ireland delivered their passengers to Saint John. Here too a few vessels appear to have been regularly commuting between south-western Ireland and Saint John, notably the *Dealy* which made 8 voyages, and the *Leviathan* which completed 5 trips. The impact of the Great Famine was heavily felt in that corner of Ireland and there were 28 emigrant voyages from there to the Maritimes during the years 1846 - 1849, compared to a dozen in the years 1834 - 1845. Indeed, until 1841, there had only been two direct trips between that part of Ireland and Saint John.

A further cluster of emigration ports were those along the central south coast of Ireland: Cork, Kinsale, Youghal, and Dungarvan. They served central and eastern County Cork, the largest and most populous county in Ireland, as well as the western half of County Waterford. Although no ship is recorded arriving in Saint John with passengers from Cork until 1819 and traffic did not really get underway until 1833, Saint John was the recipient of over 75% of the emigrant vessels from those ports. The traffic from Limerick and Galway, which together served counties Limerick, Clare, Galway, and north-western Tipperary, followed a similar pattern, with Saint John gaining more ascendancy towards the 1840s.

---

[1] "There was in the geography of Irish trade a set of constraints that funneled emigrants from particular origins to particular destinations." - Houston and Smyth, p. 90.

[2] Houston and Smyth, p. 90.

East of the Cork grouping was the traffic out of Waterford Harbour, sometimes referred to as "The Confluence" because the waters of the rivers Suir, Nore and Barrow all empty into it before rounding Cheek Point and Passage East into the Atlantic. The south-eastern corner of Ireland (counties Wexford, Carlow, Kilkenny, Leix, and much of Tipperary and Waterford) used this as their major emigration route. Since most of this is the same area as supplied crews to the Newfoundland fishery from the eighteenth century into the first decades of the nineteenth, we find many descendants of those counties in Atlantic Canada. Many, probably most, of those arriving in the Maritimes via Newfoundland, originate in that corner of Ireland. "[T]he southeastern harbours of Ireland, Waterford and Youghal, had a more geographically restricted set of contacts. They were engaged in trade with Newfoundland, Nova Scotia, and Québec."[3]

The eastern side of Ireland, Leinster, utilized ports at Dublin and Drogheda. Passengers in vessels from those harbours were drawn from the counties of Dublin, Wicklow, Kildare, Meath and Louth. Saint John did not prevail, as that part of Ireland seems to have sent emigrants to a variety of ports in the Maritimes, of which Saint John was just one. Halifax, Prince Edward Island, and St. Andrews proved just as attractive. "Dublin was not part of Saint John's network."[4]

A final grouping is that found in north-eastern Ireland where the ports of Belfast, Newry/Warrenpoint, Donaghadee, Larne, and Strangford served the eastern counties of Ulster: Antrim, Armagh, Down, and Monaghan. Some people from counties Louth and Cavan appear occasionally in vessels from these Ulster ports as well.

These patterns of emigration are reflected in the prevalence of people from different parts of Ireland in different host communities in eastern Canada. Toronto, in Upper Canada, had people drawn from counties Clare, Limerick, Tipperary, Cork and Wexford, while Québec, Lower Canada, saw the arrival of people from the ports of Belfast, Dublin, Sligo, Cork and Limerick.[5] Prince Edward Island, by comparison, had large numbers from counties Monaghan, Cork and Wexford, and Saint John, New Brunswick, had a good number from Ulster, Cork and Louth. Halifax, the major concentration of Irish in Nova Scotia, drew more than half its Irish in the nineteenth century from counties Kilkenny (18.5%), Cork (16.5%), and Waterford (15.2%). A further band of southern counties – Tipperary, Kerry, Wexford and Carlow – supplied a further 29.7%. The other twenty-five counties accounted for just 20% of the total.[6]

With the caveat that generalizations must allow for exceptions, the overall picture of Irish emigration that emerges is that the people generally set off to the New World on vessels which sailed from ports most accessible from their home community. Whether poor or not, they were all constrained by the need to find their way to seaports, and most would follow the most convenient route to get there. One of the features of knowing what ships were leaving which Irish ports is that it serves as a pointer to place of origin. In the absence of the great majority of passenger lists, knowledge of the port through which an ancestor emigrated at least narrows down the search area.

---

[3] Houston and Smyth, p. 90.

[4] Houston and Smyth, p. 90.

[5] Houston and Smyth, pp. 33, 70.

[6] Terrence M. Punch, *Irish Halifax*, p. 12. Statistics based on 7,440 Irish Catholics in Halifax, 1825 - 1900, with identified counties of origin. Even counting in a couple of hundred Irish Protestants, which boosts the share of the Ulster counties, the group of southern counties still represent more than three quarters of the whole.

IX - TONNAGE AND THE PASSENGER ACTS

Until 1803 Britain had no laws governing conditions on board emigrant ships, People went to North America in an unregulated situation. The earliest American passenger acts did not take effect until 1819. In neither case were the rules, such as they were, notably well enforced. Only gradually during the first half of the nineteenth century did regulations come to be observed and the conditions endured by emigrants slowly improve. Since much of the thrust of navigation laws addressed the ratio of passengers to the size of the vessel, it may be useful to discuss the matter of tonnage or burthen first, and then recapitulate some of the provisions of the several laws.

TONNAGE EXPLAINED[1]

Deadweight Tonnage expresses the number of tons of 2,240 pounds of cargo, passengers and stores that a vessel can transport. *Deadweight* is the difference between the number of tons of water a vessel displaces *light* (empty) and the number of tons it displaces *loaded.*

Displacement of a vessel is the weight of the vessel and contents in tons of 2,240 pounds. Displacement *light* is the weight of the vessel without stores, passengers or cargo. Displacement *loaded* is the weight of the vessel, plus cargo, fuel and stores.

Cargo Tonnage is either "weight" or "measurement." The "weight" ton in British countries is the English long or gross ton of 2,240 pounds. A "measurement" ton is usually 40 cubic feet, but in some instances a larger number of cubic feet was taken for a ton.

Gross Tonnage applies to vessels, not to cargo. It is determined by dividing by 100 the contents, in cubic feet, of the vessel's closed-in spaces. A vessel ton is 100 cubic feet. The register of a vessel states both gross and net tonnage. Surprisingly, it was only starting in 1836 that a vessel's depth as well as its breadth and length was included in the formula used to calculate tonnage.

Net Tonnage is a vessel's gross tonnage less deductions of space used as accommodations for crew, and navigational machinery. A vessel's net tonnage expresses the space available to accommodate passengers and to stow cargo. This was called the ship's *burden* or *burthen.*

WHO WAS A "PASSENGER"?

One reason why it is difficult to accumulate reliable statistics concerning the number of Irish immigrants is the system used in reckoning what constituted a "passenger" under the rules which governments established from time to time. While people today would say one person was one passenger, early passenger acts were not so forthright and we find officials reporting passengers in quantities of thirds and halves.

The Passenger Vessel Act of 1803 established the standard of 1 passenger per 2 tons burden, if the ship were going to British North America, but only 1 passenger per 5 tons if bound to the United States. The net effect of this was to direct emigration vessels towards ports in mainland British America (but not to Newfoundland which could not support its existing population once the post-war depression took hold after 1815) since the ships could carry many more people than if they were bound to a port in the United States. Under the British Passenger Act of 1817, 3 children under the age of 14 years were to be reckoned as one passenger.

---

[1] A succinct definition of tonnage may be seen in Lucille H. Campey, *Planters, Paupers, and Pioneers; English Settlers in Atlantic Canada* (Toronto: Natural Heritage Books, 2010), p. 304.

Then, in 1819, the United States decided that 2 children below the age of 8 would count as 1 passenger, and that vessels could carry 2 "passengers" per 5 tons burden, and required captains to make a passenger list to be presented to the collector of customs upon arrival in the United States. The British Act of 1823, however, permitted vessels to convey 1 "passenger" per 5 tons burden, only half as many as the American regulation called for. A merchant could ask for a licence to allow him to match the American requirement, but the British Act of 1823 seems to have been pretty well disregarded in this particular. That Act also mandated that each ship with more than 50 passengers was to have a surgeon aboard. This clause was repealed in 1827, as it was proving impracticable, and mercantile interests succeeded in repeal of the entire Act of 1823.

A new British Act was passed in 1828 which made the yardstick 3 "passengers" per 4 tons burden, and stipulated that each "passenger" was to be allotted 5½ square feet between decks. As with many laws at the time, the quantity, nature and quality of provisions for the passengers was mentioned, but in real terms little changed for many years.

An Act in 1835 tightened the space requirements somewhat and ordained 3 "passengers" per 5 tons burden and that each "passenger" was to have 10 square feet of deck. A further Act, in 1842, required the licencing of passenger agents and brokers. Children under the age of 1 were not to be counted at all.

The United States brought an amended Passenger Act into effect in March 1847. This Act changed the old standard of 1819 where 2 children under the age of 8 had been 1 "passenger". Now, every person above the age of 1 year counted as a full "passenger". Finally, in 1848, the United States ordered ships to provide ventilation between decks.[2]

It is readily apparent that the various regulations could cause confusion and that at various times, ships were carrying passengers reckoned in thirds and halves. Sometimes the rule drew distinctions at age 1, or 8, or 14, and at either end of a voyage the systems of reckoning might be different. It was probably fortunate for the shippers of that day, if not the immigration historian, that some of these rules were honoured, "more in the breach than in the observance".

X - CONFUSION IN THE PASSENGER LISTS

Early records tend to offer researchers variations in the spellings of names. Sometimes such anomalies produce no difficulty. For instance, it is easy enough to reconcile Magee with McGee, or O'Neil with O'Neal or even Neil. At other times, vagaries of spelling occur in transcriptions of older records because the copyist writes down what the document appears to say. In old handwriting it can be exceedingly difficult to be sure of what one is reading. Also we naturally tend to associate what is written down with names and places we already have encountered. When more than one copyist tackles the same list it is not uncommon to discover that each has read some of the words differently from the other.

To the usual issues confronting researchers we must add the realization that tens of thousands of Irish people were fleeing the potato famine and its attendant diseases, e.g., dysentery, typhus and other fevers to which people, already weakened by malnutrition, were particularly vulnerable. Officials at both ends of voyages from Ireland at that time were overworked and harassed by circumstances beyond their control. Some who spoke standard English would have misheard names uttered in thick brogues or even in Gaelic. They wrote down what they

---

[2] The Passenger Acts are discussed in Coleman, pp. 347 - 352, and Guillet, pp. 10 - 19.

heard. Along we come generations later and we try to decipher what may have been written in haste and confusion. Little wonder, then, that two sets of transcribers did not wind up with lists identical in every detail. Some of the differences matter, as when a name is completely omitted and that name happens to be the quarry of a genealogist seeking to learn when his ancestor arrived in North America, and in what vessel.

To illustrate this point for present purposes, the passenger list of the *Envoy* will be used. the *Envoy* sailed from Londonderry to Saint John, New Brunswick, during the famine year 1847. One list was edited by Dessie Baker, and published in 1985 as *Emigration from Derry Port, 1847-49 (Apollo, PA: Closson Press)*, pp. 42 - 44. The other version is found on pages 32 - 34 of Brian Mitchell's *Irish Passenger Lists 1847 - 1871 (Baltimore: Genealogical Publishing Co., Inc., 1988)*.

The list follows in three columns The first is the entry as it appears in Mitchell; the second as per Baker; the third column notes differences.

Mitchell's Transcription		Baker's Transcription		Comments
DOUGHER, Patrick, Strabane		**DOHERTY**, Patrick, Strabane		Surname spelling
McCOY, Neil, Limavady		**McCOY**, Neil, Limavady		
Jane		Jane		
John	11	John	11	
REED, Catherine, Limavady		**REED**, Catherine, ...		Baker omits place
SELFRIDGE, Thomas, Limavady		**SELFRIDGE**, Thomas		Baker omits place
Anne		Anne		
Mary	13	Mary	13	
Margaret	11	Margaret	11	
Catherine	9	Catherine	9	
William	7	William	7	
Elizabeth	4	Elizabeth	4	
John	4	John	4	
Alexander	2	Alexander	2	
Julia	3m	Julia	3m	
DOHERTY, Hugh, Ballymoney				Not in Baker
Elizabeth				Not in Baker
GALLAGHER, William, Strabane		**GALLAGHER**, William		Baker omits place
McDIVETT, Elizabeth, Strabane		**McDIVETT**, Elizabeth, Strabane		
HAFFORTY, Michael, Derry		**HAFFERTY**, Michael, Derry		Surname spelling
Susan		Susan		
Jane		Jane		
Sarah	12	Sarah	12	
John	7	John	7	
Daniel	6	Daniel	6	
Rebecca	2	Rebecca	2	
Thomas	1	Thomas	1	
BROWN, William, Newtownstewart		**BROWN**, William, Limavady		Different places
Rebecca				Not in Baker
David				Not in Baker
Rebecca	12	Rebecca	12	
Matilda	10	Matilda	10	
SPEER, Thomas, ...		**SPIER**, Thomas, ...		Surname spelling
Eliza		Eliza Jane		Added name
Samuel	13	Samuel	13	
Mary	9m	Mary J.	9m	Added initial

BEATTY, John, ...	**BEATTY**, John, ...	
OWENS, James, Dromore	**OWENS**, James, Dromore	
John 13	John 13	
Patrick 11	Patrick 11	
Mary 9	Mary 9	
Nicholas 4	Nicholas 4	
MOORE, Elleanor, Ballymagory	**MOORE**, Elleanor, Strabane	Different places
Elizabeth	Elizabeth	
MAGEE, Susan, Donegal	**MAGEE**, Susan, Donegal	
Mary Ann	Mary Ann	
SLAVIN, Ann, Fintona	**SLEVIN**, Ann, Fintona	Spelling of surname
Fanny	Fanny	
QUIGLEY, Elizabeth, Limavady	**QUIGLEY**, Elizabeth, Limavady	
GILLOGLEY, James, Ederny	**GILLOGLEY**, James, Ederny	
James		Not in Baker
Ellan	Ellen	Spelling of given name
Hugh	Hugh	
Bell	Bell	
Susan 12	Susan 12	
Matilda 9	Matilda 9	
Christopher 6	Christopher 6	
Sally 3	Sally 3	
Mary 9m	Mary 9m	
GALLAGHER, Francis, Ederny	**GALLAGHER**, Francis, Ederny	
James	James	
KERRIGAN, Patrick, Donegal	**KERRIGAN**, Patrick, Donegal	
McGRORTY, Michael, Donegal	**McGRORTY**, Michael, Donegal	
Michael	Michael	
Catherine	Catherine	
Patrick 12	Patrick 12	
Dennis 3	Dennis 13	Age differs
HARVEY, Catherine, Donegal	**HARVEY**, Catherine, Donegal	
McELROY, Phelix, Dromore	**McELROY**, Phelix, Dromore	
Mary	Mary	
Ellen 13	Ellen 13	
Margaret 12	Margaret 12	
Catherine 5	Catherine 5	
Mary 2	Mary 2	
John 6m	John 6m	
NELIS, James, Derry	**NELIS**, John, Derry	Different given name
KIERAN, William, Donegal	**KIERAN**, William, Donegal	
Catherine	Catherine	
Jane	Jane	
Ellan	Ellen	Spelling of given name
Barbara 10	Barbara 10	
Catharine Ann 8	Catherine Ann 8	Spelling of given name
BUSTARD, Charles, Donegal	**BUSTARD**, Charles, Donegal	
Margaret	Margaret	
William 12	William 12	
Ann Jane 10	Ann Jane 10	
Margaret 8	Margaret 8	
Hannah 6m	Hannagh 6m	Spelling of given name
CRAWFORD, Henry, Castlederg	**CRAWFORD**, Henry, Castlederg	
WILKISON, Ketty Ann, Ballymoney	**WILKISON**, Ketty Ann, Ballymoney	

MURPHY, Thomas, Ballymoney		**MURPHY**, Thomas, Ballymoney		
DOHERTY, Ann, Carn		**DOHERTY**, Ann Rosanna, Carndonagh	Place name differs	
Rosanna	8		Not in Baker	
McGLINCHY, Patrick, Donegal		**McGLINCHY**, Patrick, Donegal		
McGETTIGAN, Bernard, Ederny		**McGETTIGAN**, Bernard, Ederny		
NEELY, Thomas, Maghera		**NEELY**, Thomas, Maghera		
Margaret		Margaret		
Hugh	7	Hugh	7	
Mary	6	Mary	6	
James	4	James	4	
Margaret	2	Margaret	2	
FRYER, Mary, Ramelton		**FRYER**, Mary, Ramelton		
William	13	William	13	
Mary	7	Mary	7	
ARMSTRONG, David, Limavady		**ARMSTRONG**, David, Limavady		
Letitia		Letitia		
John James	12	John James	12	
Letitia	9	Letitia	9	
GILLESPIE, Ellan, Ballybofey		**GILLESPIE**, Ellen, Ballybofey		
CARY, George Thomas, Glendermott		**COEY**, George Thomas, Glendermott	Surnames differ	
McGILAWAY, Magy, Ballygorman		**McGILAWAY**, Magy, Ballygorman		
DOHERTY, Mary, Ballygorman		**DOHERTY**, Mary, Ballygorman		
Owen		Owen		
Mary		Mary		
Biddy		Biddy		
Thomas		Thomas		
Owen	12	Owen	12	
Edward	9	Edward	9	
John	7	John	7	
Philip	4	Philip	4	
DOYLE, Alexander, Ballygorman		**DOYLE**, Alexander, Ballygorman		
Jackey		Jackey		
Thomas		Thomas	8	Baker gives age
Mary	8	Mary	8	
John		**DOYLE**, John, Ballygorman		Baker has new family
Mary		Mary		
Mary		Mary		
Nancy		Nancy		
Alexander	12	Alexander	12	
Biddy	10	Biddy	10	
Nilly	8	Nelly	8	Spelling
Kitty	5	Kitty	5	
Ned	3	Ned	3	
DOHERTY, John, Ballygorman		**DOHERTY**, John, Ballygorman		
Grace		Grace		
LOGUE, Hugh, Rosnakill		**LOGUE**, Hugh, Rosnakill		
COYLE, John, Rosnakill		Sarah	Sequence	
LOGUE, Sarah, Rosnakill		**COYLE**, John, ...	Sequence	
PORTER, Samuel, Elagh		**PORTER**, Samuel, Elagh		
		DOHERTY, Alexander, Fannett	Not in Mitchell	
BRADLEY, John, Buncrana		**BRADLEY**, John, Buncrana		
DEVINE, James, Ballyconnoll		**DEVINE**, James, Ballyconnell	Spelling of place name	
McGEE, Bernard, Ballyconnoll		**McGEE**, Bernard, Ballyconnell	Spelling of place name	
McCHRISTLE, Peter, Omagh		**McCHRISTLE**, Peter, Omagh		

BEGLEY, Fanny, Ramelton	**BEGLEY**, Fanny, Ramelton	
McGLOON, James, Markethill	**McGLOON**, James, Markethill	
NEWMAN, Ann, Queens County	**NEWMAN**, Ann, Queens County	
Patrick	Patrick	
McCUE, Hannah, Castlederg	**McCUE**, Hannagh, Castlederg	Spelling of given name
Joseph	Joseph	
BAXTER, Thomas, Ballyconnell	**BAXTER**, Thomas, Ballyconnell	
Margaret	Margaret	
RAINBERT, Catherine, Maguires Bridge	**RAINBERT**, Catherine, Maguiresbridge	Written as one word
McFADDEN, Charles, Kilmacrenan	**McFADDEN**, Charles, Kilmacrenan	
Rose	Rose	
Nancy 12	Nancy 12	
Mary 8	Mary 8	
Magy 4	Magy 4	
Hugh 1	Hughy 1½	Spelling; age
DOHERTY, James, Carrygart	**DOHERTY**, James, Carrigart	Spelling of place name
CASSIDY, Margaret, Fintona	**CASSADY**, Margaret, Fintona	Spelling of surname
HIGGINS, Sarah, Drunon	**HIGGINS**, Sarah, Drunon	
McNELLY, Rose, Kildress	**McNELLY**, Rose, Kildress	
LITTLE, Edward, ...	**LITTLE**, Edward, ...	
Elizabeth	Elizabeth	
Margaret	Margaret	
William	William	
Anne	Anne	
Jane	Jane	
Mary	Mary	
Elizabeth	Elizabeth	
Dolly 13	Dolly 13	
Susan 8	Susan 8	
Robert 7	Robert 7	
SCALLON, Owen, Ballynamallard	**SCALLON**, Owen, Ballynamallard	
PHILLIPS, Robert, Loutherstown	**PHILIPS**, Robert, Loutherstown	Spelling of surname
McSHERRY, Terence, ...	**McSHERRY**, Terence, ...	
CONOLY, Terence, Manor Hamilton	**CONOLY**, Terence, Manorhamilton	Written as one word
Bridget	Bridget	
Margaret	Margaret	
Francis	Frances	Gender different ?
Mary	Mary	
LITTLE, Charles 13, Manor Hamilton	**LITTLE**, Charles 13, Manorhamilton	Written as one word
John 7	John 7	
Eliza 6	Eliza 6	
Thomas 4	Thomas 4	
Terence 1	Terence 1½	Age
Fanny 3m	Fanny 3m	
DRUMMOND, Hugh, Manor Hamilton	**DRUMMOND**, Hugh, Manorhamilton	Written as one word
RORKE, John, Manor Hamilton	**RORKE**, John, Manorhamilton	Written as one word
DOHERTY, George, Carn	**DOHERTY**, George, Carndonagh	Place name differs
McGAGHEY, Catherine, Loughash	**McGAGHEY**, Catherine, Loughash	
PHILLIPS, Samuel, Dromore	**PHILIPS**, Samuel, Dromore	Spelling of surname
William 7	William 7	
Alexander 4	Alexander 4	
Jane 3	Jane 3	
CLANCY, Terence, Ballyshannon	**CLANCY**, Terence, Ballyshannon	

OWENS, Biddy, Dromore	**OWENS**, Biddy, Dromore	
Rosey 6	Rosey 6	
Bridget 1m	Bridget 1m	
MURRAY, Margaret 9, Coleraine	**MURRAY**, Margaret 9, Coleraine	
Mary 7	Mary 7	
KELLY, Neally, Muff	**KELLY**, Neally, Muff	
CARNEY, Nicholas, Ederny	**CARNEY**, Nicholas, Ederny	
FISHER, Mary, Ardara	**FISHER**, Mary, Ardara	
FERRY, Catherine, Gortinleave	**FERRY**, Catherine, Gortinleave	
Eliza 12	Eliza 12	
John 10	John 10	
Mary 8	Mary 8	
Catherine 4	Catherine 4	
Ann 9m	Ann 9m	
GLASS, Henry, Eden	**GLASS**, John, Eden	Different given name
BROWN, William, Glengorland	**BROWN**, William, Glengorland	
BLACK, George, Alaugh	**BLACK**, George, Alaugh	
David	David	
KERR, Michael, Duran	**KERR**, Michael, Duran	
BURNS, John, Duran	**BURNS**, John, ...	Baker omits place
DOOHER, James, Strabane	**DOOHER**, James, Strabane	
DONAGHY, Elizabeth 12, ...	**DONAGHY**, Elizabeth 12, Strabane	Mitchell omits place
SHARKEY, Mary, ...	**SHARKEY**, Mary, ...	
MURRAY, Mary, ...	**MURRAY**, Mary, ...	
Daniel 6m	Daniel 6m	
STANTON, Ann, ...	**STANTON**, Ann, ...	
MURRAY, Michael, ...	**MURRAY**, Michael, ...	
BLAIR, William, ...	**BLAIR**, William, ...	
MONTGOMERY, George, Enniskillen	**MONTGOMERY**, George, Enniskillen	
Elizabeth	Elizabeth	
Ann	Ann	
MAGIN, James, Enniskillen	**MAGIN**, James, ...	Baker omits place
Alice	Alice	
McHUGH, Ann, Enniskillen	**McHUGH**, Ann, ...	Baker omits place
COSGROVE, Mary Ann 9, Enniskillen	**COSGROVE**, Mary Ann 9, ...	Baker omits place
McMANUS, Rose, Enniskillen	**McMANUS**, Rose, Enniskillen	
Kitty	Kitty	
Mary 13	Mary 13	
MORTON, Margaret, Eniskillen	**MORTON**, Margaret, Enniskillen	
MAGUIRE, Biddy, Enniskillen	**MAGUIRE**, Biddy, Enniskillen	
Ann 7	Ann 7	
Patrick 5	Patrick 5	
BEATTY, John, Enniskillen	**BEATTY**, John, Enniskillen	
Archy	Archy	
BURKE, James, Dungiven	**BURKE**, James, Dungiven	
Catherine	Catherine	
Biddy 11	Biddy 11	
Charles 9	Charles 9	
Patrick 7	Patrick 7	
Jane 5	Jane 5	
Mary 3	Mary 3	
James 9m	James 9m	
GUY, John, Derry	**GUY**, John, Derry	

DONAGHY, Biddy, Fintona	**DONAGHY**, Biddy, Fintona	
QUINN, Edward, Dromore	**QUINN**, Edward, Dromore	
Michael	Michael	
DUNBAR, Fanny, Newtownstewart	**DUNBAR**, Fanny, Newtownstewart	
IRWIN, Edward, Enniskillen	**IRWIN**, Edward, Enniskillen	
Jane	Jane	
John		Not in Baker
Catherine	Catherine	
Jane	Jane	
Mary Ann 13	Mary Ann 13	
Edward 8	Edward 8	
James 5	James 5	
Margaret 2	Margaret 2	
CALLAGHAN, Hannah, Glenswilly	**CALLAGHAN**, Hannagh, Glenswilly	Spelling of given name
DOHERTY, Ellen, Strabane	**DOHERTY**, Ellen, Strabane	
CLARKE, William, Moville	**CLARKE**, William, Moville	
(266 names)	(260 names)	

COMMENTARY

The most conspicuous difference between the two versions of the list is the fact that seven people in Mitchell's roster are not mentioned by Baker, while in one case the reverse is noticed. That adds eight names to the passenger list. In eight instances Mitchell supplies a place name where Baker does not. The converse occurs just once. By having both lists, therefore, the researcher has more complete information to hand.

In six instances the surnames of the passengers are not spelled identically. In some cases the variation is minimal, e.g., Philips/Phillips; Speer/Spier; Cassady/Cassidy; Hafferty/Hafforty. The first name in the lists is spelled either Dougher or Doherty; it is likely that the name was Dougherty, but we cannot be sure. In all but two instances, differing versions of given names pose no problems. No one should be troubled by Hannah/Hannagh; Catharine/Catherine; Ellan/Ellen; or Hugh/Hughy. More perplexing is the gender of the Conoly child: was this a boy named Francis or a girl named Frances? The most troublesome name problems are with the surname Coey or Cary, and the first name of Mr. Glass. Was he Henry or John?

Unless Carndonagh has been abbreviated twice to Carn, the locations do not match. Was Elleanor Moore from Ballymagory or Strabane? The former may be a fine tuning of her origin, since both are in the civil parish of Leckpatrick, County Tyrone. Was William Brown from Newtownstewart or Limavady? That difference matters appreciably to anyone attempting to focus their search because the places are miles apart and in two different counties. The different spellings of Carrigart/Carrygart should pose no problems, nor should it matter whether it reads Manor Hamilton or Manorhamilton, since clearly they refer to the same place.

Baker gives Thomas Doyle's age (8), and tells us that Terence Little and Hugh McFadden were 1½ years old, where Mitchell has them aged 1 year. Dennis McGrorty is 3 in Mitchell, but 13 in Baker. Baker breaks the Alexander Doyle family into two, with the second half being that of John Doyle. By rearranging the Logue and Coyle entries, Baker implies that the Logues were a couple, a suggestion absent from Mitchell's reading of the list.

The *Envoy* has been chosen for this exercise because there exist three other sources of information concerning the passengers who may have been in the vessel during its voyage in the summer of 1847. These add to the impression that neither version of the passenger list tells the whole story.

The first item appeared in the *New Brunswick Chronicle*[1], when 33 "passengers on board the Barque *Envoy* owned by Messrs. J. & J. Cook, merchants of Londonderry, Ireland, do hereby offer to Captain Laidler, Master of said vessel, and to his first mate, Mr. Gibson, our . . . thanks for their great kindness during the passage . . . and for the attention paid by them to our comfort . . . [W]e also bear testimony to the great care taken by them to prevent any infectious disease in the vessel, by enforcing cleanliness and order.' This encomium is dated 23 July, the date the ship reached Saint John following a voyage of five weeks.[2] In alphabetical order, the signatories were:

BLAIR, William	**IRWIN**, Edward
BRADLEY, John	**IRWIN**, John
BUSTARD, Charles	***KEANS**, Hugh
***CAMPBELL**, Edward	**KEARNEY**, Nicholas
CAREY, George Thomas	**KIERANS**, William
CLARKE, William	**LITTLE**, Edward
CONOLLY, Terence	**McCOY**, Neil
DOHERTY, John	**McELROY**, Phelix
DOUGAN, James [Dooher]	**McGOTTIGAN**, Bernard
DOUGAN, Patrick [Dougher]	**MAGIRR**, James
GALLAGHER, Francis	***MAGUIRE**, James
GALLAGHER, James	***MITCHELL**, Hugh
GALLAGHER, William	**NEALY**, Thomas
GILLOGLEY, James	**NELIS**, James
GLASS, Henry	**OWENS**, James
GUY, John	**PORTER**, Samuel
	SELFRIDGE, Thomas

Four of the 33 are marked with an asterisk (*), as their names do not appear in either version of the passenger list. Since many of the signatories headed families, we cannot be sure whether only four men are absent from the listing, or whether there were wives and children with one or all of them. At a conservative estimate, count this as 6 people missed in the original lists.

Our second group of names is comprised of 11 people who died in Quarantine at Partridge Island between the ship's arrival in late July and the autumn[3]:
BOURKE, James, 3 - this must be the James Burke, age 9 months
BOURKE, Patrick, 24 - in the list the only one of this name was a boy 7 years old
BURKE, Mary, 5 - this would be Mary Burke, age 3

---

[1] *New Brunswick Courier*, 21 August 1847. This was a newspaper in Saint John, NB.

[2] The ship departed Londonderry on 19 June 1847 and reached Saint John on 23 July 1847.

[3] Cushing *et al.*, pp. 37 - 54, *passim*.

DUNBAR, James, 2 months - died late August probably born at sea, a son of Fanny Dunbar
McELROY, Catherine, 7 - her age given as 5 in passenger list
McELROY, Jane, 6 - not listed on either passenger list; add 1 to the total complement
McELROY, Peggy, 12 - listed as Margaret McElroy (see p. 115)
McELROY, Phelim, 60 - called Phelix in the list above
MURRAY, Mary, 32 - matches lists
MURRAY, Thomas, 2 - either the Daniel Murray, 6 months old, or Thomas Mur*ph*y, an adult
QUINN, Michael, 21 - matches lists

Allowing for discrepant ages or names, we can add a baby, James Dunbar, born en route, and a child, Jane McElroy, to the total complement; two more passengers.

The third group of 11 names is found in the records of the Alms House in Saint John:[4]
BAR, Ellen, 16, Derry - not in either version of the passenger list; add one to the complement
CARNEY, Nicholas, 33, Fermanagh - shown in lists as Kearney
COLEMAN, Widow, 46, Cork - not in either version of the list; origin seems out of place; add one
DOHERTY, Biddy, 19, Derry - origin given in list as Ballygorman, which is in Donegal!
DOHERTY, James, 20, Derry - origin given in list as Carrigart, i.e., Carrickart, in Donegal!
DORAN, Susan, 38, Donegal - no match in the lists at all; add one to the complement
GALLAGHER, James, 20, Fermanagh - a match
GLASS, Henry, 20, Derry - appears to confirm his given name was Henry and not John
GRIFFIN, William, 25, Donegal - not in either version of the list; add one to the complement
LOGUE, Hugh, 60, Donegal - a match
McGLINCHE, Patrick, 14, Donegal - a match

Again we can add names to the published lists. This time we have four – Ellen Barr, Widow Coleman, Susan Doran, and William Griffin. If we add 6 from the testimonial list, 2 from the deaths in quarantine, and 4 from the Alms House lists, we have 12 to add to the numbers in the published lists. From comparing the Mitchell and Baker versions of the lists, we can add 1 person to the roster, totaling 13 further passengers identified. I believe it would be accurate to say that the emigrants in the vessel numbered 279 souls. Taken together, we can see the need for care in accepting a passenger list as being necessarily one hundred percent correct and complete. The researcher is fortunate here because there are two published versions of the passenger list, a testimonial signed by some of the passengers, a quarantine record and the register of admissions to the Alms House. When a genealogist has only one contemporary source, it would be prudent to seek means of corroborating details of spelling, origin and age if at all possible.

---

[4] Daniel F. Johnson, *Irish Emigration to New England Through the Port of Saint John*, p. 133.

APPENDIX I - IRISH AMONG THE FOUNDERS OF HALIFAX, 1749

The first organized settlement by people from the British Isles in the Maritime Provinces was that made at Halifax, Nova Scotia, in the early summer of 1749. It is apparent from the outset that great numbers of unsuitable colonists fled the arduous task of establishing a town and a ring of protective forts. More than once the governor threatened to penalize both settlers who left and the obliging ship masters who transported them from the settlement without licence to do so. We find a few hundred Irish people mentioned among the passengers in the founding fleet. It is difficult to be certain that every person selected was, in fact, a native of Ireland. In such cases the balance of probability has been applied, which means that some people who were Irish have been missed, and others were included who may not have been Irish-born. I have selected 210 people as being actually or very probably Irish.

In the *Alexander* (13):

MAGEE, William[1]; wife; 5 man servants; 3 maidservants (10)
O'NEAL, Francis, mariner; wife   (2)
O'NEAL, James, mariner (1)

In the *Baltimore* (21):

BRANAGAN, John, cooper (1)
BRITT, Thomas, labourer (1)
BRYAN, Lieut. William, Leighton's Regiment; wife; 2 man servants; 1 maidservant (5)
CARNEY, Barney, carpenter; wife; 1 boy (3)
COLEMAN, William, shoemaker[2]; wife (2)
HALEY, Pierce George, private, Powlett's Regiment; wife (2)
HURLEY, William, husbandman (1)
McSHEAN, Thomas, mariner[3]; wife (2)
PLUNKETT, John, mariner[4]; wife; 1 girl   (3)
REDMAN, Michael, mariner (1)

In the *Beaufort* (15):

CORNLEY, John, private, Beauclerk's Regiment[5]   (1)
DEVEREAUX, William, private, Foot Guards[6]; wife; 1 boy; 2 girls (5)

---

[1] William and Mary **MAGEE** were victualed at Halifax in May and June 1750 - NSA, RG 1, Vol. 32.

[2] Mary and . . . **COLEMAN** were victualed at Halifax in May and June 1750 - NSA, RG 1, Vol. 32.

[3] The wife, Alis **McSHEEN**, was victualed at Halifax in May and June 1750 - NSA, RG 1, Vol. 32.

[4] John **PLUNKETT** was buried 9 March 1750/51 at St. Paul's, Halifax, NS.

[5] John **CORNLEY** was victualed at Halifax in May and June 1750 - NSA, RG 1, Vol. 32.

[6] William, Mary, Elizabeth and Edey **DEVEREUX** were victualed at Halifax in May and June 1750 - NSA, RG 1, Vol. 32.

DOYLE, James, mariner[7]; wife (2)
DUNAHOO, Stephen, mariner; wife (2)
FLYNN, John, mariner[8]; wife (2)
HARROLD, John, labourer (1)
NEAL, James, mariner[9]; wife (2)

In the *Canning* (16):

BARRY, James, mariner; wife; 1 girl (3)
CHERRY, Edward, mariner (1)
CORBETT, Thomas, fisherman; 1 male servant (2)
DORAN, Edward, mariner[10] (1)
FINLEY, John, mariner[11] (1)
FORD, Michael, fisherman (1)
HACKET, Richard, tailor (1)
PENROSE, George, mariner (1)
PIERS, Lewis, gentleman[12] (1)
ROOK, Lawrence, mariner; wife (2)
SULLIVAN, Daniel, shipwright; 1 male servant (2)
SULLIVAN, Michael, fisherman; wife (2)

In the *Everley* (2):

DANOLY, John, smith (1)
GUNAN, Thomas, joiner (1)

In the *London* (46):

BURNE, Michael, mariner (1)
BUTLER, Joseph, mariner (1)
BYRNE, Peter, mariner (1)
CASEY, Daniel, husbandman (1)
CAVANAH, Barnaby, mariner (1)

---

[7] James **DOYLE** was victualed at Halifax in May and June 1750 - NSA, RG 1, Vol. 32. His wife's name was Margaret.

[8] The wife, Mary **FLING** was victualed at Halifax in May and June 1750 - NSA, RG 1, Vol. 32.

[9] James **NEAL** was victualed at Halifax in May and June 1750 - NSA, RG 1, Vol. 32. His wife's name was Hannah.

[10] Edward **DORAN** was victualed at Halifax in May and June 1750 - NSA, RG 1, Vol. 32.

[11] John **FINLY** was victualed at Halifax in May and June 1750 - NSA, RG 1, Vol. 32.

[12] Lewis and Mary **PIERS** were victualed at Halifax in May and June 1750 - NSA, RG 1, Vol. 32. Piers was a native of County Meath. A return of inhabitants in July 1752 mentions him with a household of four: 1 man, 1 woman, 1 boy, 1 girl, "within the town". Piers was that rarity, a member of a titled family who emigrated. His grandfather, Henry Piers, was the second son of the first Piers baronet of Tristernagh, County Meath.

CONNOLLY, Philip, labourer[13]; wife; 1 girl (3)
DAILEY, Garret, mariner[14]; wife (2)
FARRELL, Patrick, mariner (1)
FARRELL, Richard, labourer (1)
FITZGERALD, Frederick, cooper; wife; 1 boy (3)
FLEMMING, James, mariner (1)
FOX, Barnaby, husbandman (1)
GOLDING, Thomas, mariner[15] (1)
HARNEY, John, mariner (1)
JORDAN, James, husbandman[16]; wife; 1 boy; 2 girls (5)
KENNEDY, John, private, Prince's Regiment (1)
LAMB, Patrick, brickmaker; wife (2)
MALONE, Daniel, carpenter, Deptford Yard[17]; wife; 1 boy (3)
MOON[EY], Matthew, sawyer (1)
SAVAGE, John, mariner (1)
SKELLEY, James, husbandman; wife; 1 girl (3)
SMITH, James, husbandman[18]; wife; 3 boys (5)
SWYNNY, John, mariner[19]; wife (2)
TOOL, John, mariner[20]; wife; 1 girl (3)
WALSH, Bartholomew, mariner (1)

In the *Merry Jacks* (47):

BARRETT, Thomas, mariner; wife; 1 boy; 1 maid servant (4)
BLAKE, William, mariner[21]; wife (2)

---

[13] Philip, his wife Rose, and daughter Jane **CONLEY** were victualed at Halifax in May and June 1750 - NSA, RG 1, Vol. 32. The couple had two daughters baptised at St. Paul's, Halifax.

[14] Garret **DALEY** was victualed at Halifax in May and June 1750 - NSA, RG 1, Vol. 32.

[15] Thomas **GOLDEN** was victualed at Halifax in May and June 1750 - NSA, RG 1, Vol. 32. He married 1 July 1751 (St. Paul's, Halifax), Ann **HEILD**. They were still in Halifax in 1753 when their son John was born.

[16] James, Phoebe, Phoebe, and Samuel **JORDON** were victualed at Halifax in May and June 1750 - NSA, RG 1, Vol. 32. In July 1752 James Jordan lived in the south suburbs of Halifax in a household consisting of one man, 2 women and one boy.

[17] Daniel and Elis **MALONE** were victualed at Halifax in May and June 1750 - NSA, RG 1, Vol. 32.

[18] James, Martha, William, Thomas and Alexander **SMITH** were victualed at Halifax in May and June 1750 - NSA, RG 1, Vol. 32. James SMITH was born in 1698 in Londonderry, Ireland, and died at Hillsborough, New Brunswick, in 1797. The son William died in 1759.

[19] John **SWINEY** was victualed at Halifax in May and June 1750 - NSA, RG 1, Vol. 32.

[20] John and Mary **TOOL** were victualed at Halifax in May and June 1750 - NSA, RG 1, Vol. 32.

[21] William **BLAKE** was victualed at Halifax in May and June 1750 - NSA, RG 1, Vol. 32.

CHRISTIAN, John, mariner[22]; wife (2)
COLLINS, John, mariner; wife (2)
CONNOR, John, mariner[23] (1)
DALEY, John, mariner[24]; wife (2)
DELANEY, Patrick, mariner (1)
FLANIGAN, George, mariner (1)
FOX, Daniel, mariner[25] (1)
HAGARTY, Michael, mariner (1)
JORDAN, Andrew, sawyer[26] (1)
KANE, Timothy, mariner[27]; wife (2)
KELLY, James, mariner (1)
KENNEDY, John, mariner[28] (1)
LACEY, Matthew, mariner (1)
MAGEE, Robert, mariner; wife (2)
MAGRAH, James, mariner (1)
MOONEY, Lawrence, mariner (1)
O'NEAL, Charles, mariner[29]; wife; 1 girl (3)
QUINN, Michael, mariner (1)
QUINN, Thomas, mariner (1)
RYAN, James, mariner; wife (2)
SAVAGE, Matthew, baker (1)
STAFFORD, Thomas, shoemaker[30] (1)
TERRY, David, mariner; wife; 1 man servant (3)
TYRRELL, Robert, mariner (1)
WARREN, John, mariner; wife; 1 man servant; 1 maid servant (4)

---

[22] James and Esther **CHRISTIAN** were victualed at Halifax in May and June 1750 - NSA, RG 1, Vol. 32.

[23] John **CONNOR** was listed as an inhabitant of the south suburbs of Halifax in July 1752, but had moved across the harbour to Dartmouth by the time he was permitted to operate the first harbour ferry, 3 February 1753.

[24] John and Alice **DAYLEY** were victualed at Halifax in May and June 1750 - NSA, RG 1, Vol. 32.

[25] Daniel **FOX** was victualed at Halifax in May and June 1750 - NSA, RG 1, Vol. 32.

[26] Andrew **JORDIN** was victualed at Halifax in May and June 1750 - NSA, RG 1, Vol. 32.

[27] Timothy, Jane and Mary **CANE** were victualed at Halifax in May and June 1750 - NSA, RG 1, Vol. 32. Timothy and Jane had daughters Maria and Esther baptised at St. Paul's, Halifax. Timothy was buried from that church, 16 Nov 1763.

[28] John **KENNEDY** was victualed at Halifax in May and June 1750 - NSA, RG 1, Vol. 32.

[29] Charles, Elizabeth, and Eleanor **O'NEAL** were victualed at Halifax in May and June 1750 - NSA, RG 1, Vol. 32.

[30] Thomas **STANFORD** was victualed at Halifax in May and June 1750 - NSA, RG 1, Vol. 32.

WHELAN, Charles, mariner (1)
WHELAN, Robert, mariner; wife (2)

In the *Wilmington* (17):

BARRETT, Michael, joiner; wife; 1 man servant (3)
FORD, Jeremiah, mariner; wife (2)
GEARY, Dennis, mariner[31]; wife; 1 man servant (3)
GOLDEN, John, carpenter; wife; 1 boy (3)
HALY, John, mariner[32]; wife (2)
McWADE, Daniel, mariner (1)
MALONE, Patrick, mariner[33]; 1 maid servant (1)
REDMAN, William, mariner; wife (2)

In the *Winchelsea* (33):

BARRET, John, mariner (1)
BARRY, Thomas, mariner[34]; 1 man servant (2)
BRYAN, John, mariner (1)
CASEY, James, mariner[35]; wife (2)
CAVANAGH, Owen, mariner; wife (2)
COLLINS, Peter, mariner (1)
DOLIN, Brian, private, Churchill's Regiment;[36] wife (2)
FITZGERALD, Richard, mariner; wife; 3 girls (5)
FITZGIBBON, John, mariner; wife (2)
FLYNN, Terence, mariner; wife; 1 man servant (3)
LOWRY, Philip, mariner (1)
McCARDIE, Alexander, mariner (1)
MOORE, John, mariner (1)
RYAN, Cornelius, – (1)
SHEEN, John, mariner (1)
WALL, John, edge toolmaker; wife; 2 boys (4)
WARREN, James, ensign, Duke of Bolton 's Regiment; wife; 1 maid servant (3)

---

[31] Denis **GEARY** was buried from St. Paul's, Halifax, 26 Dec 1749.

[32] John and Ann **HALEY** were victualed at Halifax in May and June 1750 - NSA, RG 1, Vol. 32.

[33] Patrick **MALONEY** was victualed at Halifax in May and June 1750 - NSA, RG 1, Vol. 32.

[34] Thomas **BARRY** and another Barry were victualed at Halifax in May and June 1750 - NSA, RG 1, Vol. 32. Thomas was buried from St. Paul's, Halifax, in October 1755.

[35] James and Ann **CASEY** were victualed at Halifax in May and June 1750 - NSA, RG 1, Vol. 32. Their sons John and Felix were baptised at St. Paul's, Halifax, in 1750 and 1752.

[36] Bryan **DOLAN** and his wife Margaret had three children baptised at St. Paul's, Halifax: Mary in 1752, John in 1754, and Honora in 1757.

APPENDIX II - ULSTER IRISH ARRIVALS BEFORE 1773

The emigration directed to the Maritimes from Ulster in the period between 1761 and 1773 was owing mainly to the efforts of emigration promoter Alexander McNutt, himself a native of the north of Ireland.[1] Ten voyages from Londonderry, Ireland, purportedly brought settlers to Halifax, Nova Scotia. From there the larger part proceeded to the area around the head of Minas Basin, the more southerly arm at the head of the Bay of Fundy. The area now found in Colchester (Truro, Londonderry and Onslow townships), Cumberland (Amherst and Cumberland townships) and Hants (Douglas, Windsor and Falmouth townships) counties received most of those arrivals. A smaller share proceeded to New Dublin, west of Lunenburg on the south shore of the province or to Granville township on Annapolis Basin. A few remained in Halifax where their trades were in demand, while a handful ended up in what, in 1784, became New Brunswick.

We have passenger lists for none of the ten voyages. Since only the *Hopewell* brought out Ulster folk in 1761, we can assume that people of that origin who show up in credible sources as being in those settlement areas may well have come out in that voyage. Since several families of Ulster Scots removed to the region in 1760, after living from several to as many as forty years in New Hampshire, care must be taken to distinguish between these and the people coming directly from Ireland.

Some families were of childbearing age. Without being absolutely certain in which year the migration occurred or when a child was born, a certain amount of estimation has been employed to decide which children were Irish-born and which were born in North America.

With these cautions in mind, these emigrants have been ranked according to their earliest appearance in the records viewed. This means that a family shown as possible arrivals in 1766 might, in fact, have emigrated one, four, or even five years previous to their being noticed in one of the sources consulted. About one-third of the total migration before 1767 is accounted for here.

The Belfast Newsletter item of 11 March 1762 was a favorable report from a group who had gone to Nova Scotia in the *Hopewell* the previous year. At least forty people definitely formed part of that group:

1761

BARNHILL, Robert, Leck Parish, Co. Donegal; his wife Letitia **DEYARMOND**; children:
    John, b. 1730, d. 12 Nov 1813, and his wife
    Margaret, b. 1736, and her husband Thomas **BAIRD** and their 4 children, of whom only
        Dorcas Baird survived the voyage.
    Rebecca
    Sarah, b. ca. 1745 [married Thomas **CROWE**]
CLARK, John, Tamlaght Finlagan Parish, Co. Londonderry (at Windsor, NS, by 1765)
COCHRAN, Daniel, Derrykeighan Parish, Co. Antrim
CRAWFORD, Joseph, Rathmelton Town, Co. Donegal
HENDERSON, William, Rathmullen Parish, Co. Donegal

---

[1] Alexander McNutt became a large land-owner in Nova Scotia, the size of his grant being based on the assumption that he would bring large numbers of reliable settlers onto those holdings. He "found it difficult to compete for emigrants because of the good reputation Pennsylvania had gained among potential settlers" - Wokeck, p. 197, n. 68.

McCLEAN, Anthony, Creeve, near Letterkenny, Co. Donegal, d. 1800 at Londonderry, NS;
    his wife Margaret; children:
    John
    Mary
McNUTT, Benjamin, Mevagh Parish, Co. Donegal
McNUTT, John, Ballymacscreen Parish, Co. Londonderry
McNUTT, William, Mevagh Parish, Co. Donegal; his wife Elizabeth; child:
    Mary
MAHON, John, b. 1726, Drumhome Parish, Co. Donegal; his wife Sarah, b. 1732; daughter.
MOORE, William, b. 1740 Fahan Parish, Co. Donegal, d. 1820 at Economy, NS
MORRISON, John, Tullaghabegly Parish, Co. Donegal
PATTON, Mark, Faughanvale Parish, Co. Londonderry; his wife; children:
    Mary
    Letitia
    William
ROSS, Andrew, Ballyrashone Parish, Co. Antrim
SMITH, Robert, Drumnachose Parish, Co. Londonderry
SPENCER, Robert, Clondahorky Parish, Co. Donegal, d. 1794; his wife; children
    son
    Mary [married Jacob **O'BRIEN**]

The following people must also have been aboard the *Hopewell* for the 1761 voyage:
COCHRAN, Joseph, b. 1703 in Ulster, d. 22 Dec 1787: his wife Mary **KINNEAR**; children:
    Thomas, b. 1733, d. 26 Aug 1801
    James, b. 1742, d. 18 Oct 1819
    William, b. 1750, d. 1 June 1820
        (Amherst and Halifax, NS)

CREELMAN, Samuel, cooper, b. ca. 1728 Ulster, d. ca. 1810; his wife Isabel **FLEMING**; sons:
    Samuel, b. 1751, d. Oct 1835 at Stewacke, NS
    Francis, b. 1759, d. 3 May 1836 at Otter Brook, NS
        (Truro and Stewiacke, NS)

CROWE, James, Co. Londonderry; his wife (name not known); children:
    Margaret
    Joseph, b. 1738, d. 15 Apr 1810, and wife Esther, b. 1738, d. 6 Jan 1818, dau. of Robert
        BARNHILL
    James, b. 1740 (removed later to Philadelphia)
    Aaron, b. 1743, d. 20 Oct 1818
    Thomas, b. 1746, d. 25 Feb 1801
    John, b. 1748, d. 6 Oct 1825
    Nicholas, b. 1750
        (Truro, NS)

FALKNER, Robert, Ulster
        (Londonderry, NS)

FORBES, William, house carpenter, Ulster; his wife Elizabeth and family of four
(included his brother Robert and their father)
(Londonderry and Halifax, NS)

FULTON, James, b. 1726, Co. Londonderry; his wife Ann **CALDWELL**, b. 1728; children:
Ann
Elizabeth
Jane
Samuel
Joseph
John, b. 1754
William, b. 1757, d. 11 Dec 1812 at Upper Stewiacke, NS
(Colchester County, NS)

HILL, Robert, b. ca. 1722, County Donegal; his wife (name not known); children:
Patrick, b. 1743, d. 1 Oct 1839 at Economy, NS
Robert, b. 1747, d. ca. 1777
Jane, b. 1749, d. 29 Oct 1827; m. David **VANCE**
Charles, b. 1751, d. 16 Aug 1825 at Halifax, NS
(Economy, NS)

HUNTER, Robert, b. 1733 Ulster, d. Feb 1810; wife Esther **MOORE**, b. 1733, d. 14 Oct 1807
[sister of Hugh, William and Daniel **MOORE**]; children:
Letitia
Elizabeth
(Truro, NS)

JOHNSON, John, b. 1711 Ulster, d. 2 Dec 1793; wife Sarah **HOGG**, b. 1712, d. 8 Aug 1796;
children:
Mary, b. 1738
John, b. 1741
James, b. 4 June 1743
Sarah, b. 1745
Rachel, b. 1746
Adam, b. 1748, d. 27 June 1771.
JOHNSON, James, b. 1719 (brother of John); wife Elizabeth **PATTERSON**, b. 1726, d. 3 Dec
1776; children:
Adam, b. 1745
Robert, b. 1747
Mary, b. 1749
Margaret, b. 1751
Rachel, b. 1752
Elizabeth, b. 1754
Matthew, b. 1756
James, b. 16 Oct 1758
William, b. 1759, d. 16 Dec 1830 at Upper Stewiacke, NS
John, b. autumn 1760
(Colchester County, NS)

LOGAN, Hugh, County Antrim; son Hugh, b. 1749, d. 31 Aug 1832 at West Amherst, NS
(Amherst, NS)

LOGAN, Janet, widow, County Londonderry; children:
John, b. 1727, and wife Mary, d. Dec 1778, and *their* children:
Robert, William, Esther, Jennet
William, and wife Janet **MOORE**
two daughters
(Truro, NS)

McCURDY, Alexander, b. 1734, d. 9 Aug 1808 at Onslow, NS, son of Daniel McCurdy, Ulster;
his wife Jennet **GUTHRIE**, b. 1733, d. 21 May 1800 at Onslow, NS; son:
David
Alexander's sister Peggy
(Londonderry, then Windsor, NS)

McDORMAND, William, Ulster
(Annapolis, NS)

MOORE, Hugh, b. 1738, County Londonderry, d. 10 Dec 1820 at Truro, NS; his wife Janet
LOGAN, b. 1746, d. 28 Nov 1818 at Truro, NS, daughter of Janet Logan
MOORE, Daniel, b. 1752, d. 14 Feb 1826 at Brookfield, NS, brother of Hugh
MOORE, William, brother of Hugh
(Truro, NS)

PALMER, John, western Ulster; his wife Jane; daughters:
Eleanor
Mary   [later married John Thomas **HILL**]
(Windsor, NS)

SCOTT, George, b. 1717, Ulster; his wife Elizabeth; daughter Esther, b. 1759/60
(Colchester County, NS)

(134 in the Hopewell in 1761)

1762

The following 102 people traveled in 1762 in either the *Nancy* which did come to Nova Scotia, or possibly in the *Hopewell*, although I doubt it made a voyage to Nova Scotia that year.

BERRY, Robert, b. 1733 Ulster, d. 21 May 1781; his wife and four children
(West Amherst, NS)

BURNS, William, b. ca. 1733, d. May 1818
BURNS, Francis, Ulster, d. ca. 1812
BURNS, John
(Wilmot, NS)

CAGAN, Malachy, Ireland, innkeeper at Falmouth, NS
(Falmouth, NS)

CALDERWOOD, Robert, Ulster, d. 1781; his wife (name not known)
 (Londonderry, NS)

CAMPBELL, James, County Londonderry; his wife (name not known); daughter:
 Margaret, b. 1754 [later m. James **FULTON**, Esq., from Belfast]
 (Colchester County, NS)

COX, Charles, Ulster; his wife Eleanor **STEWART**; children:
 William b. 1757
 Eleanor, b. 1759
 Charles, b. 1761
 (Colchester County, NS)

DENNY, John, Ulster; his wife Rebecca; daughters:
 Mary, b. 27 Apr 1755 [married Isaac **O'BRIEN**]
 Margaret, b. Oct 1757 [married Andrew **O'BRIEN**]
 Janet
 Martha
 Sarah
 two others
 (Londonderry, NS)

FORREST, David, b. 1709 Ulster, d. 12 Mar 1796; wife Rosanna, b. 1713, d. 18 Mar 1798;
 children:
 David, b. 1759, d. 12 Aug 1798
 Isaac, b. 1761, d. 22 Jan 1792
 two others
 (West Amherst, NS)

GRAHAM, David, Ulster; wife and two children
 (Londonderry, NS)

HENRY, James, Ulster; wife and two children
 (Amherst, NS)

HILL, Christian Jane, d Ulster, 24 Jan 1798, widow of . . . Hill, and of . . . **MONTGOMERY**
 children:
 John Thomas, b. 1751, d. 23 Aug 1800 at Grand Pré, NS [married Mary **PALMER**]
 Jane, b. 1755
 (Horton, NS)

KARR, Archibald, Ulster; his wife Jane and child
 (Londonderry, NS)

LAW, James, Ulster; his wife
 (Cumberland, NS)

McBRIDE, Edward, Ulster; his wife Lois
NEILY, Joseph, b. ca. 1745, son of John, Ulster
NEILY, Robert, son of John
REAGH, James, Ulster, and wife Martha **NEILY**, dau. of John
 (Annapolis County, NS)

McDONNELL, Henry, Ulster; his wife
     (Cumberland, NS)

McDORMON[D], Cormac, Ulster; his wife, d. 1791
     (Granville, NS)

McLEOD, John, Newtown Limavady, Londonderry
     (New Dublin, NS)

MEE, Thomas, Ulster; his wife, d. 1803, age 78, at Cornwallis, NS
     (Cumberland, NS)

O'BRIEN, Timothy, b. 22 Jan 1725 Anglinlow, Londonderry, drowned 19 Nov 1777 at Tenecape
     Bay, NS, son of William and Esther (**LINTON**) **O'BRIEN**; his wife Margaret **GILMORE**
     m. 17 Apr 1746 in Ayrshire, Scotland, d. 25 July 1803 at Noel, NS; children:
     William, b. 14 July 1747
     Robert, b. 25 Mar 1749, d. 11 May 1818 at Noel, NS   [married Janet **McCLELLAN**]
     Isaac, b. 18 Apr 1752 [married Mary **DENNY**]
     Andrew, b. 8 Oct 1754, d. 10 Feb 1832 at Noel, NS   [married Margaret **DENNY**]
     Elizabeth, b. 20 Feb 1756   [married Joseph **McCLELLAN**]
     Eleanor, b. 20 Apr 1758
     Jacob, b. 15 June 1761, d. 1844 at Noel, NS [married Mary **SPENCER**]
     (Noel, NS)

RAY, Moses, Belfast
     (Annapolis County, NS)

RAY, James, Ulster; his wife and one other
     (Granville, NS)

ROACH, Patrick, Ulster; his wife Jane; daughter Martha, b. ca. 1761 in Ireland
     (Granville, NS)

RODGERS, John, Ulster; his wife; two others (one was named Robert **RODGERS**)
     (Londonderry, NS)

SPROUL, Robert; his wife Sarah, d. 24 July 1766; children:
     John, b. 1757, d. 31 May 1820 at Paradise, NS
     Robert
     Andrew
     (Granville, NS)

STEWART, John, Ulster; wife and one son John, b. Nov 1747 in Ireland
     (Amherst, NS)

TRAHEE, Thomas, Ireland; his wife
     (Granville, NS)

VANCE, David, b. 1747 Ulster, d. 31 Jan 1832 at Londonderry, NS
VANCE, Alexander, brother of David
VANCE, John, Ulster, d. 1808 at Londonderry, NS
  (Londonderry, NS)

WILSON, James [or Joseph], Ulster; wife; two daughters; one other person
  (Londonderry, and Windsor, NS)

WILSON, Thomas, Ulster
  (Londonderry, NS)

    (102 people in the *Nancy* or *Hopewell* [?] in 1762)

1765

The following thirty-three people seem to have emigrated in the *Admiral Hawke* in 1765:

DENSMORE, James, Londonderry; his wife Letitia MOORE; children:
  Francis, b. 11 May 1760, d. 31 Aug 1831 at East Noel, NS
  John
  William
  James
  Samuel
    (Hants County, NS)

DICKIE, Mathew, Ulster, d. Jan 1803; his wife Janet M. NISBETT, b. 1728, d. 1811; children:
  James
  David
  William, b. 1759, d. 16 June 1838 at Chipman Corner, NS
  John
    (Amherst and Cornwallis, NS)

ELLIOTT, Samuel (parents died), Ulster
  (Annapolis County, NS)

FLETCHER, Thomas, Londonderry; his wife; son:
  Thomas, b. 1758, d. 17 Jan 1844
    (Londonderry, NS)

NESBITT, William, Ulster
  (Halifax, NS)

PEPPARD, Laurence, millwright, b. 1737 Drogheda, County Louth, d. 22 Jan 1819 at Belmont
  (Londonderry, NS)

SALTER, Robert, b. 17 Aug 1730 Bandon, County Cork, d. 16 Aug 1810 at Newport, NS;
his wife Margaret, b. 10 Nov 1737 Bandon, County Cork, d. 2 Jan 1820; children:
William, b. 1757, d. 22 July 1830 at Newport, NS
Mary 'Polly'
Ann
Elizabeth
Michael
(Newport, NS)

SHARP, Matthew; wife; 2 sons and 3 daughters, b. Ulster
One dau, Martha, b. July 1751, m. 12 July 1775 at Amherst, John, son of John **STEWART**
(Amherst, NS)

SUTHERLAND, William, Ulster
(Halifax, NS)

(33 people in the *Admiral Hawke* in 1765)

1766

The following 177 people appear to have arrived in either the *Hopewell* or the *Falls* in 1766:

CAMPBELL, Patrick, Ulster
(Amherst, NS)

COOK, James, Ulster, d. 23 June 1794; his wife Martha, d. 1807; children:
James
Ralph, d. 1827
Jenny
Margaret
(Londonderry, NS)

CRATH, Samuel, Ulster; his wife
(Amherst, NS)

CRAUFORD, Mathew, Ulster; his wife and two children
(Amherst, NS)

DEYARMOND, Alexander, near Leck, Co. Donegal; his wife Mary, b. 1732/33,
dau of Robert **BARNHILL**; children:
Robert, b. 1761, d. 11 Feb 1814 at Upper Stewiacke, NS
Rebecca
John, b. 1764
(Truro, NS)

DUNLAP, David, b. 1740, County Antrim; his wife Bridget; son David
(New Dublin, NS)

FLEMING, James, b. 1740 County Londonderry, d. 31 Dec 1828; his wife Isabel
(Londonderry, NS)

GIFFIN, John, Ulster; wife Margaret, dau. of Hubert **MASON**
GIFFIN, William, probably his brother
    (New Dublin, NS)

GRACE, John, Ulster; his wife Mary, d. 1778
    (Amherst, NS)

HALL, John, Ulster; his wife, one son, two daughters
    (Horton, NS)

JOHNSTON, Robert, County Tyrone; his wife Elizabeth; children:
    Samuel
    Alexander
JOHNSTON, William, brother
    (New Dublin, NS)

LITTLEJOHN, John, Grange of Doagh, County Antrim; children:
    Jane
    Tilly
    Simon
    Sarah
    (New Dublin, NS)

McCLANE, Samuel, Ulster; wife and family of three
    (Londonderry, NS)

McCLELLAN, Peter and wife, Ulster
McCLELLAN, John
McCLELLAN, Joseph and wife Isabel
McCLELLAN, Michael
McCLELLAN, Janet, b. 8 Apr 1752 [married Robert **O'BRIEN**]
    (Londonderry, NS)

McCLENNAN, John, Ulster; his wife and son
    (Londonderry, NS)

McELHINNEY, Robert, b. ca. 1747 Ulster, d. 1831
    (Londonderry, NS)

MUCKLEMAN [McElmon], Robert, Ulster, d. 1816 at Londonderry, NS; wife and two sons
    (Amherst, NS)

McGOWAN, Robert, schoolmaster, Ulster, d. 1779; his wife Jennet; children:
    Joan
    Martha
    John
    and two others
    (Amherst, NS)

McGREGOR, Thomas, Ulster; his wife
    (Granville, NS)

McGYER, Mathew, Ulster
    (New Dublin, NS)

McNUTT, George, Ulster; his wife
    (Londonderry, NS)

MASON, Hubert, Ulster; his wife; two sons; three daughters [Margaret, Lois, –]
    (New Dublin, NS)

MORISON, Archibald, Ulster, d. 1821 at Granville, NS; his wife, five sons, one daughter
    (Annapolis, NS)

MORRISON, John, Ulster; his wife and three children
MORRISON, John, Jr., trader, d. 1798; his wife and son
MORRISON, Hugh, Ulster; his wife
    (Granville, NS)

MURDOCH, John, flax grower, b. 1718 Killygordon, County Donegal, d. 18 Dec 1790;
    his wife Margaret **DRYDEN**, b. 1718, d. 3 Dec 1790; children:
    James, b. 1745; Rev. James Murdoch, as this boy became, was drowned
        in the Musquodoboit River, 21 Nov 1799.
    Elizabeth, b. ca. 1748 [married Matthew **FRAME**]
    two others
        (Horton, NS)

NICHOLSON, William, Ulster; his wife and family of four
    (Londonderry, NS)

PARK(S), Matthew, County Antrim; his wife Mary; children:
    James, b. 1747, d. 25 Jan 1843 at Port Medway, NS
    John
    William
PARK(S), James, County Antrim; his wife Jane; children:
    James
    William, b. 1752, d. 12 Nov 1838 at Lunenburg, NS
    Rebecca
    John
    Robert, d. 1818 at Lunenburg, NS
    Joseph, d. 1814 at New Dublin, NS
    Jane
    Thomas
        (New Dublin, NS)

QUIGLEY, William, Ulster; his wife Elizabeth
    (Granville, NS)

REED, Francis, Ulster; his wife and family of four
(Londonderry, NS)

ROBERTS, James, Ulster, d. 1808/09 at Amherst, NS
(Amherst, NS)

SHARP, Mathew, Ulster; his wife and five children
(Amherst, NS,)

SIMPSON, John, Ulster; his wife, one son, one daughter
(Amherst, NS)

SIMPSON, John, Ulster
(Falmouth, NS)

SMITH, John, miller, b. 2 Feb 1723 Londonderry, d. 23 Apr 1806, son of
William and Jane (**GRIFFITH**) **SMITH**; his [second] wife Isabella,
b. 16 June 1741, d. 8 Dec 1829, dau of Rev. **HOLMES**, Templemore;
children (older ones by his first wife, Martha, m. 9 Jan 1743, d. 1758, dau of
Richard **MORRIS**):
Jane, b. ca. 1748
Alice
William
Margaret
Richard
Rebecca
Elizabeth
Joshua
Mary
Elizabeth [2nd]
(Newport, NS)

STARK, John, Ulster; his wife and four others
(Granville, NS)

WADE, Philip, b. 1748 Ulster, d. 13 Mar 1836
(Gagetown, NB)

WILSON, Claude, weaver, Ulster, d. 1800 at Londonderry, NS
(Londonderry, NS)

WILSON, William, Ulster; wife and two children; one other
(Londonderry, NS)

(177 people in the *Hopewell* or the *Falls* in 1766)

ARRIVED BY SHIPS UNKNOWN (Pre-1773)

The people listed below reached the region before 1775. Tonge was an officer at the capture and occupation of Louisbourg, 1745-1749, and remained in Nova Scotia. James Roche served the garrison at Annapolis Royal as an artificer, perhaps for several years before 1749. Lawrence Kavanagh was a merchant trader in Cape Breton following the British conquest in 1758 and probably came out in his own vessel. The others arrived from Ireland by various unknown ships over the period between 1749 and 1775. With the foregoing list, Irish arrivals adding up to 632 souls are included, together with the year of their earliest known appearance in the Maritimes.

1745   **TONGE**, Winckworth, naval officer at siege and occupation of Louisbourg
b. 4 Feb 1728 Wexford, d. 7 Feb 1792 at Halifax, NS
(Cumberland, NS)

by 1749   **ROCHE**, James, artificer, Limerick, d. 1752; his wife; children:
James
Thomas
(Annapolis Royal, NS)

by 1750   **FITZGERALD**, James; his wife Mary
(Halifax, NS)

by 1752   **FITZPATRICK**, Terence, blacksmith, d. 1774 age 46
(Halifax, NS)

by 1752   **HEFFERNAN**, Dennis, cooper; his wife Mary
(Halifax, NS)

by 1752   **MURPHY**, John, farmer, b. 1712 Ireland, d. 7 Oct 1802; his wife Mary
(Halifax, NS)

by 1754   **CRONEEN**, Thomas, b. Ireland
(Halifax, NS)

1754   **MULLOWNEY**, John, b. ca. 1725 Ireland, to NS 1754, to Philadelphia 1764,
to Britain 1773, back to Halifax in Sep 1775; his wife
Margaret **SMITH**, b. ca. 1729 Ireland
(Halifax, NS)

by 1758   **NEAL**, Henry, cooper, County Kilkenny, d. 1773
(Halifax and Chester, NS)

by 1759   **HEAD**, Michael. surgeon, b. ca. 1741 Waterford or Dublin, d. 1 June 1805
(Chignecto, then Halifax, NS)

ca. 1759   **RYAN**, Daniel, b. ca. 1741 Ireland, d. Oct 1804
(Cumberland, NS)

ca. 1760   **FENERTY**, William, b. ca. 1735 Connaught, d. 21 June 1816
(Sackville, NS)

by 1760   **NEGUS**, William, cooper, b. ca. 1719 Ireland, d. 22 Oct 1777; his wife
Elizabeth **DOHERTY**, b. ca. 1730 Ireland, married 19 Nov 1760 in NS
(Chester, NS)

by 1760   **SHEY**, William, Ulster, lost at sea, 1772;
also his brother, Peter, b. 1748 Ulster, d. 7 Sep 1818
(Newport, NS)

by 1761   **KAVANAGH**, Lawrence, trader, Waterford, d. 1774 in a shipwreck
            wife Margaret **FARRELL**, Waterford
            son James, b. 1756 Waterford, d. 1804 Halifax
            (Louisbourg and St. Peters, NS, 3 people; probably others)

by 1761   **LYNCH**, Timothy, blacksmith, b. ca. 1735 Ireland, d. 1796;
            wife, Bridget **BUCKLEY**, b. ca. 1739 Ireland, married 29 Sep 1761 in NS
            (Chester, NS)

by 1761   **MURPHY**, Timothy, b. 1731 Ireland, d. 10 Apr 1797; his wife Ann **ORR**,
            b. 1735 Ireland, married 29 Nov 1761; widow of Jeremiah **CONNER**, Halifax

by 1762   **RILEY**, James, fisherman, b. ca. 1735 Ireland
            (Blandford, NS)

by 1763   **CULLERTON**, James, b. 1726 southern Ireland, d. 1 Dec 1801; his wife
            Ann **ROACH**, b. 1742 Ireland, married 18 May 1763 at Halifax, NS.
            (Halifax, NS)

by 1765   **COCHRAN**, George, Ulster; his wife
            Elizabeth 'Betsy' **SMITH**, b. 1739, d. 24 Nov 1826 at Newport, NS
            (Londonderry and Newport, NS)

by 1765   **PHEALON**, Edmund, Sr., b. ca. 1727 Waterford or Kilkenny, d. 2 Jan 1802
            PHEALON, Thomas, b. 1729, d. 11 Feb 1784, his brother
            Thomas's wife Alicia, b. 1739, d. 23 Nov 1810; children:
            Edmund, Jr., d. 1796
            Patrick
            Alicia
             Margaret
            (Halifax, NS)

by 1765   **PORTER**, Patrick, Ulster; his wife; children:
            Jane
            Ellen
            William
            Robert
            (New Dublin, NS)

by 1767   **DILL**, David, b. 1735 Springfield, Parish of Clondavaddog, County Donegal,
            d. 25 Jan 1816 at Windsor, NS; also his brothers or half-brothers:
            DILL, Mungo, b. 1760, d. May 1843 at Windsor, NS
            DILL, John
            (Windsor, NS)

by 1767   **LACEY**, Richard, b. ca. 1740 Ireland, d. 30 Oct 1772
            (Chester, NS)

by 1768   **ALLISON**, James, b. 1743 County Londonderry, d. 1820 at Windsor, NS
            (Windsor, NS)

by 1768   **SHERLOCK**, Foster, b. 1749 Waterford, d. 12 Apr 1811 at Manchester, NS
        His brother George William, d. 1816
        (Halifax and Guysborough, NS)

by 1768   **SMITH**, Caleb, b. 1724 Mountmellick, Co. Leix, son of William and Jane
        (**GRIFFITH**); his wife Catherine **REYNOLDS**; children:
        John A., b. 1762
        Margaret
        (Falmouth, NS)

ca. 1769   **CUNNINGHAM** brothers from County Roscommon:
        John, b. ca. 1745
        Richard, b. 1748, d. 20 Oct 1823 at Antigonish, NS
        Michael, b. 19 Feb 1756, d. 1 Aug 1815 at Antigonish, NS
        (Halifax and Antigonish, NS)
Their ship, bound for Philadelphia, was wrecked on Sable Island.

1769   **ALLISON**, Joseph, b. 1720, Drumnaha, Londonderry, d. 21 Nov 1795; his wife
        Alice **POLK**, widow **CALDWELL**, d. 23 July 1808 at Grand Pré, NS;
        children:
        Rebecca, b. 1751, d. 1842
        William, b. 1753, d. 23 May 1831
        John, b. 1753, d.1 Mar 1821
        Joseph, b. 1755, d. 23 Nov 1806
        James, b. 1765, d. 7 Mar 1849
        Nancy, b. 1768, d. 27 Oct 1858
        (Horton, NS)
Their ship, bound for Philadelphia, was wrecked on Sable Island.

1769   **HUNTER**, David, b. Aghadowey, County Londonderry; his wife
        Margaret, dau of Lodowick **MARTIN**; possibly a child or two
        (Hants County, NS)
Their ship, bound for Philadelphia, was wrecked on Sable Island.

1769   **McHEFFEY**, Richard, b. 1733 Ulster, d. 26 Jan 1790; his wife Mary **CAULFIELD**;
        children:
        Robert, b. 22 Feb 1758, d. 20 Nov 1838 at Windsor, NS
        Daniel, b. 19 Feb 1763
        William, b. 10 Aug 1765
        (Windsor, NS)
Their ship, bound for Philadelphia, was wrecked on Sable Island.

ca. 1769   **FRAME**, Matthew, b. 1748, d. 24 May 1830, son of Archibald and Mary
        (**CROWE**) **FRAME**, Castlefinn, County Donegal
        (Shubenacadie, NS)

1769   **McCORMICK**, Samuel, b. 1741, d. 12 June 1823, son of Hugh and Mary
        (**McDONOUGH**) Ulster to Halifax, NS, from a ship bound to Philadelphia
        (Annapolis County)
His ship, bound for Philadelphia, was wrecked on Sable Island.

1769   **WALLACE**, John, b. 1737 County Donegal, d. 18 Jan 1835
            (Albert County, NB)

by 1770   **NORWOOD**, William, b. ca. 1725 County Cork, d. 27 Dec 1795
            wife Sarah, b. 1723 County Cork, d. Jan 1787; children:
            Susannah, b. ca. 1750, d. 18 Mar 1825
            Mary, b. ca. 1755
            Edward, b. ca. 1759, d. 31 Jan 1817
            Winckworth, b. ca. 1764, d. 30 Aug 1821
            Charity, b. ca. 1766, d. 22 May 1839
            (Chignecto and Halifax, NS)

1771   **HAMILTON**, Robert, b. 8 Nov 1734 County Armagh, d. Dec 1814; his wife
            Agnes **FERGUSON**, b. 5 Mar 1739 County Armagh, d. Mar 1835; children:
            William, b. 18 Dec 1758
            Mary, b. 21 Jan 1761
            Margaret, b. 4 Oct 1763
            Robert, b. 16 Feb 1765
            John, b. 31 July 1768
            Archibald, b. 19 Mar 1771 on the passage out
            (Upper Stewiacke, NS; came either in the *Hopewell* or the *Nancy* in 1771)

by 1773   **DILL**, Robert, b. 1740 County Donegal, d. April 1812
            (Londonderry, NS)

(193 people)

A number of other northern Irish families settled in Nova Scotia before 1773, but were not directly out from Ireland. Most had lived for a few years or even a generation or two in New England before taking up the land grants being offered by the government to entice Protestant settlers to take up lands vacated by the expelled Acadian population. The prevalent opinion in official circles at the time was that Protestant inhabitants would be loyal subjects. The wisdom of that assumption was severely tested during the opening years of the American Revolutionary War when some settlers rebelled and attempted to seize Fort Cumberland situated on the Isthmus of Chignecto, where Nova Scotia and New Brunswick meet. Others, notably in the townships at the head of Minas Basin where many of the Ulster Irish had been granted land, refused to sign an oath of allegiance.[2]

Some family names of the New England Irish coming into the province between 1760 and 1773 were Archibald, Blair, Caldwell, Denson, Dickey, Dunlap, Fisher, Lynds, McCabe, McGee, McKeen, McNutt, Manning, Miller and Taylor. Several descendants of these families have been prominent in the public life and professions of the region and beyond.

---

[2] There is a useful chapter, "Response to Revolution" in Gordon Stewart and George Rawlyk, *A People Highly Favoured of God; The Nova Scotia Yankees and the American Revolution* (Toronto: Macmillan of Canada, 1972), pp. 45 - 62. A more recent work gives further detail. - cf., Carol Campbell and James F. Smith, *Necessaries and Sufficiencies; Planter Society in Londonderry, Onslow and Truro Townships, 1761 - 1780* (Sydney: Cape Breton University Press, 2011), chapters 18 and 19. See page 2, n.8 (above) for other instances of pro-revolutionary sentiment among the Ulster and New England settlers in 1775 - 1777.

APPENDIX III - IRISH EMIGRANT PETITIONERS FOR LAND IN NOVA SCOTIA

No ship from Ireland is recorded as having left Irish emigrants in Nova Scotia or Cape Breton between 1790 and 1812. The *Polly* (1799) had just nine passengers and they all went to Québec. In 1812 two vessels, the *Margaret* and the *Prudence*, were bound for New York but were captured by the Royal Navy at the onset of the War of 1812 and brought into Halifax. A few people from these ships remained in Nova Scotia, though most did not. Irish people reaching the province between 1813 and 1815 are among those for whom no information exists to indicate the vessel in which they came or from what port they had sailed. Yet, Irish people reached the province during that period, according to information contained in petitions for land grants filed between 1808 and 1830.[1] One hundred and thirty-two petitioners in 125 petitions covering at least 430 people offer a representative sample. The petitioners all identified themselves as being Irish and stated the length of time they had been in the province. These, and people like them, represent the many for whom we lack not only passenger lists, but even the names of the vessels that brought them. Years are necessaily approximate.

Arrived 1792 - 1802

BOOTH, John, Windsor, Hants Co., in 1812 had wife, 3 children, here 14 years [1797/98]

BURK, Richard, Salmon River, Guysborough, age 63 in 1819, emigrated in 1796[2]

CALLAGHAN, Owen, Chester Road, with wife, 6 children in 1821, here 24 years [1796/97][3]

CARROLL, Patrick, Shubenacadie in 1811, here 16 years [1794/95][4]

CARROLL, William, in 1813 had been here 17 years via Newfoundland [1795/96]

CASEY, Jeremiah, Cumberland Co., with wife, 7 children in 1817, here 20 years [1796/97][5]

CATON, Patrick, west side, Grand Lake, in 1817 had wife, 6 children, here 17 years [1799/1800][6]

CLANCEY, Pierce, Halifax, in 1811 had been here for 18 years [1792/93]

CONNEL, Jeremiah, Lunenburg, in March 1814 had wife, 4 children, here 17 years [1796][7]

---

[1] NSA, RG 20, Series "A".

[2] "Record" **BURK** headed a household of 7 at Guysborough in 1817 (census).

[3] Owen **CALLAHAN** married 4/5 Dec 1805 at Chester, NS, Anne Margaret, dau of George and Elizabeth **COLLICUTT**, Chester, and had 6 children born at Chester (township record): Charles (b. 17 May 1803), Elizabeth (b. 25 Sep 1806), Eleanor (b. 8 Feb 1809), Daniel (b. 7 June 1811), Allen Tupper (b. 10 July 1813), and Thomas (b. 22 Apr 1817).

[4] Patrick and Anne (**LANGILLE**) **CARROLL**, Shubenacadie, had 5 children baptised at St. Peter's Catholic Church, Halifax, NS: Michael (7 Sep 1824, age 7 years), James (1 Feb 1821), Matthew (8 July 1823), Edward (20 July 1825), and Terence (12 Aug 1827).

[5] Jeremiah **CASEY**, Catholic, farmer, headed a family of 6 males and 4 females at Nappan, Cumberland County - 1827 census. Casey was among the first grantees at West Leicester, Cumberland County, in 1817.

[6] Patrick, son of Thomas and Mary (**WALSH**) **CATON** [KEATING], Co. Wexford, married 18 Oct 1810, Alice Elizabeth, dau of Michael and Eleanor **BUTLER**, Co. Kilkenny - St. Peter's Catholic Church, Halifax, NS. Patrick died 18 Aug 1818 at Halifax, age 38. Alice died 24 Aug 1824 at Halifax, age 33.

[7] Jeremiah and Ann (**CROKER**) **CONNELL** had a son baptised at St. Peter's Catholic Church, Halifax, NS: Joseph (21 July 1809).

CONNELLY, Patrick, Windsor, Hants Co., in 1813 had 4 children, here 15 years [1797/98][8]
CONNER, Dennis, barber, Halifax, in 1816 had wife, 2 daughters, here 20 years [1796][9]
COSTIGAN, John, in 1814 had a wife, here 14 years [1799/1800][10]
COYLEY [KILEY], Lawrence, fisherman, Prospect, in 1814 had wife, 3 sons, here 14 years via
      Newfoundland [1799/1800]
CUTTS, Michael, St. Margarets Bay, Halifax Co., in 1807 had wife and a child, emigrated in 1800
DEALY, Patrick, Baddeck River, Cape Breton, age 60 in 1826, bachelor, here 24 years [1801/02]
DIGGINS, Thomas, Gut of Canso, age 40 in 1821, here 25 years [1795/96][11]
DOYLE, James, blacksmith, Rawdon, Hants Co., in 1808 had wife, 5 children, here 7 years [1800/01][12]
DOYLE, John, blacksmith, Rawdon, in 1808 had wife, 4 children, here 13 years [1794/95][13]
DULHANTY, Richard, trader, Halifax, in 1813 had wife and family, here 14 years [1798/99]
DWYER, Cornelius, Onslow/River John, in 1809 had wife, 3 children, here 7 years [1801/02]
ENGLISH, John, Halifax, in 1813 had wife, 4 children, here 13 years [1799/1800][14]
FITZGERALD, Michael, fisherman, Portuguese Cove, in 1810 had wife, 4 children, here 1797[15]
FITZMAURICE, John, Windsor Road, Halifax Co., in 1813 had wife, 7 children, here 22 years [1791][16]
FITZPATRICK, James, Pictou, in 1809 had wife, 3 children, here in 1802

---

[8] Patrick, surgeon, son of Felix and Mary (**QUINN**) **CONNELLY** of Co. Tyrone, married 19 Oct 1808, Mary Catherine, dau of Dr. James and Mary (**MAGRATH**) **CALDWELL**, Harbour Grace, NL - St. Peter's Catholic Church, Halifax, NS.

[9] Denis **CONNER** married 13 June 1809, Anne **BARTLING** - St. Paul's Anglican Church, Halifax. Their 2 daughters were baptised in that church: Julie Ann (11 June 1810); Matilda Elizabeth (5 July 1812).

[10] John and Jane (**DICKENS**) **COSTIGAN** had two sons baptised at St. Peter's Catholic Church, Halifax, NS: Edward (9 May 1802) and John (8 Apr 1804).

[11] Thomas "**DIGGONS**" headed a household of 7 at Manchester Township in 1817 (census).

[12] James **DOYLE**, Catholic, mechanic, Windsor Road, headed a household of 5 males, 4 females and 1 male servant - 1827 census. He was a native of County Kilkenny.

[13] John, son of Michael and Alice (**MALONEY**) **DOYLE**, Aghaviller, Co. Kilkenny, married 15 Oct 1801, Elizabeth, dau of William and Freelove (**POTTER**) **SMITH**, Newport, NS - St. Peter's Catholic Church, Halifax, NS. They baptised 6 children in that church: Alice (13 July 1803), Michael (1 Feb 1805), John (2 Oct 1808), Stephen (13 July 1811), Donal (20 Nov 1813), and Elizabeth (22 Dec 1815).

[14] John and Anne (**MACKEY**) **ENGLISH**, Hammonds Plains, Halifax County, had 4 children baptised at St. Peter's Catholic Church, Halifax, NS: John (5 Apr 1807), Joseph (29 June 1809), Mary Ann Eliza (8 July 1811), and Eleanor Johanna (14 May 1822). Another child was Mary Anne, born ca. 1818. John English, Anglican, farmer, Hammonds Plains, headed a family of 2 males and 3 females - 1827 census. John **ENGLISH** was a native of Clonmel, County Tipperary.

[15] Michael and Charlotte (**PENNELL**) **FITZGERALD** had a son, Matthew, baptised 22 Dec 1803 at St. Peter's Catholic Church, Halifax, NS.

[16] John, son of John and Mary (**O'KEEFF**) **FITZMAURICE**, Monagay Parish, Co. Limerick, married 22 Jan 1801, Mary, dau of Armistead **FIELDING**, Windsor Road, NS - St. Peter's Catholic Church, Halifax, NS. They had 5 children baptised there: James Armistead (28 Mar 1802), Thomas (20 Feb 1804), Maria Elizabeth (5 June 1808), John Charles and William Henry (18 Nov 1810).

GAUBE, David, near Windsor, Hants Co., in 1812 had been here 15 years [1796/97]
GRADY, James, Dartmouth, in 1810 had wife, 6 children, here 11 years [1798/99][17]
HOGAN, James, Windsor Road, in 1813 had wife, 4 children, here 14 years [1798/99][18]
HOLLEY, Dennis, Windsor, Hants Co., in 1812 had wife, 4 children, here 14 years [1797/98]
JADIS, Charles, Windsor, Hants Co., in 1809 had wife, 2 children, emigrated in 1801[19]
JOHNSON, John, Onslow Township, Colchester District in 1815, emigrated in 1800
KELLY, William, Antigonish, in 1817 had wife, 6 children, out from Waterford 23 years [1793/94][20]
KEOUGH, Thomas, Halifax Co., in 1809 had wife, 6 children, here 9 years [1799/1800][21]
LAMEY, James, Cape Breton Island in 1810, out via Newfoundland in 1798
LOCKMAN, Thomas, River Inhabitants, age 48 in 1821 with wife, 8 children, here 22 years [1799]
LOMBARD, William, Tatamagouche, Colchester District, in 1818 had wife, 3 children, here in 1799
LONG, William, Windsor-Chester Road, in 1810 had wife, 4 children, here 12 years [1797/98]
McMAIN, James, Musquodoboit District, in 1818 had wife, 3 children, here 17 years [1800/01]
McQUILKIN, Henry, in 1808 had wife, 5 children, emigrated from County Down in 1802[22]
MORISEY, David, in 1813 had been here 17 years [1792/93]
MURRAY, Richard, Stewiacke River, 1812, had wife, 2 children, here 14 years [1797/98]
NASH, James Dwire, Truro, in 1813 had wife, 5 children, here 11 years [1801/02][23]
NASH, William, Guysborough, in 1813 had wife, 7 children, here 15 years [1797/98][24]

---

[17] James **GRADY**, Chezzetcook, NS, and his wife Jane, dau of Alexander and Margaret (**ROBERTSON**) **NELSON**, Colchester County, NS, had 6 children baptised at St. Peter's Catholic Church, Halifax: John (27 Nov 1804), James (13 Nov 1806), William (9 Oct 1808), Jane (20 Sep 1810), Edward (12 June 1813), and Joshua James (7/10 Feb 1816). James "Gready", Catholic, farmer, headed a family of 3 males and 3 females at Chezzetcook, Halifax County - 1827 census.

[18] James, farmer, and Catherine (**PREEPER**) **HOGAN** had 5 children baptised at St. Peter's Catholic Church, Halifax, NS: Patrick (13 Oct 1802), James (20 Sep 1806), Eleanor (29 Mar 1809), Elisa (July 1813), and Bridget (17 July 1816).

[19] Charles **JADIS**, Esq., married 24 July 1802, Sarah, youngest dau of Peter **HALL**, Windsor, NS - *Nova Scotia Royal Gazette*, 29 July 1802.

[20] William **KELLY** was a native of the Parish of Ballygunner, County Waterford.

[21] Thomas and Sarah (**CASSIDY**) **KEHOE** had 6 children baptised at St. Peter's Catholic Church, Halifax, NS: Mary (5 Dec 1801), Sarah (12 Feb 1805), James and Thomas (26 Oct 1806), George (13 Nov 1808), and Patrick (20 Jan 1811).

[22] Henry **McQUILKIN** appears to have returned to Ireland between 1799 and 1802. He married (1) 27 Sep 1794, Charlotte **HOLMAN**, and (2) 4 Aug 1823, Mrs. Isabella **MACKEY**, both marriages at St. Paul's Anglican Church, Halifax. He died in July 1824 - *Acadian Recorder*, 31 July 1824. He had 5 children baptised at St. Paul's: Henry (8 May 1797), Hannah Maria (28 June 1799), Jane Cochran (3 Dec 1814, age 10 years), Isabella Hill (3 Dec 1814, age 5½ years), and Mary (27 July 1821, age 18½ years).

[23] James D. **NASH** married 15 Aug 1805 at Truro, Sarah **HUGH[E]S**.

[24] William **NASH** married 1 Oct 1799 at Guysborough, Eliza, dau of Samuel and Elizabeth **AIKINS**. Nash died ca. 1816, as Widow Nash headed a household of eight at Manchester Township in 1817 (census). By 1819 she had married Daniel **OATS**, whose petition that year states that he had come from Ireland in 1816, and mentions all the children: Ellen, 19, John, 16, Thomas, 14, William, 12, Eliza, 10, Tobias, 8, Catherine, 6, Robert, 4, all surnamed **NASH**, and Maria **OATS**, 1.

NIXON, James, Douglas, Hants Co., in 1813 a single man, here "15 or 16 years" [1797/98]
O'CONNOR, Michael, Yarmouth, in 1808 had wife, 6 small children, here 7 years [1800/01]
POWER, Edmund, Halifax, in 1813 had wife, 2 children, here 15 years [1797/98][25]
PURCELL, Patrick, fish dealer, Upper Prospect, Halifax Co., in 1816 had been here 25 years [1791][26]
REDDEN, James, Windsor Township, in 1820 had wife, 11 children, here 25 years [1794/95]
SKERRY, John, Dartmouth, ferryman, in 1816 had been here 18 years [1797/98][27]
SLATTERY, James, Louisbourg, Cape Breton, age 25, in 1811 here for 17 years [1793/94]
STAPLETON, Michael, Canso, Guysborough, in 1815 had been here 16 years [1798/99][28]
SULLIVAN, Patrick, Halifax, with wife, 2 children in 1817 had been here 20 years [1796/97][29]
TOBIN, James, Sydney County, in 1810 had been here 9 years [1800/01]
TOBIN, Thomas, grocer, Halifax, in 1813 had wife, 4 children, here 18 years [1794/95][30]

Arrived 1803 - 1812

BYRNE, Owen, Tracadie, Antigonish, age 18 in 1807, by 1821 had been here 14 years [1807]
BYRON, Michael, trader, Halifax, in 1819 was 36 years old, here 9 years [1809/10][31]
CASEY, John, Port Pisway [Petpeswick], in 1812 had wife, 6 children, here 15 months [1810/11]
CLEARY, Peter, in 1812 had been here 6 years [1805/06]
CURTIS, William, Stewiacke, Colchester District, in 1810 had been here 2½ years [1807/08][32]

---

[25] Edmund, son of Thomas and Margaret (**LARKIN**) **POWER**, Ringagonagh Parish, Co. Waterford, married 30 June 1803, Mary, dau of Luke and Catherine (**MORRISY**) **MCGRAH**, Ross, Co. Wexford, widow of Thomas **WATSON** - St. Peter's Catholic Church, Halifax, NS.

[26] Patrick and Mary (**MARTIN**) **PURCELL** had 6 children baptised at St. Peter's Catholic Church, Halifax, NS: Patrick (1 Oct 1803), Johanna (12 Dec 1805), Eleanor (7 July 1808), Thomas (22 Dec 1809), Philip (3 Jan 1813), and William (10 Mar 1818). Patrick Purcell, Jr., Catholic, fisherman, Upper Prospect, headed a household of 1 male and 1 female, while Patrick Purcell, Catholic, farmer, Upper Prospect, had a household of 5 males, 2 females, 1 male servant and 1 female servant - 1827 census.

[27] John, son of Luke and Mary (**LARISSY**) **SKERRY**, Knocktopher, Co. Kilkenny, widower of Bridget **SHEA**, married 28 May 1807, Maria, dau of Capt. Martin and Maria (**BATCHELOR**) **MEAGHER**, Jeddore, NS. Their dau Mary was baptised 26 Apr 1809 - St. Peter's Catholic Church, Halifax, NS. She died in infancy. John Skerry, Catholic farmer, Dartmouth, had a household of 2 males, 1 female, 6 male servants, and 4 female servants - 1827 census. John died 1 Sep 1838, age 74, at Dartmouth, NS.

[28] Michael, son of Thomas and Bridget (**RYAN**) **STAPLETON**, Co. Tipperary, married 9 Aug 1811, Anne, dau of Colin and Mary (**MEAHER**) **McNERE**, Manchester, NS - St. Peter's Catholic Church, Halifax. Michael "Stappleton" headed a household of seven at the Gut of Canso in 1817 (census).

[29] Patrick, son of Denis and Catherine (**MURPHY**) **SULLIVAN**, Co. Kerry, married 17 Sep 1813, Catherine, dau of Nicholas and Alice (**LONG**) **MURRAY**, Co. Wexford. - St. Peter's Catholic Church, Halifax, NS. They had two daughters baptised there: Margaret (30 Aug 1814) and Catherine (29 Oct 1815).

[30] Thomas and Catherine (**SHORTIS**) **TOBIN** had a daughter baptised at St. Peter's Catholic Church, Halifax, NS: Mary Anne (21 May 1803).

[31] Michael, son of Richard and Ann (**HEATON**) **BYRON** of Dublin, married on 15 Feb 1810, Ann, dau of John and Catherine (**SIMMONDS**) **COUSINS** of England - St. Peter's Catholic Church, Halifax, NS. Michael Byron died 26 Aug 1848 in Halifax, age 67.

[32] William **CURTIS** was a native of the City of Cork.

DELANEY, Timothy, East River of Pictou, in 1808 was recently married and here 3 years [1804/05][33]
DOYLE, Patrick, in 1813 had a wife and had been here 3 years [1809/10]
DREW, Daniel, Mabou River, Cape Breton, age 32 in 1810 and had been here 5 years [1804/05][34]
DUGGAN, John, Dartmouth, in 1810 had a wife and family, and had been here 2 years [1807/08]
DWYER, Patrick, Dorchester, Guysborough, in 1813 had been here 8 years [1804/05][35]
ENGLISH, Patrick, East River of Pictou in 1819, emigrated in 1811
FENNELL, Thomas, Antigonish, in 1817 age 26 with a wife, had been here 8 years [1808/09][36]
FULTON, John, Economy, Colchester District, by 1816 had been here 8 years [1807/08]
       His nephews, James and Samuel **LONG**, emigrated in 1815 to join him
GIBBS, John, Petite Riviere, Lunenburg Co., age 28 in 1821 and had been here 10 years [1810/11][37]
GLENN, Thomas, Guysborough in 1829, emigrated in 1807[38]
GRAHAM, John, Parrsboro, in 1815 was 48, with wife, 9 children, here 2 years [1812/13]
GRAY, Samuel, Mabou River, Cape Breton, in 1816, emigrated in 1809
HARRISON, Robert, Pugwash, Cumberland Co., in 1830 was 27, and here 22 years [1807/08][39]
HATTON, Henry, merchant, and Robert, attorney, Pictou in 1816, emigrated in 1812[40]
HATTON, James, New Lairg, Pictou, in 1815 had been here 2 years [1812/13]
HEALEY, John, Musquodoboit, in 1821 had wife and family, here 16 years [1804/05]
HENDERSON, John, Musquodoboit, born 1768, with wife, 4 children; Samuel Henderson, born 1773;
       Jean Henderson, with 4 children; Robert **IRVINE**, born 1762, with wife, 3 children; and George
       BELL, born 1765, with wife and a child, emigrated from County Antrim in July 1812[41]
JOHNSON, William, Manchester, Guysborough, age 43 in 1829, here 25 years [1803/04]
KEENAN, Dennis, Cape George, Antigonish, in 1816, emigrated in 1810

---

[33] Timothy **DELANEY** was a native of County Kilkenny.

[34] Daniel **DREW**, a native of County Wexford, died 9 Sep 1829 at Mabou, NS, age 75.

[35] Patrick "**DWYRE**" headed a household of 7 at Antigonish in 1817 (census).
He was a native of County Waterford.

[36] Thomas, son of Thomas and Elizabeth (**BUTLER**) **FENNELL**, Co. Tipperary, married
21 Apr 1814, Eleanor, dau of Michael and Alice **FLEMING**, Halifax - St. Peter's Catholic Church,
Halifax, NS. Their son James was baptised in that church, 21 Oct 1810, when one day old.

[37] John **GIBBS** married 18 Dec 1821 at Petite Riviere, Ruth **PARKS**
- *Acadian Recorder*, 29 Dec 1821.

[38] Thomas **GLENN** married 18 Oct 1808, Mary **McKENZIE** - Christchurch Anglican,
Guysborough.

[39] Robert **HARRISON**, carpenter, Presbyterian, headed a household of 1 male and 4 females
at Wallace, Cumberland County - 1827 census. Robert was a son of Thomas Harrison, who emigrated
from County Sligo with his wife and 6 children about 1807.

[40] Robert **HATTON** was a native of Gorey, County Wexford. Henry was his eldest son. They
emigrated to Prince Edward Island in 1812 and crossed to Pictou the following year

[41] Samuel **HENDERSON** married 23 Oct 1817, Jean **McDORMOND** - by Col. Purdy, J.P.,
Cumberland County, NS. Samuel Henderson, farmer, Presbyterian, one male; John Henderson,
Presbyterian, farmer, 2 males and 2 females; John **HENDERSON** died 20 July 1852 at Middle
Musquodoboit, in his 85th year (headstone).

LYNCH, Matthew, Fergusons Cove, Halifax Co., in 1818 had 5 children, here 15 years [1802][42]
McCABE, James, in 1812 had been here 4 years [1807/08]
McCONNELL, Peter, Liscomb, age 24, had wife and child by 1814, from Belfast in 1810/11[43]
McDADE, Charles, Cumberland Co., age 20, emigrated 6 months before [1812]
McKIM, Andrew, Cumberland Co., in 1809 had wife, 4 small children, here 5 years [1801/02][44]
McKIMM, Thomas, Londonderry, Colchester, 1814, out from north of Ireland 8 years ago [sic][45]
MAHAR, Thomas, butcher, River John, Pictou, in 1812, here 2 years [1809/10]
MEAGHER, Thomas, Cape John, Pictou, 1809, here last year after 6 years in Newfoundland [1808]
MOORE, John, Musquodoboit River, Halifax Co., 1818, here 6 years [1811/12]
MULCAHY, John, shoemaker, Petite Riviere, Lunenburg Co., single, 28/29 in 1823, here 12 years [1810/11]
NOWLAN, James K., New Dublin, Lunenburg Co., 1818, here 7 years [1810/11]
O'BRIEN, John, Havre Boucher, Antigonish, 1823, had wife, 10 children, emigrated in 1802
OLIVER, Francis, mason, Sydney, Cape Breton, 38 in 1825, here 14 years [1810/11]
O'MALLEY, John, farmer, Musquodoboit, 1813, had wife, 3 children, here 3 years [1809/10]
PATTERSON, Samuel, Musquodoboit, age 24 in 1815, had wife and child, from Donegal in 1812
ROACH, John, St. Marys River, Guysborough, 1817, had wife, 3 children, here 9 years [1807/08]
SHEA, James, Upper Prospect, Halifax Co., 35 in 1816, married, here 13 years [1802/03][46]
SHEA, Walter, Antigonish, 48 in 1818, had wife, 8 children, here 8 years [1809/10][47]
SKERRY, James, Dartmouth, 1816, here 10 years [1805/06][48]
STACK, James, Pictou, 1811, here 7 years [1803/04][49]

---

[42] Matthew and Mary (**QUINTAN**) **LYNCH** had 4 children baptised at St. Peter's Catholic Church, Halifax, NS: Michael (21 Nov 1802), John (17 Feb 1806), Bridget (Apr 1813), and Mary (9 June 1816). Matthew Lynch was buried from that church, 26 Feb 1826, age 73. Mary Lynch, widow, Catholic, fishing, Fergusons Cove, headed a household of 3 males, 4 females and a male servant - 1827 census.

[43] Peter **McCONNELL** married 9 Feb 1813 at St. Marys River, Experience **MILLS**.

[44] Andrew **McKIM**, Baptist, farmer, Wallace, Cumberland County, headed a household of 4 males and 9 females - 1827 census.

[45] Thomas **McKIM** was here more than eight years by 1814, since he married Mary **DILL** in the Presbyterian Church, Londonderry, NS, on 11 Mar 1802.

[46] James **SHEA**, Catholic, fisherman, Upper Prospect, headed a household of 2 males, 1 female, 1 male servant - 1827 census.

[47] Walter **SHEA** was a native of County Tipperary who emigrated to St. John's, Newfoundland, and about 1800 to Parrsboro, Nova Scotia, from where he moved to Antigonish about 1810. He had four daughters and three sons: Thomas (Halifax, NS), John (San Bernardino, CA), and Maurice (Chicago) - D. J. Rankin, *A History of the County of Antigonish, Nova Scotia* (Toronto, 1929), pp. 357 - 359.

[48] James was a younger brother of John Skerry from Knocktopher, Co. Kilkenny. James and Barbara (**BOWDEN**) **SKERRY**, Lake William, Halifax County, had 8 children baptised at St. Peter's Catholic Church, Halifax, NS: John (3 Dec 1812), Catherine (25 Jan 1815), James (3 Apr 1817), William (13 Dec 1819), Mary (16 Apr 1822), David (2 Aug 1824), Barbara (13 Aug 1827), and Michael (21 Jan 1829).

[49] James, son of Michael and Margaret (**DAILY**) **STACK**, Tralee, Co. Kerry, married 2 June 1813, Ellen, dau of Thomas and Mary (**SCANNEL**) **KEEFE**, Castlelyons, Co. Cork - St. Peter's Catholic Church, Halifax, NS. They had two sons baptised there: Michael (3 May 1814, buried 12 July 1816) and Thomas (20 May 1817).

SULLIVAN, John H., merchant, Sissiboo, Digby, 1813, emigrated in 1811
THOMPSON, Thomas, Pugwash Harbour, Cumberland Co., 1817, married, here 10 years [1806/07]
WREN, William, Chezzetcook, Halifax Co., 1813, here 8 years [1804/05]

<u>Arrived 1813 - 1815</u>

BURKE, Nicholas, Antigonish, 22 in 1818, here 4 years [1813/14]
BYRNE, Timothy, Halifax County, 1819, emigrated in 1815
DALY, Laurence, Antigonish, 25 in 1818, here 4 years [1813/14]
DAVEY, James, Digby Neck, 30 in 1825, had wife, 2 children, here 10 years [1814/15]
DELANY, Michael, Antigonish, 21 in 1818, emigrated in 1813
FERGUSON, John, grocer, Musquodoboit, 1821, had wife, 5 children, here 6 years [1814/15][50]
FITZGERALD, William, Pictou, single man in 1818, here 3 years [1814/15]
FLYNN, Edward, Antigonish, 30 in 1818, had wife and family, emigrated in 1813
HENNEBERY, Thomas, Greenfield, Stewiacke, 40 in 1821, from Dungarvan, Waterford, Feb 1815
HENRY, John, Antigonish, 24 in 1817, from north of Ireland 2½ years ago [1814]
KEEFE, John, Antigonish, 21 in 1818, emigrated in 1813
LYNCH, Edward, Pictou, 1818, emigrated in 1815
LYNCH, James, Hants County, 1840, emigrated from County Cork in 1815
McCARTHY, Charles, Pictou, May 1819, here 4 years [1815]
McDADE, John, wife, 2 children; William McDade, single, 1814, from Donegal "last summer" [1813]
McMULLIN, John, Cape Lewis, Antigonish, single man, 1814, "recently out" [1813/14]
MANNIX, John, Lake Ainslie, Cape Breton, 1819, emigrated in 1813
MARTIN, Peter and John, Gut of Canso, 1821, here 6 years [1814/15]
MEAGHER, Edward, Pictou, 1816, emigrated from Waterford in autumn 1815
MOORE, William, Cumberland County, single man, 1814, from Donegal last summer [1813]
MULCAHY, Patrick, Musquodoboit, 1822, had wife, 2 children, here 7 years [1814/15][51]
MULCAHY, Thomas, Musquodoboit, 1822, single man, here 6 years [1815/16][52]
RUSSELL, John, Clam Harbour, Halifax Co., 1824, here 10 years [1813/14][53]
RYAN, Thomas D., Musquodoboit, 25 in 1830, emigrated in 1813
TORPEY, John, Little River, Sydney Co., 32 in 1822, married, here 7 years [1814/15][54]

---

[50] John **FERGUSON**, Presbyterian, farmer, Chezzetcook, headed a family of 3 males, 6 females - 1827 census. John and Christiana (**PENTZ**) **FERGUSON**, Chezzetcook, had their eighth child baptised at St. Paul's Anglican Church, Halifax: Mary Ann Magdalene (11 May 1818).

[51] Patrick **MULCAHY** married 26 Aug 1819, Elizabeth **LYTON** - Christchurch Anglican, Windsor, NS.

[52] Thomas, son of Thomas and Joanna (**FORD**) **MULCAHY**, City of Waterford, married (1st) 31 Aug 1827, Margaret, dau of Patrick and Mary (**RYAN**) **WASHINGTON**, Powerstown, Co. Kilkenny, and had a son John baptised 28 Oct 1829, age 4 months. He married (2nd) 12 May 1836, Judith **MULLALY** of Co. Tipperary - St. Peter's Catholic Church, Halifax, NS. Thomas Mulchahy [sic], manufacturer, Catholic, Chezzetcook, headed a household of 2 males and 3 females - 1827 census.

[53] John and Betsy **RUSSELL**, Clam Harbour, had a son William baptised 6 July 1833 at St. Paul's Anglican Church, Halifax.

[54] The surname Torpey is associated strongly with County Clare in western Ireland.

Arrived 1822 - 1825

A further group of 40 petitioners includes 83 people from Ireland who claim to have arrived between 1822 and 1825. No recorded ships left Irish emigrants in Nova Scotia during the years 1822-23-24, while in 1825 the *Brothers* and the *Resolute* brought only 50 people between them. It appears likely that many petitions were filed in the calendar year *after* their being submitted. If that were the case, two ships arriving in 1821, the *Amicus* out of Cork and the *Rob Roy* from Belfast, landed 237 Irish emigrants at Halifax. Since some of the passengers from those vessels mentioned the ship that brought them, it is probable that many of those named below were among those emigrant shipmates.

BARRY, David, New Annan Road, 23 in 1826, emigrated in 1821/22
BROOKS, Robert, Amherst, Cumberland Co., 1827, emigrated in 1821/22
CAMPBELL, John, Mabou River, 32 in 1835, emigrated before 1823
CARTER, William, Cumberland County, 1829, emigrated 4 years before from Donegal [1824/25]
CASEY, John, Antigonish, 1828, emigrated 3 years before from the north of Ireland [1824/25]
COLEMAN, Walter, Knoydart, Antigonish, 1827, emigrated 3 years before [1823/24]
COLLINS, Joseph, Musquodoboit Valley, 32 in 1824, with wife, 4 children, emigrated in 1823
DAVIS, Patrick, Canso, 30 in 1825, with wife, 1 child, emigrated one year ago [1823/24]
EAGAN, Michael, Guysborough, 40 in 1823, with wife, 4 children, emigrated 6 months ago [1822/23]
FARRELL, Edward, Ohio, Antigonish, 22 in 1822, with wife, 1 child, emigrated 3 months ago [1822]
FLINN, Michael, Guysborough, 25 in 1829, emigrated from Sligo in June 1822[55]
GILLIN, John, Tatamagouche, Colchester, 1825, with wife, emigrated in 1823
HANRAHAN, Patrick, Hallowell Grant, 39 in 1823, with wife, 4 children, here one year [1821/22]
HEFFERNAN, Michael, Tracadie, Antigonish, 24 in 1827, emigrated 4 years before [1822/23]
HODGES, Jonathan, Dalhousie Settlement, Annapolis Co., 1826, with wife and mother, emigrated
      from the south of Ireland 3 years before [1822/23]
JONES, Thomas, Liverpool, Queens Co., 1825, emigrated 3 years before [1821/22][56]
KEARNEY, James and Patrick, Salmon River, 1828, emigrated from 3 to 5 years before [1822/25]
KELLY, Martin, South River, Antigonish, 38 in 1823, with wife, 2 children, arrived Dec 1822
KENNA, Lawrence, South River, Antigonish, 27 in 1822, single man, emigrated in autumn 1822
LACEY, Patrick, Liverpool, Queens Co., 1825, emigrated 3 years before [1821/22]
MADDEN, James, South River, Antigonish, 21 in 1825, single man, emigrated a year ago [1823/24]
MAGUIRE, James, 24, and Patrick, 33, Antigonish, 1825, "out recently" [1824/25]
MONAHAN, Edward, Antigonish-Guysborough Road, 50 in 1822, with wife, 1 child, out July 1822[57]
MOORE, William, River Philip, Cumberland Co., 27 in 1827, had wife, 3 children, out 4 years [1822/23]
MULLIN, James, Gut of Canso, 24 in 1822, "recently out" [1821/22]
MURRAY, James, Antigonish-Guysborough Road, 1822, with wife, 1 child, out 5 months [July 1822]
NOWLAN, Edward, Tracadie, Antigonish, 38 in 1822, with wife, 6 children, emigrated in July 1822
O'BRIEN, Robert, Knoydart, Antigonish, 1827, emigrated 3 years before [1823/24][58]
O'GORMAN, Richard, Guysborough Road, single man, 21 in 1823, out 6 months ago [1821/22]
POWER, James, Mabou River, Cape Breton, 34 in 1823, emigrated a year ago [1821/22]

---

[55] Michael **FLINN** headed a family of three at Melford, Guysborough Co. - 1838 census.

[56] **LACEY** and **JONES** were associated in the petition. Thomas Jones married 4 May 1826, Eliza **MOSER** - St. John's Anglican Church, Lunenburg, NS.

[57] **MURRAY** and **MONAHAN** were associated in the petition.

[58] **O'BRIEN** and **COLEMAN** were associated in the petition.

PURCELL, Edward, Milford Haven, Guysborough, married in NS, 31 in 1826, out one year [1824/25][59]
RACKET, Peter, Tracadie, Antigonish, single man, 26 in 1822, out "recently" [1821/22]
ROCHE, Michael, Manchester, Guysborough, single man, 26 in 1823, out 4 months [1822/23][60]
ROGERS, John and Thomas, Guysborough-Antigonish Road, 1829, emigrated in 1823[61]
RONAN, Peter, Antigonish, 23 in 1824, emigrated 2 years before [1821/22]
RYAN, Michael, Guysborough-Antigonish Road, married, 26 in 1825, emigrated in 1825
TATE, Henry, Guysborough County, 1829, emigrated 5 years before [1823/24][62]
TINNEY, Patrick, Fundy Shore [Minudie], Cumberland Co., 1828, emigrated in 1823
WHEALON, Patrick, Tracadie, Antigonish, single man, 24 in 1825, out 3 years before [1821/22]
WOODLANDS, Richard, Cumberland Co., 1828, emigrated in 1825

APPENDIX IV - EMIGRANTS TO THE MARITIMES IN THE ORDNANCE SURVEY MEMOIRS

In the 1830s a systematic attempt was made to map Ireland. The field officers of the survey were to gather brief descriptions of each parish, including topographic, social and economic information. The series of memoirs proved very expensive and that part of the project had to be abandoned in 1840. Before that happened, field teams had collected considerable material about two counties in particular: Antrim and Londonderry. For the historian of Irish emigration the bonus found among those working notes were lists of about three thousand people who had emigrated from certain parishes between 1833 and 1839. Of these, 244 people left for destinations in Maritime Canada. The great majority were bound to Saint John, New Brunswick, but a few went to St. Andrews, NB, and to Sydney, Nova Scotia. The following list of these is extracted from the work of a team led by Brian Mitchell and published under his name as *Irish Emigration Lists 1833 - 1839* (Baltimore: Genealogical Publishing Company, Inc., 1989).

The most surprising thing about the people listed as going to New Brunswick is that, with a very few possible exceptions, they do not turn up among the passengers named by the records kept at Saint John for 1833-34, 1837-38. However, four vessels brought 870 passengers to Saint John from Londonderry in 1833 and 1834 for which no nominal list of passengers has been preserved, and many of our "missing" emigrants may have traveled in one or other of those.[1] It is equally possible that many of these emigrants left home with the stated intention of going to Saint John or St. Andrews but, upon reaching Londonderry, took ship for another destination. Not all Irish emigrants at that period had an accurate sense of where various cities were situated in America.

---

[59] "Edmund" **PURCELL**, farmer, headed a family of seven at Guysborough - 1838 census.

[60] Michael **ROACH**, merchant, wife, and 2 sons under the age of 6 in Wilmot Township, Guysborough County - 1838 census.

[61] Thomas **ROGERS** married 21 Nov 1828, Jennet **McNAIR** - Anglican Church, Guysborough, NS

[62] Henry **TATE** married 25 Jan 1827 at St. Marys River, Sarah **JORDAIN** - *Acadian Recorder*, 7 Apr 1827. Henry Tate, farmer, his wife and 5 children lived in St. Mary's Township - 1838 census.

---

[1] These vessels were the *Active* and *Ellergill* which arrived in June 1833 with 273 and 321 passengers, respectively, the *Jane Vilet* which brought out 255 people in July 1833, and the *William* with 21 passengers in September 1834.

A) 237 people intending to emigrate to Saint John, New Brunswick, 1833 - 1839

NAME	AGE	TOWNLAND	PARISH	COUNTY	YEAR
ADAMS, Samuel	25	Ballyscullion West	Ballyscullion	Londonderry	1834
Jane	23	Ballyscullion West	Ballyscullion	Londonderry	1834
ANDERSON, David	22	Ar[d]varness	Macosquin	Londonderry	1833
Margaretanne	1	Ar[d]varness	Macosquin	Londonderry	1833
BARR, Samuel	28	Seygorry	Aghadowey	Londonderry	1835
BLACK, Sibby	45	Blind Gate Street	Coleraine	Londonderry	1833
James	17	Blind Gate Street	Coleraine	Londonderry	1833
Stewart	14	Blind Gate Street	Coleraine	Londonderry	1833
Joseph	10	Blind Gate Street	Coleraine	Londonderry	1833
Mary Anne	4	Blind Gate Street	Coleraine	Londonderry	1833
Eliza	3	Blind Gate Street	Coleraine	Londonderry	1833
Robert	3	Blind Gate Street	Coleraine	Londonderry	1833
Matty	1½	Blind Gate Street	Coleraine	Londonderry	1833
BLAIR, William	31	Ballyvernstown	Glynn	Antrim	1839
Jane	30	Ballyvernstown	Glynn	Antrim	1839
William, Jr.	7	Ballyvernstown	Glynn	Antrim	1839
Sarah	4	Ballyvernstown	Glynn	Antrim	1839
Mary	2	Ballyvernstown	Glynn	Antrim	1839
BOOTH, Thomas	26	Cam	Macosquin	Londonderry	1833
BRADLEY, Isabella	32	Leitrim	Ballyscullion	Londonderry	1835
James	12	Leitrim	Ballyscullion	Londonderry	1835
James	3	Leitrim	Ballyscullion	Londonderry	1835
BRAWLEY [Brolly], John[2]	24	Drummond	Drumachose	Londonderry	1834
CAMPBELL, John[3]	46	Magheramore	Tamlaght Finlagan	Londonderry	1834
Mary	44	Magheramore	Tamlaght Finlagan	Londonderry	1834
Maryann	9	Magheramore	Tamlaght Finlagan	Londonderry	1834
CAMPBELL, Robert	24	Lisnagroat	Tamlaght O'Crilly	Londonderry	1834
CAMPBELL, John	25	Drumnacanon	Tamlaght O'Crilly	Londonderry	1834
Ann	29½	Drumnacanon	Tamlaght O'Crilly	Londonderry	1834
CHRISTIE, Andrew	21	Ballyrobin	Killead	Antrim	1835
Samuel (tailor)	27	Ballyrobin	Killead	Antrim	1835
CLARKE, Mathew	45	Drumballyhagan	Kilcronaghan	Londonderry	1834
COLEMAN, Cochran	18	Articlave	Dunboe	Londonderry	1833
Mary	30	Articlave	Dunboe	Londonderry	1833
CONNOR, Matilda[4]	22	Ballykelly	Tamlaght Finlagan	Londonderry	1833
CONNOR, William	24	Ardgarvan	Drumachose	Londonderry	1833
CONWAY, William	10	Drummond	Drumachose	Londonderry	1834
COOK, James	40	Drummond	Drumachose	Londonderry	1834
Jane	38	Drummond	Drumachose	Londonderry	1834
Daniel	20	Drummond	Drumachose	Londonderry	1834
Ann	18	Drummond	Drumachose	Londonderry	1834

---

[2] A labourer of this name, age 21, from Cam, Co. Derry, arrived in the *Robert Burns* in 1834.

[3] A Campbell family from "Newton", Co. Derry, arrived in the *Robert Burns* in 1834: John, labourer, 40; Mary, 38; and Mary Ann, 9. They may be this family.

[4] Matilda Conner from Ballykelly, 23, arrived in the *Salus* in 1833.

NAME	AGE	TOWNLAND	PARISH	COUNTY	YEAR
Jane	14	Drummond	Drumachose	Londonderry	1834
Bell	10	Drummond	Drumachose	Londonderry	1834
Kittyann	8	Drummond	Drumachose	Londonderry	1834
James	6	Drummond	Drumachose	Londonderry	1834
COUGHLIN , Ann	26	Derrylane	Bovevagh	Londonderry	1834
CRAWFORD, James	45	(not stated)	Ahoghill	Antrim	1836
CROSSET, Martha	30	Garvaghy	Ahoghill	Antrim	1835
Jane	10	Garvaghy	Ahoghill	Antrim	1835
Elizabeth	8	Garvaghy	Ahoghill	Antrim	1835
James	6	Garvaghy	Ahoghill	Antrim	1835
DEVANNY, William	21	Killcranny	Killowen	Londonderry	1833
DIXON, Francis	40	Ballymacombs More	Ballyscullion	Londonderry	1835
William	30	Ballymacombs More	Ballyscullion	Londonderry	1835
John	28	Ballymacombs More	Ballyscullion	Londonderry	1835
DOHERTY, Robert	30	Gortycloghan	Desertoghill	Londonderry	1834
DONA[G]HY, Nancy	25	Articlave	Dunboe	Londonderry	1833
DOUGHERTY, Robert	24	Magheramore	Desertoghill	Londonderry	1833
DOUGLAS, George	20	Leck	Drumachose	Londonderry	1833
Margaret	21	Leck	Drumachose	Londonderry	1833
DOUGLAS, William	22	Drumsaragh	Tamlaght O' Crilly	Londonderry	1835
Margaret	25	Drumsaragh	Tamlaght O' Crilly	Londonderry	1835
DUNBAR, Mary, Sr.	60	Mynock[5]	Kilrea	Londonderry	1835
Mary, Jr.	30	Mynock	Kilrea	Londonderry	1835
Mary	40	Mynock	Kilrea	Londonderry	1835
Margaret	6	Mynock	Kilrea	Londonderry	1835
Jane	4	Mynock	Kilrea	Londonderry	1835
DUNLOP, Ellen Jane	22	Mynock	Kilrea	Londonderry	1835
Matilda	19	Mynock	Kilrea	Londonderry	1835
EVANS, Hugh	20	Articlave	Dunboe	Londonderry	1834
FARGEY, John	20	Farranlester	Macosquin	Londonderry	1834
FLEMING, Andrew	24	Ballymacross	Maghera	Londonderry	1834
James	17	Ballymacross	Maghera	Londonderry	1834
Sarah	15	Ballymacross	Maghera	Londonderry	1834
FULGRAVE, Robert	24	Fermoyle[6]	Dunboe	Londonderry	1833
GALLAGHER, Patrick	22	Drummond	Drumachose	Londonderry	1833
GALLOWAY, James	22	Craigs[7]	Ahoghill	Antrim	1836
Robert	20	Craigs	Ahoghill	Antrim	1836
GARVEN, Patrick	20	Drumramer	Drumachose	Londonderry	1833
GILDERSON, William	40	Magheramore	Tamlaght Finlagan	Londonderry	1834
Ann	40	Magheramore	Tamlaght Finlagan	Londonderry	1834
Thomas	8	Magheramore	Tamlaght Finlagan	Londonderry	1834
William	6	Magheramore	Tamlaght Finlagan	Londonderry	1834
Mary	4	Magheramore	Tamlaght Finlagan	Londonderry	1834
John	2	Magheramore	Tamlaght Finlagan	Londonderry	1834

[5] "Mynock" is correctly Moyknock.

[6] This townland is Formoyle.

[7] This appears to refer to the townland of Craignageeragh in the parish of Ahoghill.

NAME	AGE	TOWNLAND	PARISH	COUNTY	YEAR
GORDON, George	18	Glasveagh[8]	Tamlaght Finlagan	Londonderry	1834
GORDON, James	28	Killure	Macosquin	Londonderry	1834
GRAHAM, Andrew	30	Drumsaragh	Tamlaght O' Crilly	Londonderry	1835
Eliza	28	Drumsaragh	Tamlaght O' Crilly	Londonderry	1835
GREER, William	24	Rathbrady Beg	Drumachose	Londonderry	1833
GREY, Eleanor	30	Drummond	Drumachose	Londonderry	1834
HAGHERTY, Joseph	28	Drummond	Drumachose	Londonderry	1833
HAMPSEY, Elizabeth	24	Cuilbane	Desertoghill	Londonderry	1833
HEALEY, Neil	28	Ballyking[9]	Tamlaght Finlagan	Londonderry	1833
Margaret	26	Ballyking	Tamlaght Finlagan	Londonderry	1833
Maryann	4	Ballyking	Tamlaght Finlagan	Londonderry	1833
Eliza	2	Ballyking	Tamlaght Finlagan	Londonderry	1833
John	50 days	Ballyking	Tamlaght Finlagan	Londonderry	1833
HILL, Archibald	30	Long Commons	Coleraine	Londonderry	1833
Margaret	31	Long Commons	Coleraine	Londonderry	1833
HUTTON, James	32	Derrylane	Bovevagh	Londonderry	1833
IRVINE, Ann	18	Walworth	Tamlaght Finlagan	Londonderry	1834
JOHNSTON, Mary Anne	20	Craigs	Ahogill	Antrim	1836
JOHNSTON, Thomas	26	Drunagully	Dunboe	Londonderry	1834
JOHNSTONE, Ritchard	38	Drumane	Tamlaght O'Crilly	Londonderry	1835
Eliza	36	Drumane	Tamlaght O'Crilly	Londonderry	1835
James	8	Drumane	Tamlaght O'Crilly	Londonderry	1835
Henry	6	Drumane	Tamlaght O'Crilly	Londonderry	1835
Jane	4	Drumane	Tamlaght O'Crilly	Londonderry	1835
Ritchard	2	Drumane	Tamlaght O'Crilly	Londonderry	1835
KENNEDY, Robert	30	Gortycloghan	Desertoghill	Londonderry	1834
KENNY, James	20	Craigs	Ahoghill	Antrim	1836
KIRKWOOD, John	21	Moneysallin	Tamlaght O'Crilly	Londonderry	1835
LAFFERTY, Thomas	18	Ballyquinn	Balteagh	Londonderry	1834
LAGAN, Mary	20	Kilhoyle	Balteagh	Londonderry	1834
LITTLEWOOD, Ann	24	Drummond	Tamlaght Finlagan	Londonderry	1834
LOGUE, John	18	Kilhoyle	Balteagh	Londonderry	1834
Bernard	15	Kilhoyle	Balteagh	Londonderry	1834
LYNCH, Michael	40	Kiltest	Aghadowey	Londonderry	1835
LYNN, David	20	Drummond	Drumachose	Londonderry	1833
LYNN, David	19	Rathbrady Beg	Drumachose	Londonderry	1834
McALLISTER, Robert	18	Rathbrady Beg	Drumachose	Londonderry	1833
McATYRE [McAteer], John	25	Ballysally	Coleraine	Londonderry	1834
McCAGUE, Nancy	22	Clooney	Magilligan	Londonderry	1833
McCAHEY, Nathaniel	21	Mynock	Kilrea	Londonderry	1835
McCAHY, Samuel	50	Ballyscullion West	Ballyscullion	Londonderry	1834
Jane	48	Ballymacombs More	Ballyscullion	Londonderry	1835
Ann	25	Ballymacombs More	Ballyscullion	Londonderry	1835
Margret	20	Ballymacombs More	Ballyscullion	Londonderry	1835
John	18	Ballymacombs More	Ballyscullion	Londonderry	1835
Eleanor	16	Ballymacombs More	Ballyscullion	Londonderry	1835

[8] The modern spelling of this townland is Glasvey.

[9] This is properly the townland of Ballykeen.

NAME	AGE	TOWNLAND	PARISH	COUNTY	YEAR
Charles	14	Ballymacombs More	Ballyscullion	Londonderry	1835
Jane	12	Ballymacombs More	Ballyscullion	Londonderry	1835
Sarah	6	Ballymacombs More	Ballyscullion	Londonderry	1835
McCAULEY, James	30	Ballyking	Tamlaght Finlagan	Londonderry	1833
Ann	28	Ballyking	Tamlaght Finlagan	Londonderry	1833
(Girl)	4	Ballyking	Tamlaght Finlagan	Londonderry	1833
(Girl)	2	Ballyking	Tamlaght Finlagan	Londonderry	1833
McCAULEY, Robert	30	Glasveagh	Tamlaght Finlagan	Londonderry	1834
McCAY, Mary	26	Drummond	Drumachose	Londonderry	1834
McCLEMENT, Robert	19	Drunagully	Dunboe	Londonderry	1833
McCLOSKEY, John	25	Ballintemple	Errigal	Londonderry	1833
Ann	19	Ballintemple	Errigal	Londonderry	1833
McCLOWD, James	30	Drummond	Drumachose	Londonderry	1833
McCLOY [McClay], William	20	Ballymacpeake[10]	Tamlaght O'Crilly	Londonderry	1835
McCOLLIAN, William	30	Drumsaragh	Tamlaght O' Crilly	Londonderry	1835
Eliza	26	Drumsaragh	Tamlaght O' Crilly	Londonderry	1835
John	3	Drumsaragh	Tamlaght O' Crilly	Londonderry	1835
McELVAN, John	19	Rathbrady Beg	Drumachose	Londonderry	1834
McENTIRE, Margaret	18	Drummond	Tamlaght Finlagan	Londonderry	1834
McFAULL [McFall], Daniel	23	Rathbrady Beg	Drumachose	Londonderry	1834
McGAUNEY, Francis	30	Articlave	Dunboe	Londonderry	1833
James	22	Articlave	Dunboe	Londonderry	1833
McGAUY, Ann	50	Ballykelly	Tamlaght Finlagan	Londonderry	1834
Maria	20	Ballykelly	Tamlaght Finlagan	Londonderry	1834
Ann	8	Ballykelly	Tamlaght Finlagan	Londonderry	1834
McGEE, Margaret	45	Ballykelly	Tamlaght Finlagan	Londonderry	1834
Matty	32	Ballykelly	Tamlaght Finlagan	Londonderry	1834
Eliza	1	Ballykelly	Tamlaght Finlagan	Londonderry	1834
McGOWEN, Ann	20	Killowen	Killowen	Londonderry	1833
James	16	Killowen	Killowen	Londonderry	1833
McGOWEN, Henry[11]	22	Ballyquinn	Balteagh	Londonderry	1834
McKEE, William	19	Ballysally	Coleraine	Londonderry	1834
Ann	22	Ballysally	Coleraine	Londonderry	1834
McKENDRY, James	25	Moboy	Ahoghill	Antrim	1836
Peggy Anne	20	Moboy	Ahoghill	Antrim	1836
McKINNEY, James	21	Killyless	Ahoghill	Antrim	1836
McLAUGHLIN, Edward	24	Drumreghlin[12]	Tamlaght Finlagan	Londonderry	1834
McLAUGHLIN, James	30	Rathbrady Beg	Drumachose	Londonderry	1834
Patrick	26	Rathbrady Beg	Drumachose	Londonderry	1834
Maryanne	24	Rathbrady Beg	Drumachose	Londonderry	1834
William	18	Rathbrady Beg	Drumachose	Londonderry	1834
McLAUGHLIN, John	28	Killcranny	Killowen	Londonderry	1833

---

[10] This is the townland of Ballymacpeake Lower. Ballymacpeake Upper is in the adjacent parish of Maghera.

[11] Henry McGowan died 9 Sep 1871 at Hartt's Mills, York County, NB, age 60
- *Colonial Farmer*, 23 Oct 1871.

[12] This townland is more properly written as Drumraighland.

NAME	AGE	TOWNLAND	PARISH	COUNTY	YEAR
McLAUGHLIN, John	50	Ballykelly	Tamlaght Finlagan	Londonderry	1834
Ann	50	Ballykelly	Tamlaght Finlagan	Londonderry	1834
Catherine	24	Ballykelly	Tamlaght Finlagan	Londonderry	1834
Martha	22	Ballykelly	Tamlaght Finlagan	Londonderry	1834
McMACKEN, John[13]	22	Drummond	Drumachose	Londonderry	1834
MAHARG, William	30	Gortycloghan	Desertoghill	Londonderry	1834
MARTIN, Thomas	22	Drummond	Drumachose	Londonderry	1833
MILLER, Jane	20	Ar[d]varness	Macosquin	Londonderry	1833
MILLER, Margaret	18	Finlagan	Tamlaght Finlagan	Londonderry	1834
MOONEY, Henery [sic]	65	Drumane	Tamlaght O'Crilly	Londonderry	1835
Mary	75	Drumane	Tamlaght O'Crilly	Londonderry	1835
MORRISON, Mathew	27	Crossgare	Macosquin	Londonderry	1834
MULLAN, James	20	Grannagh	Aghanloo	Londonderry	1834
MULLAN, Jane	20	Old Town Deer Park	Ballyscullion	Londonderry	1834
MULLIN, Docia	22	Drummond	Drumachose	Londonderry	1834
MULLIN, Molly	30	Drummond	Drumachose	Londonderry	1834
Marcus	10	Drummond	Drumachose	Londonderry	1834
John	8	Drummond	Drumachose	Londonderry	1834
Edward	6	Drummond	Drumachose	Londonderry	1834
Patrick	4	Drummond	Drumachose	Londonderry	1834
Robert	2	Drummond	Drumachose	Londonderry	1834
NODWELL, Mathew	30	Glenkeen	Drumachose	Londonderry	1834
Catherine	28	Glenkeen	Drumachose	Londonderry	1834
Maryann	5	Glenkeen	Drumachose	Londonderry	1834
Eliza	3	Glenkeen	Drumachose	Londonderry	1834
O'KANE, Ellen	20	Clooney	Magilligan	Londonderry	1833
Margaret	18	Clooney	Magilligan	Londonderry	1833
O'KANE, John	26	Tartnakelly	Tamlaght Finlagan	Londonderry	1834
O'NEILL, James	18	Derrylane	Bovevagh	Londonderry	1834
PAUL, William	50	Articlave	Dunboe	Londonderry	1833
Elizabeth	45	Articlave	Dunboe	Londonderry	1833
Sarah	16	Articlave	Dunboe	Londonderry	1833
QUINN, John	30	Bovedy	Tamlaght O'Crilly	Londonderry	1835
Mary	25	Bovedy	Tamlaght O'Crilly	Londonderry	1835
Bridget	3	Bovedy	Tamlaght O'Crilly	Londonderry	1835
Mary Jane	1½	Bovedy	Tamlaght O'Crilly	Londonderry	1835
RAMSAY, Samuel	38	New Row	Coleraine	Londonderry	1833
Jane	21	New Row	Coleraine	Londonderry	1833
Catherine	7	New Row	Coleraine	Londonderry	1833
John, Jr.	5	New Row	Coleraine	Londonderry	1833
Samuel	3	New Row	Coleraine	Londonderry	1833
Eliza	1 mo	New Row	Coleraine	Londonderry	1833
RICHY, James	50	Ballycrum	Drumachose	Londonderry	1833
Molly	48	Ballycrum	Drumachose	Londonderry	1833
Samuel	20	Ballycrum	Drumachose	Londonderry	1833
James	18	Ballycrum	Drumachose	Londonderry	1833
SCULLION, Daniel	20	Ballyscullion West	Ballyscullion	Londonderry	1834

[13] John McMACKEN, 21, labourer, arrived in the *Robert Burns*, in 1834.

NAME	AGE	TOWNLAND	PARISH	COUNTY	YEAR
SHEAGOG, William	25	Brackaghrowley[14]	Kilcronaghan	Londonderry	1834
SIMPSON, Jane	50	Killyless	Ahoghill	Antrim	1836
Margaret Anne	22	Killyless	Ahoghill	Antrim	1836
James	14	Killyless	Ahoghill	Antrim	1836
William	12	Killyless	Ahoghill	Antrim	1836
SMITH, James	25	Ballyagan	Desertoghill	Londonderry	1834
SMITH, William	22	Fermullan	Dunboe	Londonderry	1833
STERLING, Cochran	28	Knockmult	Dunboe	Londonderry	1833
STEWART, Margaret	30	Clintagh	Aghadowey	Londonderry	1835
Mary	4	Clintagh	Aghadowey	Londonderry	1835
THORPE, Stephen	18	Articlave	Dunboe	Londonderry	1833
USHER, John	24	Killure	Macosquin	Londonderry	1834
WHITE, John[15]	19	Ballyking	Tamlaght Finlagan	Londonderry	1834
WORKMAN, Sarah	24	Drumnacanon	Tamlaght O'Crilly	Londonderry	1834
Ann	21	Drumnacanon	Tamlaght O'Crilly	Londonderry	1834
WRIGHT, Hugh	64	Bovally	Drumachose	Londonderry	1834

B) Two people intending to emigrate to St. Andrews, New Brunswick, 1835

NAME	AGE	TOWNLAND	PARISH	COUNTY	YEAR
CHRISTIE, Andrew	21	Ballyrobin	Killead	Antrim	1835
Samuel (tailor)	27	Ballyrobin	Killead	Antrim	1835

C) Five people intending to emigrate to Sydney, Nova Scotia, 1836

NAME	AGE	TOWNLAND	PARISH	COUNTY	YEAR
JOHNSTONE, William	35	Whiteabbey	Carmoney	Antrim	1836
Margaret	30	Whiteabbey	Carmoney	Antrim	1836
David	12	Whiteabbey	Carmoney	Antrim	1836
Isabella	10	Whiteabbey	Carmoney	Antrim	1836
McKINNEY, John	22	Mullinsallagh	Ahoghill	Antrim	1836

[14] This may refer to Bracaghreilly townland, which is in adjacent Maghera parish.

[15] An 18-year-old labourer of this name landed from the *Ambassador* in 1834.

APPENDIX V - A COFFIN SHIP: THE *ALDEBARAN*, 1847

During the flight of thousands of frightened and hungry Irish at the time of the Great Famine of the 1840s some voyages were so unfortunate in terms of human suffering and death that people spoke of such vessels as "coffin ships". One vessel that could be nominated for that dubious distinction would have been the barque *Aldebaran,* 492 tons[1], whose first crossing in 1847 was disastrous for the suffering souls in steerage.[2]

The *Aldebaran*, **BARRASS**, master, sailed from Sligo with 418 passengers, and arrived at Partridge Island, Saint John, New Brunswick on 16 May 1847.[3] On 26 April 1847 the Emigration Office at Saint John received a list of passengers in the ship which cleared Sligo on 22 March with 383 passengers, 262 adults and 121 children under 14 years of age.[4]

A couple of days after the ship reached Saint John, it was reported that the *Aldebaran* left Sligo with 418 passengers, "36 of whom died on the passage, and 105 are now sick with fever and dysentery. We learn that the passengers complain bitterly of the bad quality of the provisions and water served out to them during the passage. Since writing the above, we learn that two more have died since arriving at the Quarantine station."[5]

That was not the end of the story. During the summer a further 84 passengers from the *Aldebaran* perished at the Quarantine station on Partridge Island. They were natives of Connaught. the westernmost province of Ireland. Three passengers who survived the quarantine were admitted to the Alms House in Saint John, namely, James **BRANNEN**, 55, from Mayo; Catherine **BRANNEN**, 12, from Mayo, perhaps a daughter of James; and John **FINAN**, 20, from Sligo.[6]

Since many of the passengers were traveling in family groups, the following list of deaths in the Quarantine station may serve as an indication of the names of others who were passengers on this voyage. The prevalence of people aged 10, 20, 30, 40, 50, 60 indicates that ages were rounded to the nearest ten. Another feature to note is the scarcity of people upwards of 40, just five among the 84.

---

[1] Under the terms of the British Passenger Act of 1835, the vessel could carry 3 passengers per 5 tons register, and three children under 14 were to be counted as one adult passenger. The *Aldebaran*, by that measure, could carry 295 adult passengers. One quarter of the deaths in quarantine were of children below the age of 13. If that proportion obtained throughout the passenger list, this was a clear case of overcrowding. There is no indication that the master or the ship owner were fined for this violation. In fact, the *Aldebaran*, sailing from Dublin, returned to Saint John with more passengers in October 1847. This time, no record mentions the number of passengers.

[2] The vessel's name – *Aldebaran* – is Arabic, from *al-debaran*, meaning a follower. It is a red star in the Hyades, a V-shaped cluster in the head of the constellation Taurus.

[3] David Dobson, *Ships from Ireland to Early America*, Vol. I, pp. 4 - 5; Vol. III, p. 5.

[4] New Brunswick Courier, *1 May 1847.* It appears that the vessel added 35 passengers *after* clearing the port of Sligo.

[5] *The Weekly Observer* [Saint John], 18 May 1847.

[6] Johnson, p. 116.

Seventy-one deaths were reported between the vessel's arrival in mid-May and 2 July 1847:[7]

ALLAN, Catherine, 12
BOYCE, Ann, 6
BRANNAN, Sarah, 25
BRAY, Honora, 26
CLARKE, Martin, 22
CLIFFORD, Michael, 23
COIL, Bridget, 18
CONLEY, Patrick, 40
    Winny, 40
COOPER, Peter, 35
CORRAGAN, Con., 10
COUGHLIN, Owen, 10
CRONIN, Jerry, 27
CULGIN, Patrick, 28
DEVITT, Andrew, 50
DOHERTY, Bridget, 23
DOUGAN, Henry, 13
    John, 60
    Thomas, 13
    John. 30
DYER, James, 27
FLYNN, Charles, 24
FORD, Philip, 20
FOX, Catherine, 20

GILL, Ann, 36
GILLAN, Michael, 18
GILLESPIE, Francis, 13
GRAY, Unity, 23
GREEN, John, 22
GUNNING, Mary, 9 mos.
HARRINGTON, Mary, 30
    Mary, 9
    Mary, 8
JUDGE, Thomas, 40
KELLEY, Bernard, 30
KELLY, Mary, 27
KENNON, Michael, 20
KILMARTIN, James, 40
LAHEY, Michael, 30
LAYMAN, Charles, 30
LEAR(E)Y, Mary, 3
McCALEE, John, 32
McCUE, Larky, 25
McDERMOTE, Patrick, 10
McGEE, Honora, 25
    James, 4
    Mary, 30

McMANUS, Jerry, 4
    John, 33
McMORRISY, Rody, 33
MACK, Mary, 8
MALONEY, Mary, 25
    Patrick, 20
MANTAN, Bartley, 30
    Mary, 25
MARTIN, John, 15
MORIN, Lawrence, 30
MORRISEY, Mary, 25
MORRISON, John, 23
    Margaret, 25
MULLANEY, Michael, 20
MURRAY, John, 26
OPERAN, Mary, 9
PRESTON, Barbara, 60
RAFTER, Catherine, 25
    Thomas, 30
    William, 50
SHEA, Mary, 2
    Peggy, 1½
SULLIVAN, Jerry, 10
TUMMANY, Conly, 23

Eight more of the passengers died between the second of July and the end of that month:[8]

COLEMAN, Ann, 5
DUGAN, Hugh, 33
    Thomas, 19

JOLLY, Martha, 22
McLYNN, John, 50

McMANUS, Nora, 40
PARAT, Thomas, 60
    Winney, 13

There were five further deaths among the passengers from the *Aldebaran*:[9]
John **GILLESPIE**, 14 (31 July - 7 Aug); John **JENNINGS**, 15 (6 - 20 Aug); William **BYRNE**, 20, and Thomas **MAGEE**, 20 (27 Aug - 3 Sep); and Patrick **MAHADY** (17 - 25 Sep).

---

[7] *New Brunswick Courier*, 10 July 1847.

[8] *Ibid.*, 7 Aug 1847.

[9] *Ibid.* 7 Aug 1847, 28 Aug 1847, 4 Sep 1847, and 25 Sep 1847.

Of 418 passengers, 36 died at sea and 84 died in quarantine, in all 120, a mortality of over 28%. This was more than double the mortality rate of ships from Ireland reaching New Brunswick in 1847. Most of the survivors quickly departed Saint John to enter the United States.[10]

In contrast to the *Aldebaran* was the J. & J. Cooke vessel, *Marchioness of Clydesdale,* which departed from Londonderry with 380 passengers on 5 April and arrived at Saint John on 17 May 1847 in good condition. "Nine deaths took place on board the Barque *Marchioness of Clydesdale* which arrived at Quarantine from . . . on Monday. We presume the others were all in good health, as she was allowed to come up to the town on Wednesday and discharge."[11] Only one passenger – Charles **DUFFY**, 40 – died at Partridge Island Quarantine.[12]

Ten passengers were admitted to the Alms House in Saint John, where three died, and the records again present the sorts of discrepancies discussed elsewhere.[13]

Becky **McMONEGAL**, 17, from Donegal - Biddy **McGONIGLE**, from Ballygorman
Dimnock **McCULLOGH**, 40, from Tyrone - Dominic **McCULLOGH**, from Beragh (died 20 July)
Thomas **McCULLOUGH**, 15, from Tyrone - Thomas **McCULLOGH**, 10, from Beragh
Bernard **McCULLOUGH**, 12, from Tyrone - Bernard **McCULLOGH**, 6, from Beragh
Susan **McCULLOUGH**,14, from Tyrone - Susanna **McCULLOGH**, 8, from Beragh (died 17 Aug)
Nancy **McCULLOUGH**, 8, from Tyrone - Ann **McCULLOGH**, 4, from Beragh
Patrick **McCULLOUGH**, 4, from Tyrone - Patrick **McCULLOGH**, 2, from Beragh (died 6 Sep)
Ellen **O'DONELL**, 37, from Donegal - Eleanor **O'DONNELL**, from Carn
George **O'DONELL**, 8, from Donegal - George **O'DONNELL**, 7, from Carn
Charles **O'DONELL**, 5, from Donegal - Charles **O'DONNELL**, 4, from Carn

14 passengers died out of a total of 380, fewer than four percent which was well below the mortality rate typical among steerage passengers during the late 1840s. The *Aldebaran* was not the worst case. The *Syria* set out with 241 passengers for Québec. "All her passengers were Irish, had crossed to Liverpool to embark, and had spent one night at least in the cheap boarding-houses of Liverpool." By the time the *Syria* reached Grosse Isle, the quarantine at Québec, 9 passengers had died at sea and a tenth died on landing. There were 84 cases of fever among the survivors. The health officer, Dr. Douglas, believed that another 20 to 24 were "certain to sicken."[14]

---

[10] There were easy means of getting to Boston. For example, the Saint John *Morning News*, 10 March 1847, carried an advertisement announcing that "The steamer, *Maid of Erin*, will leave the North Wharf for Portland, touching at Eastport on Tuesday, the 16th instant, at 10 o'clock, A.M. and leave Portland for S. John on Friday, the 19th instant, after the arrival of the first Train from Boston, touching at Eastport. For Freight or Passage, Apply to Capt. **LEAVITT** on board, or to Thos. **PARKS**, Dock Street."

[11] *Ibid.* 22 May 1847. The master was Captain Ferguson.

[12] *Ibid.*, 10 July 1847. Duffy's name does not appear in the list published in Mitchell, pp. 2-5.

[13] Mitchell, pp. 2 - 5, whose version is used here, and Johnson, pp. 150 - 151.

[14] Woodham-Smith, p. 219.

Even worse was the case of the *Larch* which left Sligo with 440 passengers and had buried 108 at sea before reaching Grosse Isle with 150 cases of fever on board.[15] The *Virginius* followed the Ireland via Liverpool route. Setting out with 476 passengers, she arrived at Gross Isle having buried 158 at sea (33% mortality), with 186 of the survivors, as well as the captain, mate, and all but six of the crew, sick with fever. Dr. Douglas considered that "not more than six or eight were really healthy and able to exert themselves."[16]

The one misery these poor emigrants were spared was shipwreck or having to abandon a crippled brig in mid-Atlantic. The *Falconer* which reached Saint John in spring 1847 had aboard the captain and crew of the brig *Demerest* which had been en route from Sligo to New York, but had to be abandoned as it was in immanent danger of sinking and was too far from any port to be towed to safety. As well as the officers and hands of the *Demerest*, the *Falconer* brought 23 Irish passengers to the safety of Saint John.[17]

Whether our Irish ancestors reached the shores of America hungry, poor, or ill, the fact that they arrived and carried on with life, sometimes against the hostility of those who lived here before them, marks them as among history's great survivors. Uncounted millions of Americans and Canadians bear Irish names or had a grandmother who did. Celt, Norse, Norman, Welsh, English, Scot, Huguenot or Palatine – the mixture we call the Irish – produced a remarkable people. It is a heritage to be proud of, but one demanding that we live up to it.

---

[15] *Ibid.*, p. 225. Mortality on the crossing approached 25%, and another 34% arrived sick. It appears that about 30% of the original passengers did not survive their emigration.

[16] Guillet, p. 96. With 33% dead at sea and a further 39% seriously ill, mortality must have been well above 40% and possibly as high as 50%. Official figures for 1847 record that 17,465 of the 106,812 emigrants to British North America died on voyage, at quarantine or at hospitals, i.e., one in six - Coleman, p. 185. The ratio for New Brunswick was better, with 2,115 deaths out of 17,074 emigrants, or about one in eight.

[17] *Morning News*, Saint John, 14 Apr 1847.

SHIP INDEX

All references to a vessel's name do not necessarily refer to the same vessel. Multiple use of names for ships was common practice. As observed in the footnotes, sometimes there was confusion as to what was the proper name of a vessel, because different secondary sources offer versions at variance with one another. In those cases, the ship is indexed under both names.

INDEX OF SURNAMES

TOPICAL INDEX

CPSIA information can be obtained
at www.ICGtesting.com
Printed in the USA
BVOW04s0424171117
500200BV00014B/46/P

9 780806 319650